The SHAPE of FUTURES PAST

The SHAPE of FUTURES PAST

The Story of Prediction

CHRIS MORGAN

Webb&Bower

EXETER, ENGLAND

To Mike Rohan for getting me interested in early science fiction.

By the same author:
FUTURE MAN
FRITZ LEIBER: A BIBLIOGRAPHY 1934-1979

Published in Great Britain 1980 by
Webb & Bower (Publishers) Limited,
33 Southernhay East, Exeter, Devon, EX1 1NS

Distributed by WHS Distributors
(a division of W. H. Smith and Son Limited)
St John's House, East Street, Leicester LE1 6NE

Designed by Vic Giolitto

© Webb & Bower (Publishers) Limited 1980
Text and Illustrations © Chris Morgan 1980

British Library Cataloguing in Publication Data

Morgan, Chris
　　The shape of futures past.
　　1. Forecasting — History
　　I. Title
　　133.3'2'09034　　CB161

ISBN 0-906671-15-9 Pbk

Typeset by Advertiser Printers (Newton Abbot) Limited.

Printed and bound by Redwood Burn Limited, Trowbridge and Esher.

Contents

AUTHOR'S FOREWORD

This is a book about past predictions of the future. It is not the first such, nor will it be the last. There exists such a wealth of fascinating predictive material which has been out of print for upwards of sixty years that several more books could appear on the subject without significant overlap.

Although this book covers predictions from prehistoric times to the present day it concentrates on those made between 1800 and 1945. That was a particularly interesting period, starting when the idea of the changing future — the future formed by scientific progress — was being established and ending before the future became the commonplace subject which it is today. Most of these predictions of the future were originally written as fiction, described today as "science fiction" but in those days as "scientific romances" or "tales of the future". "Science fiction" is a more extensive label than is "tales of the future", since only a part of science fiction is set in the future — although a large part, perhaps seventy or eighty per cent depending upon one's exact definition of science fiction.

Chapter 1 deals with predictions before 1800, Chapter 10 with those since 1945. The eight chapters in between cover the tale of the future between those dates, divided up according to the authors' reasons for making their predictions. Most authors of stories about the future did not believe that their predictions would come true, but were trying to warn their readers of possible dangers, or to demonstrate how utopia might be achieved, or to satirize contemporary society; some tried to put across philosophies, others tried only to entertain; and there were a few who tried to predict what really would happen. Each of these intentions has a chapter to itself.

In addition, two common themes which these authors explored hang together so well that it would be wrong to try and divide up stories about them by intention: those themes are war and alien contact, and each has a chapter devoted to it.

This is not intended as a rigorous textbook and I want it to be enjoyed. Many more tales of the future exist than there is room to discuss in it. The choice of what to include was not easy, but I have tried to cover all categories, though not necessarily to use the obvious examples in each case: some almost unknown books, which do not appear to have been described or summarized by any previous commentator, have been included deliberately because they are good examples of points I wish to make, or simply because they are entertaining. I would rather have included descriptions of twice as many books, but there were of course constraints on space.

There is a bibliography of all nonfiction works referred to or used (except for unimportant passing references). No bibliography of fictional works is included, but the title, author and year of first English-language book publication are given in the text for each work mentioned. If anyone requires further information I would direct them to Professor I. F. Clarke's excellent bibliography *Tale of the Future* (1978) for all fictional works published in the UK. For fiction never published in the UK there is nothing totally comprehensive and dependable; Bleiler's *Checklist of Fantastic Literature* (1948) and Tuck's as yet unfinished *Encyclopaedia of Science Fiction and Fantasy* (1974, 1978) are useful though limited. No published bibliography of nonfiction prediction exists.

In selecting the accompanying illustrations I have tried, with a few honourable exceptions, to use only those which have not appeared in the commentaries or encyclopaedias of science fiction published in recent years.

Chris Morgan
Birmingham
January 1980

1 ASTROLOGY AND TRAVELLERS' TALES

THE FUTURE BEFORE 1800

The principal concern of this book is the predictive fiction and serious predictive speculation published between 1800 and 1945. There was almost none before 1800 (although this is an arbitrary date rather than one of special significance), while since 1945 so much has been published that any attempt to deal with it all in this single volume would result in a swamping of the older, obsolete — and more interesting — predictions. Besides, recent works have been extensively described, analyzed and bibliographized, and most are in any case still in print; they need no further exposure and will receive none here — except for brief mentions in my final chapter of a number of works, either because they demonstrate the continuation of earlier trends or because they show the initiation of new trends.

Yet before those books of 1800 to 1945 are analyzed something needs to be said about what went before. Predictive fiction did not just appear from a clear blue sky one day. It has roots, a long heritage, is the result of several disparate trends and external events. Prior to 1800 almost nobody thought to set a work of fiction in the future, but this does not mean that people before that time had no concept of the future or did not bother about the future; it signifies only that authors had no need to set their works in the future.

For some six thousand years mankind *has* concerned itself with the future — *via* astrology. This is what W. H. G. Armytage, in *Yesterday's Tomorrows*, has termed the "Mantic Heritage". The ancient Egyptians were the earliest, so far as is known, to develop and use the art of prophecy. Believed implicitly by Pharaohs and commoners alike, prophecy was an everyday occurrence, nearly always performed by the priests. It was part of their regular priestly training to learn the methods of divination and to practise them when asked. In particular, they were required to predict the fortunes of the kings and of the nation of Egypt.

From Egypt astrology spread to Greece, where famous oracles were founded at Delphi, Dodona and Lebadea, presided over by priestesses, through whom the gods would speak their prophecies. In a few cases, including Delphi, there was a sibyl (a wise woman, reputed to live to a great age) present to answer any question of a prophetic nature addressed to the oracle. The Jews, too, learned prophecy from Egypt, and their generations of famous prophets are known to us through the Bible — Isaiah, Jeremiah, Ezekiel and Daniel, as well as the twelve minor prophets.

Ancient China developed its own astrological system, based on a different interpretation of the zodiac. Prophecy by this and other means was considered very important — especially at the court, where there was an official astrologer — from about 2700BC. From the 9th century BC right up until the present the *I Ching* or "Book of Changes" has been used by rich and poor alike to foretell their personal future — although the standard hexagrams are all rather vague, so answers tend towards the cryptic.

The Romans possessed a complex system of oracles and professional seers. Prophecies were not universally believed (Julius Caesar disregarded his "Ides of March" warning) but there are many stories of their fulfilment. An extensive range of phenomena was made use of at one time or another in the process of divination, including dreams, fire, water, entrails, mirrors, the fall of dice and, when all else failed, divine inspiration.

In Britain the Celts established an early tradition of prophecy — often, though not exclusively, through the medium of the preChristian priesthood. Sacrifices were made, of bulls in peacetime and of men in times of war. These men, most frequently prisoners, are said to have been inserted into hollow man-shaped figures of wickerwork, which were burnt; from the sounds of their cries and of the flames the prophecy was divined.

Much later, in the 5th century AD, there was the enigmatic figure of Merlin, a famous magician and prophet who has become a firm and important part of British mythology on little more evidence than the writings of the notoriously unreliable Geoffrey of Monmouth. According to Geoffrey, Merlin made a series of cryptic predictions covering events of the next ten thousand years and more.

It is interesting that astrology — so closely akin to alchemy and the black arts — continued to exist and even gain in popularity alongside the Christian Church. No conflict seemed to exist: Christian kings and princes continued to believe in the prophecies of astrologers and, in some cases, to appoint court astrologers, such as John Dee, official astrologer to Elizabeth I of England. The standing of astrologers was normally very high; the practice was regarded as a legitimate science, indivisible from astronomy and frequently carried out by those with some training in science or medicine.

Probably the greatest of all astrological prophets, in that his precise prophecies have been proven surprisingly accurate for a number of centuries after his death, was Nostradamus. He was a Frenchman,

Michel de Notredame, and lived from 1503 to 1566. A practising physician, he found time to make prophecies of events ranging in time from his immediate future up to the year AD7000. All his long-range predictions are couched in cryptic verse, with many of the proper names in anagram or clue form, and with facts deliberately made obscure by means of *double entendres* and esoteric references. With hindsight it is possible to untangle the apparent meaning of most quatrains, obtaining references — sometimes very detailed — to (for example) Cromwell, London's great plague and fire, the French Revolution, Napoleon, the Russian Revolution and World War II (with a reference to "Hister", which seems to be astonishingly close to Hitler). His prophecies pertaining to our future are impossible to interpret with any certainty.

In the year 1999 in the seventh month,
A great king of frightfulness will come from the skies
To resuscitate the great king of Angumois,
Around this time Mars will reign for the good cause.

Although Angumois certainly refers to France the remainder is obscure. Could the "great king of frightfulness . . . from the skies" denote missiles launched from orbital satellites, or is it a warning of alien invasion? Can Mars be taken as standing for war, or more literally in reference to the planet?

There have been many other notable seers. Mother Shipton was a contemporary of Nostradamus; the rest form a clear heritage leading to present-day clairvoyants and to the daily "What Your Stars Foretell" columns in most newspapers. Since the late 19th century clairvoyancy and precognition have been regarded as one facet of the wider field of extrasensory perception. It must be remembered that almost all prophecies of this kind are short-term, personal and (in many modern instances) unspecific enough to be widely applicable. They are never an attempt to describe a future society or to set fiction in the future. Yet they are evidence of an early and continuous awareness of the existence of the future and of the fact that it will be different from the present.

Two more strands are the Mayan Long Count and the interpretation of dreams. From 3113BC in the Mayan civilization of Central America a Long Count of time was kept, day by day, for well over four thousand years. The Mayans possessed words for high numbers (such as the *kinchiltun*, equal to 3.2 million or 20^5) and were able to think in terms of an almost infinite past and future.

As for dreams, it has been believed for thousands of years that they reflect the past and future, even that while one is dreaming one's mind is actually visiting portions of one's past or future existence and experiencing them. The idea was revived and popularized by J.W. Dunne (in his book *An Experiment With Time;* 1927), who proved to his own satisfaction that a careful recording and analysis of dreams will produce detailed prophecies of one's own future — or occasionally, generally indirectly, of the futures of other people.

A trend which, at first sight, appears completely separate from predictions of the future is the writing of accounts of fantastic voyages to strange parts of the world, at a time when there still remained many areas of the globe not visited by Europeans. Often presented in the first person, some of these fictional accounts may have been believed, for they were not always — to Europeans — any more fantastic that the genuine experiences of Marco Polo in 13th-century Asia. The purpose of these tales of fantastic voyages was primarily to entertain — although sometimes it was to satirize the author's contemporary scene, sometimes to predict what might actually be discovered, and sometimes to prescribe ideal systems of government.

In the 2nd century AD the Greek satirist Lucian of Samosata wrote two fantastic voyages involving trips to the Moon. In his *True History* a boat which sails out of the Mediterranean through the Straits of Gibraltar (then known as the Pillars of Hercules and reckoned to be the furthest extent of the world's habitable area) on a voyage of discovery is picked up by a waterspout and conveyed to the Moon, which its crew first see as "a great country in the air, like a shining island". The men of the Moon are at war with those of the Sun, and Lucian describes the fantastic proceedings in detail.

The army of Endymion, King of the Moon, contains sixty million Moon-men, plus spiders the size of islands and cavalry mounted on gigantic birds and fleas. The Moon-men are strange creatures indeed, subsisting on fumes and condensed air, and dissolving into smoke when they die. The ship at length returns to Earth, where it is swallowed by a sea-monster more than a hundred miles in length.

Icaromenippus is concerned with a deliberate voyage to the Moon by Menippus, who flies there, using birds' wings, to settle an argument over the shape of the Earth. After meeting and discoursing with some spirits he finds there, Menippus flies on to Heaven but is returned to Earth by the gods.

From the 16th century, to take a great leap, fantastic voyages became more frequent. Among them was Ariosto's *Orlando Furioso* (1516) which, among other adventures, includes a chariot journey to the Moon. Cervantes' *Don Quixote* (1605) contained a variety of wonderful adventures.

But the 17th century saw the publication of quite a lot of voyages to the Moon — all set at the time of writing. The evaporation of dew, the flight of birds, the help of demons and the use of rockets (one of Cyrano de Bergerac's methods) were all schemes for reaching the Moon; they enabled mankind's fantastic voyages to be extended into space, although little use was made of the remainder of the Solar System: it was to be some time before voyages to the planets became popular.

Then, in the 18th century, a new locale was developed. In 1741 *Niels Klim's Journey Underground* by a Dane, Ludvig Holberg, was published — the first popular book to take Man's journeying into the centre of the Earth (although the idea of an inhabited subterranean country originated with early theories that the biblical Garden of Eden was located below ground; a few works of fiction appeared in the 1720s and 1730s which include journeys far underground). Klim finds a model of the Solar System in the cavernous interior of the Earth and lives for a while on the planet Nazar, meeting its strange inhabitants. The work is partly satirical, involving an inversion of many human conventions. It was quickly translated into several other languages, including English, and was instrumental in starting a vogue for hollow-Earth stories.

Only ten years later, in 1751, Robert Paltock's *Life and Adventures of Peter Wilkins* appeared, in which Wilkins lives for many years in large caverns below ground, in "the Country of the Glumms and Gawreys or Men and Women that fly", as the book's subsidiary title puts it. Peter Wilkins marries one of these flying women and they have several children. In the same year was published *John Daniel* by Ralph Morris, which includes a trip to the Moon on a mechanical airship with manually operated wings.

Slightly later fantastic voyages were Tiphaigne's *Giphantis* (1760-1) and the anonymous *The Aerostatic Spy* (1785), although the most extravagant and fantastic of them all was *The Travels and Surprising Adventures of Baron Munchausen* (1786), usually attributed to Rudolph Raspe. Mostly too broad and farcical to be termed satire, this is a parody of the genre of fantastic voyages then so popular. Some of its episodes are borrowed from older legends but all are deliberately far-fetched. Among the Baron's other exploits, he makes two journeys to the Moon — one by climbing a beanstalk, the other by the force of a hurricane — builds a single-span bridge from Africa to Britain, is swallowed by a large fish, and is transported from Margate to South America and back by a giant eagle. Yet the Baron confines himself to the time of writing, never venturing into the future — even though a few futuristic pieces, including the anonymous *The Reign of George VI 1900-1925,* had already appeared.

But these non-futuristic fantastic voyages lead on directly to the futuristic science fiction of the 19th and 20th centuries, in which the fantastic voyages written of by (for example) Jules Verne and the increasingly frequent interplanetary novels have played an important part. Alongside these, stories set in lost valleys or hollow Earths are still, at the time of writing, continuing to appear.

A number of satires were published during the period before 1800. The easiest to obtain is Jonathan Swift's *Gulliver's Travels* (1726). Presented in the guise of a travel book giving accounts of visits to several "Remote Nations" of the world by Captain Lemuel Gulliver, it is thus posing as a book of the most popular kind at the time.

The narrator is clearly intended as an everyman figure — a pleasant, honest fellow who carries with him the conventions and preconceptions of the people of his time. He observes the faulted societies he visits (each society emphasizing at least one of the failings of Swift's contemporary society) and records each with a wonderful simplicity. Because Gulliver is neither a philosopher nor a critic (although, of course, Swift was) but rather an innocent, over-credulous character, he is able to describe the most dire or ridiculous practices he encounters in a deadpan manner which adds to the fun. Being unconceited and the first to admit his own failings, Gulliver frequently heightens the satire by admitting that he is "not skilful enough to comprehend" various pieces of false logic or sheer lunacy.

A slightly later satire, Voltaire's *Micromegas* (1750), reverses Swift's approach and uses an extraterrestrial viewpoint to show up Man's shortcomings. Micromegas is a gigantic alien from Sirius who, together with a companion from Saturn, visits Earth, which had been thought uninhabited. There they observe and communicate with mankind. The extraterrestrial visitors are highly advanced creatures who are astonished and greatly amused by mankind's self-importance. The main intention of the book seems to be an attempt to show mankind's relative insignificance in cosmic terms.

There is a trail of other satirical works which involve speculative elements or fantastic locales but are not set in the future; the trail extends across the second half of the 18th century and into the 19th. *A Voyage to the Moon* (1793) by Aratus uses the Moon — reached by a recently discovered balloon — as its setting, peopling it with a society of snakes, who are intelligent and English-speaking, in order to satirize contemporary England. In *Armata* (1816-17) by Thomas Erskine a counter-Earth is postulated, attached to our own Earth at the South Pole and accessible through rock-bound channels. Armata itself is a counter-England, similar in many respects to the real one but differing in some crucial areas.

Although either of these books could have been set in the future they were not; at the time it was not yet necessary. In fact the tradition of satires being set in unusual locales in the writer's present day lasted long after it would have been quite acceptable for them to have been placed in the future. See, for example, Archibald Marshall's novel *Upsidownia* (1915), where there is a complete reversal of social and economic values. The location of the country of Upsidownia is left unspecified; though Upsidownia is reached *via* a cave this is merely a gateway to a parallel

Earth — i.e., the book is not set underground. Alternatively it might be no more than a delusion.

When all is said and done, these are merely devices for bringing a member of one culture into the environment of an opposing culture for the purpose of striking sparks. And, after L. S. Mercier's *Memoirs of the Year 2500* (1772), which is the earliest satire to be set in the future, a futuristic setting becomes possible, although by no means obligatory, for satirically intended fiction — for a long time, whether a tale was set in the future or in an unexplored part of the Earth, exactly the same function was served.

Although utopias can be said to date from the *Republic* of Plato (427-347BC) the word itself, from the Greek for "no place" and "a good place", was first used in its present meaning — an "imaginary state of ideal perfection" — by Sir Thomas More in his political satire, *Utopia* (1516). It is uncertain as to whether or not More intended his Utopia to represent an ideal. Certainly it seems harsh and puritanical to us, in the 20th century, though it embraces a form of communism, with all citizens working for the common good and all food being distributed according to need. The form of government is a cross between an elective democracy and a benevolent dictatorship, with considerable control by the authorities over the lives of the citizens — travel permits, etc. Although Utopia is basically an egalitarian society there is some slavery, and women are discriminated against to a large extent.

This would have been, in general, an improvement on 16th-century England, but the religious freedoms allowed in Utopia angered many churchmen at the time. It is never quite certain which of Utopia's elements are intended seriously and which satirically.

This was followed by Thomasso Campanella's *The City of the Sun* (1623), a mixture of eugenics and mysticism, Sir Francis Bacon's more scientific though unfinished *The New Atlantis* (1627), in which some 20th-century readers manage to find cryptic references to many areas of modern science and technology, and a handful of others, less well known. These were all visions of ideal states, claimed to be in existence in remote parts of the world at the time of writing. While this was easy enough to present convincingly in the 16th century, by the time the 19th century arrived it was clear that the store of unknown islands capable of housing advanced civilizations was running low.

If the elements so far presented are put together it will be seen that mankind had, for several thousand years, been aware of the existence of the future, *via* prophecies. It was not that any radical progress was expected: this was not considered as part of the future, because little or no progress was readily visible in the historic past. Obviously the future would be just like the present in the same way as the present was just like the past, in terms of methods and systems and customs. One got older and eventually died, but this was natural and expected. Occasionally one's country was defeated in war and a new monarchy imposed, but this would make relatively little difference at grass-roots level. Whatever happened, the future was not a qualitatively different world, only a repetition of the past and present. Yet people were ever hopeful of a personal or national improvement of fortune in the future, and predictions of specific events, including war and royal assassination, were always popular.

Some of the fiction which appeared was what *The Encyclopaedia of Science Fiction,* edited by Peter Nicholls, calls "proto science fiction": fantastic voyages, satires and utopias which were in some way speculative and which used an out-of-the-way location in the present day as their setting, when they might, had the author thought of it, have used the future. An increasing number of such works are clearly predictions of what might be or prescriptions of what should be, and so they are verging on being futuristic. By the middle of the 18th century the numbers of such works appearing had increased considerably — each year saw the publication of a few new specimens.

Other strands which must now be drawn in are geographical and industrial.

Whereas the writers of the 17th century could find plenty of areas — which the imaginative cartographers of the day marked up as *"terra incognita"* or "here be dragons" — in which to set their tales, however fantastic, things were rather different by the 1770s. During that decade the full extent of Australia became known, and New Zealand was discovered. The positions and outlines of the world's landmasses were being charted. Even a fair-sized island could not be fictionally inserted without people knowing it for what it was. Writers had to retreat to the continental interiors, to the centre of the Earth, to other worlds — thus making it rather more difficult for a sailing ship to make accidental landfall — if they wished to portray a different civilization.

The "industrial" strand refers not only to the fact that the scientific advances of the 17th century had continued but that they were being turned into the bread-and-butter form of technological innovation. Threshing and weaving machines made their appearance during the 1730s, and Watt's steam engine joined them in 1765. The Industrial Revolution was under way — it is normally presumed to date from about 1750. Throughout western society change and progress were plainly visible to all, and people began to wonder where it would all end. They began to extrapolate the advance of technology. They began to conceive a future in which the world could be radically different.

The fairly obvious result of all this is that fantastic voyages, satires and utopias tended to be set less in obscure parts of the present and more in the wide open spaces of a dynamic future.

But there was no immediate rush by writers to exploit the future. Professor I. F. Clarke, in *The Tale of the Future* (third edition; 1978), lists four tales of the future which were published in Britain before 1770, but none of these (including the anonymous *The Reign of George VI 1900-1925,* which is easily accessible due to its 1899 and 1972 editions) was either very startling as a prophecy or well enough received to merit imitation.

This was changed by the publication of Louis Sebastien Mercier's partly satirical utopia *L'An 2440,* published in France in 1771 and in Britain, as *Memoirs of the Year 2500,* in the following year. (The book is described more fully in Chapter 6.) It was swiftly translated into several European languages and went into many editions, being widely read and imitated. Its influence was considerable, although it did not lead immediately to the setting of all fantastic voyages, satires and utopias in the future. Yet Mercier's book must be regarded as a watershed and, when the tale of the future became relatively commonplace, in the 1820s and 1830s, the credit was due to him.

2 THE END OF CIVILIZATION AS WE KNOW IT

DIRE WARNINGS

Once upon a time there was a parody of the imperturbability of the British Broadcasting Corporation's radio announcers in the face of even the worst news. In part it ran: "In three minutes a bomb will explode which will cause the end of civilization as we know it. In the mean time, here is a gramophone record."

The majority of predictive stories can be interpreted as "dire warnings" of some kind. Sometimes the warning is explicit and unmistakable; it is clear that the author has written his novel as a propaganda exercise, often with the intention of saying "this is what will happen unless we take action now". All dystopian futures, indeed all futures containing dystopian elements, give warning of the way society may go in one or several centuries' time. Then there are specific disaster stories which warn of death and destruction, even if they offer neither a solution nor any hope of one.

Besides tales in these more obvious categories, many other stories of the future offer implicit cautions — sometimes obscured by the weight of allegory or satire. Even descriptions of the most marvellously progressive and utopian futures can be interpreted — if one tries hard enough — as satirical warnings of grim times to come. Of course, the terms "utopia" and "dystopia" are in some cases a matter of opinion; a conservative 19th-century vision of the heaven to come might easily be anathema to us. Almost all tales of the future, then, are open to interpretation as warnings of the future.

We will look at future wars in Chapter 3, so here we will merely note that many such tales, including some of the best known, were obvious warnings. G. T. Chesney's *The Battle of Dorking* and William Le Queux's *The Great War in England in 1897* warned against the weakness of the British army by showing it defeated (or, in the latter case, almost defeated) by European invaders; M. P. Shiel's three "yellow peril" novels *(The Yellow Danger, The Yellow Peril* and *The Yellow Wave)* were all concerned with Asian invasions of Europe, although in fact never intended to be taken as serious warnings; *The Riddle of the Sands,* by Erskine Childers, warns of German plans to invade England, rather than portraying an actual war. Only a few pre-1914 future-war novels can be interpreted as dire warnings of war itself; H. G. Wells' *The War in the Air* is one of them. During the 1930s most future-war stories were warnings not so much of war (though they were mainly pacifist in intention) as of the dreadful poison gases which it was felt were bound to be used in the next war; notable among these was Neil Bell's *The Gas War of 1940.*

Another category of warning, of alien invasion, is likewise dealt with in its own chapter. Here too the most famous novel of all, H. G. Wells' *The War of the Worlds,* is a good example. It gave the initial warning against alien invasion which led to so many tales of maleficent non-humans — Martians in particular — in books, films and comic strips, the warning being extended from alien invasion of Earth to aliens wherever they happened to be found (the recent film *Alien* is an example). *The War of the Worlds* is, of course, far more than a dire warning of alien invasion; it is also, among other things, a warning against complacency, a warning of vulnerability — the English authorities are contemptuous of Martian fighting power until they find themselves beaten; the Martians are conquerors of all they can find until laid low by humble bacteria.

Even aliens are not always alien in origin or appearance: a rather different threat was presented in *Out of the Silence* by Erle Cox, where a woman from a high-technology civilization which existed on Earth millions of years ago is woken from deep-frozen slumber. She is alien in her outlook, and potentially as dangerous as Wells' invaders from Mars.

The two most important and most frequent types of warning are those of political dystopias and against the misuse of science.

Political dystopias in predictive fiction occupy both ends of the political spectrum in about equal numbers: for every fascist dictatorship or capitalist oligarchy suppressing the workers there is an objectionably strict or violent communist régime. In some cases there is revolution or a collapse of the hated status quo; in others the opposition continues . . . or is even quashed.

A good early example of dystopias where the right wing holds power is *Caesar's Column* (1890) by Ignatius Donnelly (at first using the name Edmund Boisgilbert). It shows the USA of 1988 as a wonderful place for the rich, with unlimited electrical power ("the magnetism of the planet iself is harnessed"), some automation, TV screens with an "instant news" facility, like Prestel, air travel by balloon, and geothermal heating. But for the poor there is nothing but misery. They are forced to work very hard for very low wages, insufficient food and no hope of betterment. The few millionaire property owners control everything for their own benefit, maintaining their position as ruling oligarchs by means of widespread corruption. The whole of society is described as "a gorgeous shell . . . rotten at the core".

The author is savage in his condemnation of Jews and millionaires:

"If a community were to send to India and import a lot of man-eating tigers, and turn them loose on the streets, to prey on men, women and children, they would not inflict a tithe of the misery that is caused by a like number of millionaires." And he refers to the "uncrowned monarchs of commerce, whose golden chariots drive recklessly over the prostrate bodies of the people".

This is strong stuff, carefully calculated to upset contemporary property owners. It is a strongly class-conscious novel — much more so than any other speculation of the 19th century — and it is strange to find such class-consciousness emerging from the USA, the land of opportunity, where any poor boy could amass riches by intelligence and hard work.

In *Caesar's Column* Gabriel Weltstein, an innocent young man of Swiss extraction, journeys to New York on business for his Ugandan farm, and soon falls foul of the Plutocracy. He is helped out and befriended by Max, one of the few honest rich men in the country and one of the leaders of an anarchist group who are plotting revolution. Gabriel joins them, finds a shapely romantic interest, and participates in the revolution.

Of course, the revolution leads to enormous slaughter. One of the other anarchist leaders, Caesar Lomellini, has the bright idea of stacking up the 250,000 corpses of soldiers and citizens and using cement to build them into a vast pillar. Guess its name.

The situation in New York gets out of control, and Max, Gabriel and a few friends escape to Uganda by airship to found their own utopian state, built on a base of Marxist socialism — and faulty economics.

Jack London's obsessive socialism continually spilled over into his fiction, but nowhere more strongly than in his novel *The Iron Heel* (1907). This is very much a piece of revolutionary socialist propaganda, an outspoken warning against the complete domination of the working class by the Plutocrats. Basically, the story concerns Ernest Everhard's fight for social justice for the workers against unassailable odds. Set in the relatively close future (mainly 1910-1917), it shows the USA being taken over by the Oligarchy, who acquire trusts and monopoly powers covering most of industry and commerce. This process is reinforced by the old-boy network which rules politics and the legal system. Eventually the Oligarchy's despotism gains them the name of "the Iron Heel".

Everhard is identified as a potential danger early on, due to his absolute grasp of sociology and politics. He can win any verbal argument, but his opponents are never willing to play fair. At one point they offer him a high government appointment (US Commissioner of Labour) as a bribe, but he stands by his principles and refuses the post. He is imprisoned on a trumped-up charge, as are many of his followers, but his wife carries on the struggle.

In 1915 he is helped to escape from prison. Later he and his wife, Avis, witness the destruction of Chicago by the militia of the Iron Heel in order to forestall a socialist uprising. His death in 1932 is mentioned but not detailed.

The novel's structure is a curious one. It is obviously being written by Avis Everhard after her husband's death, but there are frequent footnotes by an editor seven hundred years in the future, more than three hundred years after a successful revolution and the establishment of a socialist democracy. While very little is futuristic in the story apart from the Iron Heel itself, some of the notes show that the author had a good imagination for future possibilities. For example: "Even as late as that period [1925] cream and butter were still crudely extracted from cow's milk. The laboratory preparation of foods had not yet begun."

H. G. Wells' *When the Sleeper Wakes* and "A Story of the Days to Come" (both 1899) portray a similar situation, set in about the year 2100, with a tiny number of immensely rich property owners who oppress the starving masses until (in *When the Sleeper Wakes*) the awakened Sleeper, Graham, becomes a symbol of awakened socialism, and a workers' revolt ensues. A very similar warning occurs in *Metropolis*, the 1926 film on which was based the novel by Thea von Harbou (first publication in English 1927). Here, too, there is a workers' revolt.

Two novels in which the tyranny of the few over the masses is very much political — a fascist dictatorship rather than purely economic control — are Sinclair Lewis' *It Can't Happen Here* (1935), set in the USA, and Andrew Marvell's *The Minimum Man* (1938), set in the UK. The latter, obviously based on Oswald Mosley's British Fascist Party of the 1930s, refers to a right-wing coup early in 1970, mentions government brutality, concentration camps, the persecution of the Jews, blackshirts and "the Party", and describes the successful left-wing counter-coup later in the year.

Although *It Can't Happen Here* is Sinclair Lewis' demonstration that a fascist dictatorship could occur in the USA, it is intended more as a warning of the corruption which the absolute power of dictatorship brings, rather than simply a condemnation of fascism.

Set in the immediate future (1936-40), it shows how Buzz Windrip, a brilliant orator, attains the presidency of the USA on a basically socialist platform. His strong nationalist and racist views become apparent only gradually, as he starts to persecute the negroes and, to a lesser extent, the Jews. "All negroes shall be prohibited from voting, holding public office, practising law, medicine, or teaching in any class above the grade of grammar school, and they shall be taxed 100 per cent of all sums in excess of $10,000 per family per year which they may earn or in any other manner receive ... Negroes shall, by definition, be persons with at least one-sixteenth coloured blood."

Windrip's régime progresses to concentration camps, suppression of the press, widespread brutality towards the common people, the elimination of political opponents, and war on allies and neighbouring states in order to "unite the country against the common foe" — not only paralleling the contemporary situation in Hitler's Germany but also anticipating developments there.

The protagonist is Doremus Jessup, a small-town newspaper proprietor and editor, who comes to realize just what Windrip is and how he has achieved his position. "The tyranny of this dictatorship isn't primarily the fault of Big Business, nor of the demagogues who do their dirty work. It's the fault of Doremus Jessup! Of all the conscientious, respectable, lazy-minded Doremus Jessups who have let the demagogues wriggle in, without fierce enough protests." Jessup does protest, and is put into a concentration camp. He escapes and helps the underground movement to stir up the people of the USA against Windrip, but the author provides no happy ending — just the prospect of a long struggle.

Certainly the warning is clear: "it" could all too easily happen here. The book must have shattered the complacency of many of its contemporary readers. But there is another warning here, too. At the time of Lewis' writing, most of the western world regarded the rise of Hitler with a fair amount of favour — concentration camps, territorial expansion, mass extermination: these were still to come. Lewis showed their inevitability once a fascist state has been set up, and cautioned against approval of such a state. His contemporaries must have felt that he was being unnecessarily harsh towards Hitler: time was to prove him right.

Among the novels which provide a dire warning of the perils of socialism or communism none is so outspoken or violent as William Le Queux's *The Unknown Tomorrow* (1910). Written in Le Queux's usual highly emotional journalistic style, this describes a socialist revolution in Britain in 1935. For some years, ever since the Anglo-German war of 1912, Britain's economic position has declined, with overseas demand for British goods at a low ebb and many workers unemployed. All sections of the population are affected, though naturally the working class are the worst hit. In several parts of the country there are strikes and demonstrations, notably at Glasgow, where seven hundred are killed by the army.

The situation is ripe for a political swing to the left. MP Henry Harland puts forward a peaceful declaration of socialist revolutionary intent, but this is taken by the workers as a license to overthrow the establishment by violent means. Atrocities begin immediately, as the working class rises up in revolt.

As in his *The Great War in England in 1897* and *The Invasion of 1910,*

Le Queux cleverly uses the names of well known streets and buildings in various parts of the country as the setting for many gory and horrifying events in which the rich are robbed and killed, their homes burned and priceless possessions deliberately destroyed, in chapters with titles like "Death to the Rich" and "London Under the Red Terror".

A revolutionary council is set up to govern the country, with Harland as its president and the brutal George Sillence as a deputy. On November 1st that year there are elections in which the socialists win every seat. Their programme of reform is very radical, and not even the socialists themselves unanimously support it, although some of the items included are obviously very worthy. There are fourteen proposals:

(1) a legal working day of seven hours;
(2) minimum legal wage of thirty shilling a week for both sexes;
(3) distribution among the people of all profits from state-owned industries;
(4) abolition of all direct taxation;
(5) free maintenance of all attending state schools;
(6) pensions for both sexes after the age of sixty;
(7) establishment of state pawnshops;
(8) establishment of state restaurants;
(9) public ownership of all hotels and the sale of alcoholic liquors;
(10) abolition of the standing army;
(11) public ownership of food and coal supply;
(12) abolition of the marriage tie;
(13) nationalisation of land; and
(14) repudiation of the National Debt.

A fifteenth proposal, to abolish the Christian faith because "we should acknowledge no master", is defeated at that point but later carried out because Christian aims conflict with those of socialism. There is much doubt over item (12) — the abolition of the marriage tie — even though its intention is to make the woman "a comrade of her husband, and not his slave". Also, all children are made state property, sweeping away family life.

Yet there is no possibility of the state being in a position to pay the minimum wage or to fund the cost of free schooling or pensions, because there is no industry or trade or taxation to provide an income. "The new Socialist State was engaged in pulling down all existing institutions, not in rebuilding them. That was to come later on, they told the country."

It becomes increasingly obvious, to the socialist leaders as to the reader, that the régime must collapse. Disillusionment sets in when the minimum wage of thirty shilling a week fails to materialize after a year of waiting, and socialist rule ends by common consent in January 1937. At this point Britain is so weak economically that Germany decides she is not worth invading! Thus Le Queux damns socialism as being violent, ruinous and impossible in practice. He does so in the most convincing manner.

A very similar pattern is followed by J. D. Beresford in his novel *Revolution* (1921). Here the socialist revolution occurs in 1922 or 1923 and is less violent. Beresford was presenting his warning (against the Russian revolution of 1917 being repeated in the UK) in terms of individual human reactions rather than casualties. It is an appeal for pacifism, but presented through the example of its protagonist rather than by sickening the reader with an excess of killing. Also, *Revolution* confines itself to a single village, in the London commuter belt, showing the effects of a general strike, the problems of food shortage, the setting up of a Bolshevist cooperative, and the eventual right-wing counter coup at the end of the year.

A different approach is to show not a socialist revolution but the iniquities of socialism or communism as present in a long-existing state. Best known of these is Yevgeny Zamyatin's *We* (1924), a clever satire on the Soviet system, and fully described elsewhere in this book. Although the presentation used in *We* is anything but straightforward, the warning against a state which maintains absolute control over its citizens is unmistakable.

Another work on this theme which is interesting, despite its inherent lack of credibility, is *Unborn Tomorrow* by John Kendall, first published in 1933. Set in the UK in 1995, this shows the world as a communist state, controlled from Moscow. This situation has prevailed since 1938, when Russian troops invaded all of Europe. Over the years everything has become state controlled.

What has evolved is almost a utopia, but one which resembles a rather restrictive boy scout camp. There is a universal three-hour working day; all poverty, hunger, illness and unemployment have vanished; and status is achieved according to merit, with frequent transfers of personnel to avoid favouritism. But social problems abound. In particular there is a falling birthrate and a great shortage of females, so most men live in blocks of rooms, eating communally and spending their leisure time in enforced activities such as rambles, physical training and lectures. There is a state ideology, with hymns and prayers every evening, although religions are not banned. As all children are raised by the state there is never any home life.

Nor is there any freedom. Only three grades exist, with the majority of people in Grade 3. There is more luxury for Grade 1 members but little more freedom. Almost everybody seems to grumble about the system (which seems virtually unworkable, although described by the author with little trace of humour). The falling population has meant that several countries — in general, those farthest from Moscow — have been abandoned, including for example Australia, China, Ireland

and Scotland. Everything seems poised for the system to collapse.

The plot follows the adventures of a rebel who is motivated by love for a particular girl rather than a conscious desire to change the system. Eventually the two of them escape to the Lake District of England where, after five years of idyllic happiness, they learn from the radio that the communist ideals are being abandoned as a failure.

Ayn Rand's *Anthem* (1938) tells a similar story but with much more bitterness and (on the part of the author, at least) greater political awareness. It is satirical, almost an allegory against communism, set in a primitive future, some centuries after the "Unmentionable Times" when war came and the great secrets of science were lost to the world.

Society is based upon collectivism to a ridiculous degree. No individuality is permitted. The word "we" is used instead of the word "I", which has been outlawed and become forgotten. Nobody is allowed to be better than anyone else. It is a very harsh and hard-working society, without leisure or joy. "Everything which is not permitted by law is forbidden." There is no family life, and men and women are habitually kept apart except for forced mating. It is, in effect, a slave society.

The narrator, Equality 7-2521 (all names are of this kind now), is tall and intelligent — both of which qualities are crimes. His teachers tell him: "There is evil in your bones. Equality 7-2521, for your body has grown beyond the bodies of your brothers." At school he tries not to show that he is always the first to understand what is taught, but even so the World Council is afraid of his potential and, when the time comes for him to be assigned his profession for life, he is made a street sweeper.

In fact it is this lowly occupation which gives him the chance to rebel. He finds a grille at ground level which leads down to a short stretch of underground tunnel. Despite the incredibly severe penalties for any crime or infringement of the laws (ten years' imprisonment for stealing a candle; burning at the stake for uttering the word "I") he sneaks off regularly to this subterranean refuge, and there keeps a diary: the book *Anthem*. Also he carries out experiments, studying science from old books and building an electrical battery.

But any form of science — or progress — is now forbidden. Also "What is not done collectively cannot be good" — "And if this should lighten the toil of men . . . then it is a great evil, for men have no cause to exist save in toiling for other men." Equality 7-2521 is forced to escape into the Uncharted Forest. There he is joined by his illicit girl friend, Liberty 5-3000. Eventually they find a long-lost house and, in books therein, rediscover the word "I". As Equality 7-2521 says, "The word 'We' is as lime poured over man, which sets and hardens to stone, and crushes all beneath it." Not only does this novel (which is little more than a novelette — unlike Rand's other predictive novel, *Atlas Shrugged* (1957), which is vast) attack the essence of communism, showing it up for what it might be, and for what Ayn Rand believed it is, it also satirizes Zamyatin's *We,* itself a satire.

A book which is not so much a dire warning of an imposed communist or fascist government as of a particular nationality of imposed government is *When William Came* by "Saki" (H. H. Munro), first published in 1913. Professor I. F. Clarke in *The Tale of the Future* calls this "the best of all the 'German invasion' stories". In fact, this fine novel deals not with war or invasion but only with their aftermath — a UK occupied by the Germans.

It is set in the immediate future: the war and invasion have come in the autumn of, presumably, 1914. Everything has been very swift, catching the UK unawares. This is all explained to an Englishman who was ill and abroad at the time, and has returned to find German occupation a *fait accompli.*

The British politicians had believed: "War between two such civilized and enlightened nations is an impossibility". But a week later it has happened, is all over. "Our half-trained and our untrained men could not master the science of war at a moment's notice, and a moment's notice was all they got."

The stranger-in-a-strange-land approach is well used here. Murrey Yeovil has been away from England for only about nine months but he returns to his country to find it already partly Germanized, with bilingual street signs (such as Regentstrasse), bilingual cab drivers, continental street cafés, and a large number of occupying Germans in an even larger number of fancy uniforms.

Yet the Germans are not shown as brutal conquerors; the author is much more subtle than that. Relatively few people have left for the colonies, which are still British. The king and his court are now in Delhi. Many things in Britain have not changed; life goes on. Murrey's wife Cicely is an important member of London society, organizing parties, fraternizing with the enemy. Her husband disapproves, but is powerless to stop her . . . or the Germans. Although the occupying forces have introduced a few rules and regulations they have done remarkably little to cause change. They want the UK to remain the UK because they like it that way — except for a few small trifles like the use of arms (the British are now forbidden any military training) and the Union Jack. At the end of the book a crumb of comfort is offered: perhaps the youth of Britain will be raised to hate the invaders, growing into a force which will keep British nationalism alive and eventually free the country.

A similar warning is contained in *If Hitler Comes* by Douglas Brown and Christopher Serpell (originally published in 1940 as *Loss of Eden*). Set in the immediate future, it shows the UK government signing a treaty of "Friendship and Mutual Assistance" with Hitler. There is immediate press censorship — "a pure formality, of course" — and the way has been paved for German troops to be stationed in the UK and for various repressive measures to be taken, as they had been in Germany.

This is a much harsher occupation than in *When William Came*.

A novel which bridges the gap between dire warnings of totalitarian régimes and those of misused science and technology is Aldous Huxley's *Brave New World* (1932). According to an author's foreword dated 1946, the theme of the book "is not the advancement of science as such; it is the advancement of science as it affects human individuals."

The setting is a high-technology totalitarian state some four hundred years in the future, where the people are kept subservient by the use of the carrot rather than the stick. Subjected to a deluge of propaganda even before their ectogenic birth, all citizens are taught to love the state and to be content with their fixed status (there are five grades, from the tall and intelligent Alphas to the small, simian, semi-moronic Epsilons; grading depends on chemical treatment at the foetal stage and is carefully planned, producing exact numbers of each). " 'I'm glad I'm not an Epsilon,' said Lenina, with conviction. 'And if you were an Epsilon,' said Henry, 'your conditioning would have made you no less thankful that you weren't a Beta or an Alpha.' "

In some ways this totalitarian future is a utopia, because all are clean, well fed and happy (and kept that way by constant indoctrination; by the psychedelic drug, *soma;* and by various leisure activities such as Obstacle Golf and a multi-sense entertainment form extrapolated from the cinema — the "feelies"). There is also plenty of casual sex without guilt or commitment, and a state religion based on Henry Ford, with the T symbol (from the Model T Ford) substituted for the cross. The Alphas, in addition, have much freedom and their own private aircraft. All grades are given work to suit their level of intelligence, so that the whole world will be content and trouble-free, whether at work or at play.

The warning here, then, is of the dehumanization of Man by science and technology. This is particularly so in the sphere of reproduction, which is divorced from sex and totally artificial. The "budding" of fertilized Gamma, Delta and Epsilon ova to produce dozens of identical embryos — a system analogous to cloning — seems particularly distasteful. There is very little privacy for anyone, because secrecy and solitude are discouraged (though not to the same extent as in Zamyatin's *We*). There is, of course, no family life, and no one knows who their parents were — the only subject where a taboo is recognized. Marriage does not occur, and long liaisons between couples are discouraged.

The system of grades is justified by the state because it provides the right quality of citizen for every level of occupation; an experimental community of Alphas proved to be a disaster, with strikes and a civil war. Similarly, the working day is fixed at seven and a half hours in order to keep people occupied, and a local experiment with a four-hour day produced "unrest and a large increase in the consumption of *soma*".

But Huxley's novel is not just a caution against totalitarianism or the misuse of science, it is also a satire of contemporary life and of the futuristic utopias of other writers. This is why, in several places, he prefers to score points off his contemporaries or to make witty asides (for example, on the "feelies": "There's a love scene on a bearskin rug; they say it's marvellous. Every hair of the bear reproduced") rather than concentrate on producing a wholly consistent and credible future prediction.

Most of the warnings of Man's capability of destroying himself and his planet by the careless testing of some new device which he does not fully comprehend or cannot properly control are intended either as satires or as escapist adventures.

Karel Čapek's play *R.U.R.* (first English translation published in 1923), about robots, artificial constructions of flesh and blood which look human and are used to perform menial tasks, was intended as a satire on the class struggle. But the robots, as they rise up and kill everybody in the world (there is one survivor), are a symbol not only of the proletariat but of technology getting out of hand. Čapek's robots are shown to be both good and bad; they serve mankind well but they also lead to his extinction. The same can be said of the motor car, and of most industrial processes.

Čapek was making the same point — perhaps more consciously — in another satire, *The Absolute at Large.* Here the Karburators, which serve man by extracting every particle of power out of fuel (thus providing very cheap power for all purposes) also release elements of God — the Absolute — upon an unprepared world, with disastrous results.

Twenty years before *R.U.R.*, a satirical dystopia involving robots was serialized in *Argosy.* This was William Wallace Cook's *A Round Trip to the Year 2000,* which did not appear in book form until 1925 and thus came to be looked upon as a copy of Čapek's work. In fact, Cook's picture of the year 2000 contains a number of original features. The robots, known as muglugs, are true automata, made of metal and built as servants; but they rise up in revolt and go on a spree of destruction with electric guns. There is a high level of technology, but life is rather difficult and dangerous. For example, air is monopolized by the Air Trust and rented out to individuals for breathing purposes, and there are always airships overhead, from which things are frequently dropped. (The idea of selling air was later used as the basis of a novel, *The Air Trust* by George Allan England (1915); however, this was a warning against monopoly powers rather than against the misuse of technology.)

In E. M. Forster's satirical story "The Machine Stops", more fully described elsewhere, the warning is aimed not at the development and use of technology but at Man's reliance on it. In a far future society the

Machine supplies all mankind's wants, and has come to supplement Man's body (though in a psychological sense only); when the Machine fails everything stops and mankind dies. It is a story concerned more with making its point than with credibility.

New and invincible weapons, which their eccentric inventor (or, if he is high-principled, somebody else who kills him for his invention) uses to make himself master of the world, are a common feature of science fiction. Although all such tales can be interpreted as an implied warning, few are intended as such.

A fairly early example is *Emperor of the World* by C. J. Cutcliffe Hyne (first published in 1910 as *Empire of the World*). This is a romantic farce, which means that the eccentric inventor of this particular ray acts with the very best of intentions and never actually kills anybody.

The inventor (also the book's hero) is Jack Bryn-Scarlett MP, brilliant and well born but impoverished (MPs were not paid a salary until 1911). He invents the "New Force", a wonder ray that reduces iron to a "yellow sludge", its "two or more constituent elements". The ray can be finely controlled at any distance (thousands of miles, where necessary). Bryn-Scarlett, using the eponymous title *"Imperator Mundi"*, manages to sink ships, melt telephone cables and destroy printing presses at will by manipulating controls in his London apartment; his object is to prevent war between the UK and Germany by causing the German states to become independent from each other again.

The farcical side to all this is that while he is styling himself *"Imperator Mundi"* he is virtually penniless. His landlady locks him out of his flat because he cannot pay the rent, so he takes a room at his club (which is just four doors along the road) and climbs across the rooftops to reach his apparatus and save the UK. At one point he even takes a job doing electrical fitting in order to earn enough money to eat. At length he marries a wealthy woman and lives happily ever after!

S. Fowler Wright's novel *Power* (1933) is a grim account of a similarly destructive ray. Its inventor intends to demonstrate its power by destroying central London, and then plans to blackmail the world into giving him all the money and alcohol and women he wants!

His friend Stanley Maitland MP kills him (after being told all the secrets of the invention) and then holds the country to ransom for various political and social changes. He is an idealist and, although he tries hard to use his power to make the UK a better place, he is still employing technology to acquire power and then misusing that power. In particular he wants to give people more freedom by stopping the proliferation of ever more complex laws. He wants to stop the slaughter on the roads, all idleness and waste, birth control, vivisection, etc. In the event he comes to an arrangement with various members of the government, allowing him to rule by order throughout the year 1934. He succeeds fairly well and does not succumb to corruption, but this in no way invalidates the book's warning.

The World Set Free (1914) by H. G. Wells is partly a caution against the development of new weapons of war. In particular it includes "atomic bombs", which are dropped by hand from open aircraft and go on exploding for ever, though their power is halved every seventeen days, leaving gold as a by-product. (In fact Wells' novel was not the first to use the term "atomic bomb" to refer to the ultimate in destructive power; the credit for that must go to Robert Cromie in his novel *The Crack of Doom* (1895), unless some even earlier challenger can be unearthed. Cromie's description of the event was no more accurate than Wells'.) But later in this novel the world does manage to control its advances in science and technology, and a kind of utopia is produced.

One of the best pre-1945 descriptions of an atomic explosion is to be found in Harold Nicolson's *Public Faces* (1932). Although primarily a political satire, this demonstrated the ease with which world war can break out as a result of misunderstandings and mistakes. Some unique mineral deposits found on an island in the Persian Gulf, and known only to the UK, enable the construction of very high-speed rocket aircraft and an atomic bomb. In June 1939 the aircraft are (with consummate idiocy) tested at low level over various foreign cities, and the atomic bomb is tested, without adequate safeguards, in the western Atlantic.

While the rocket aircraft do little more than shatter a few windows by breaking the sound barrier over Paris, Berlin, Moscow, New York, Cairo, Tokyo, etc., the atomic explosion is much more provocative. The bomb is dropped by rocket and observed from what is thought to be a safe distance — intended to be fifty miles — by HMS *Albatross*. But the explosion produces an enormous cloud of steam which engulfs the *Albatross* and also a US cruiser nearby. An aircraft sent up by the US ship escapes to tell the tale. "The sea below was hidden by the steam, which changed gradually to a thick black cloud whirling westwards with the speed of a hurricane." A long-term result is the diversion of the Gulf Stream, providentially providing the UK with a warmer climate.

An even more spectacular result from an atomic test is envisaged by Neil Bell in *The Lord of Life* (1933). Intended as a character study of a lower-class nonentity before and after a world disaster, the disaster itself is a warning against uncontrolled scientific experimentation. An archetypal mad scientist tries to extort a great deal of money from the UK government in return for details of his atomic findings.

When his request is refused he splits a succession of atoms, causing the Earth to "stop dead in its tracks, cease to revolve round its axis and cease also to move in its orbit around the Sun" — at least, for a minute or two. The result of this is that most of Earth's air, water and lifeforms go shooting off into space, never to be seen again, together with all traces of human civilization except an experimental submarine and, as is eventually revealed, a high-altitude aircraft with a girl aboard. While the setting is not particularly scientific it is at least dramatic, provides its warning and conveniently clears the decks so that the plot can go in the direction the author intends.

It is a moot point as to whether one can warn against a *natural* disaster of world-shaking proportions, such as the Moon crashing into the Earth: the caution can only be against that particular disaster occurring — and, anyway, there is little that forewarned humanity could do to prevent the Moon from spiralling down and colliding with us! Perhaps the detailing of future disaster may be interpreted as a warning or reminder of mankind's continued frailty as compared to the power of nature. Nevertheless, let us look at three typical natural disasters, respectively due to plague, ecodisaster and cosmic collision.

"The Scarlet Plague", by Jack London, first appeared in 1915. It is the story, told looking back from the year 2073, of the plague which appears in 2013, killing nearly all of humanity — eight billion of them. A very few people, perhaps one in five or ten million, are naturally immune, but no serum or other treatment is ever developed, and none who contract the disease recover. The great difficulty is in tracing carriers, since the disease has an incubation period of three weeks during which it shows no sign of its presence — then a red rash develops and death ensues within an hour.

The result, inevitably, has been a regression to barbarism. The old man who tells the story of the plague yet again to his mocking grandchild is a former professor of English at a US university; he believes himself to be the only person left on Earth who can read.

It is claimed that the story was written as a warning not of plague but of the "fascist-like plutocracy" which was controlling the USA in 2013. This seems to be overstating the case, judging from the story alone, for it includes virtually none of the revolutionary socialism of which *The Iron Heel* is so full.

Ecodisaster can spring from any of a thousand small beginnings. In *Nordenholt's Million* by J. J. Connington (1923) it springs from a fireball which brings about a mutation in a few bacteria. But these are denitrifying bacteria, which liberate nitrogen from nitrogenous compounds (such as nitrates in the soil), so that plants cannot make use of it. The mutated bacteria are much more efficient at this job, and multiply very rapidly. The effect is, of course, that plants die.

The affected area quickly spreads, aided by intercontinental aircraft, to cover the whole world. Everywhere crops are dying. While politicians call meetings and wonder where it will all end, only Nordenholt, a far-sighted millionaire, realizes the true gravity of the situation — he knows that millions in the country are bound to starve, and billions worldwide, but there is absolutely no way of saving them.

He prepares a plan for saving some of the UK's population. Assuming dictatorial powers, he establishes a community of five million around Glasgow in the Clyde Valley. He advertises for a million manual workers to join him — "Nordenholt's Million". The area is forcibly evacuated, the five million installed, and road and rail links with the rest of the country broken to avoid invasion by starving hordes. The task of this community is to produce enough nitrogenous minerals to make the soil fertile again as soon as the bacteria die out, and despite some sabotage the plan succeeds. Nordenholt dies of strain but the community goes on to build a utopia.

That example of the Moon crashing into the Earth occurs in R. C. Sherriff's *The Hopkins Manuscript* (1939; revised as *The Cataclysm*, 1958). The narrator, Edgar Hopkins, a bachelor in his mid-forties living quietly in a Hampshire village on a small private income, is among the first to learn of the impending disaster because he is a member of an astronomical society: the members are given ten months' warning but are sworn to secrecy.

The government launches a national drive to build bomb shelters, though this is not taken very seriously. After the news is broken to the general public, with about four months to go (it has to be announced because by now the Moon is visibly larger and closer), there is little panic but much more energy put into the shelter-building. There are some tidal disturbances in advance, then the cataclysm occurs, on schedule, and the Moon splashes down in the north Atlantic, filling it. Quite large numbers are killed, despite the shelters.

Hopkins does not go to the local shelter, preferring to trust to his own house. He survives the "tornado, earthquake and flood", but finds a large ship from Southampton Water occupying his field the next morning. The rest of the book is concerned with the struggle to grow enough food for the people of Britain.

Hopkins goes on a trip "to the Moon", which overlaps Cornwall "to within three miles of Penzance". He is disappointed by the "immense slag-heap of grey, broken slate stretching as far as we could see, like some gloomy, ghostly continent of primeval times".

At length a European war breaks out over the partitioning of the Moon's mineral wealth. The Asian and African nations unite to invade Europe, and the white man's doom is sealed.

There are no other common categories of cautionary predictions, but many individual novels highlight some particular doom or dystopia.

Into this rag-bag group must go Max Pemberton's 1901 novel *Pro Patria*, about a French plot to dig a tunnel under the English Channel for invasion purposes. It is one of several novels of that period which feature a tunnel as a means of invasion.

Set close to the date of writing, it has as its hero Alfred Hilliard, an English army officer on leave in France. He meets a former acquaintance, half-French and quickly identifiable as the villain of the piece, who lures him into the "coal-mines" at Calais and then, once Hilliard has seen what is obviously a tunnel pointing towards England, accuses him of being a spy. Hilliard manages to escape from the tunnel and, by much deviousness, from France, too.

But back in England no one will believe him. To substantiate his story he searches for the English mouth of the tunnel, which he expects to find close inland from Dover. He does find it, in the grounds of a large house, with French workmen digging from this end, too, but he is spotted and imprisoned in the house. As Hilliard narrates it:

> Here, three miles from the shores of my own country, in a place where no spy — no, not the shrewdest that ever breathed — might have looked for it, here were those who would go down — or it might be, already had gone down — to meet that road of steel which, minute by minute and hour by hour, France thrust out beneath the Channel-bed until it should touch the gardens of England and make her mistress of them. No dream, no hallucination, I said, but a truth so terrible that every impulse of being — my hope of career, my hope of love, my hope of home — was lost in it. For I was a prisoner in that house of mystery when I would have given all my fortune to have cried out the warning to my countrymen.

Needless to say, Alfred Hilliard is released and the plot discovered — though the author is diplomatic enough to mention that this was not a French government scheme. The English end of the tunnel is dynamited and the terrible threat of invasion lifted from British shoulders — until the next such novel.

During the 1890s writers seem to have had an obsessive need to produce novels about the terrible deeds of anarchists. Sometimes they were the heroes (as in Donnelly's *Caesar's Column* or George Griffith's *The Angel of the Revolution);* at other times they were villains.

Hartmann the Anarchist, or The Doom of the Great City (1893) by E. Douglas Fawcett is definitely in the latter category. It is the fast-moving tale of an anarchist attack on London. The date is unspecified but it seems to be about 1915. The attack is carried out by an airship (constructed of a new silver-grey metal, stronger than steel yet as light as cardboard), a type of enclosed dirigible driven by small propellers, with hydrogen and sand tanks.

Under the leadership of Hartmann and Swartz the anarchists drop bombs on the centre of London, causing great loss of life: Fawcett seems to relish destroying well known landmarks — the Houses of Parliament, the Tower of London, and so on — in the same way as does William Le Queux. The anarchists also fire machine guns at the panic-stricken crowds and drop petrol bombs. They are aided by more anarchists on the ground, said to number "12,000 in London alone". Hartmann professes no nationalist or socialist philosophy; his purpose is simply to wreck civilization: "We want no more 'systems' or 'constitutions'." In the end there is some kind of a dispute among the anarchists on the airship, and it explodes.

An outstanding prophecy which warns of the ascendancy of humanism is R. H. Benson's *Lord of the World* (1907). Set in about the year 2000 this describes nothing less than the destruction of Christianity. Already, by the time the book opens, only the Roman Catholic Church survives out of all western religions. The Church of England seems to have been disbanded and some of its places of worship put to secular use : St Paul's Cathedral is now Paul's House — a hall. Even Roman Catholicism is constantly losing members (and priests) to the Masons and the pull of materialism in general.

War threatens between the united Europe and the Eastern Empire, but the mysterious American Julian Felsenburgh visits the East and brings peace. Nothing is known of him except his phenomenal success as a peacemaker. When he appears in London he is found to be astonishingly impressive and commanding, young but with white hair and an absolute gift of oratory. He seems to be more than human and is offered the presidency of Europe, then of the world. He is made into a god, as the head of a new and nonspiritual "religion" which springs up. This is a form of humanism, its rituals based on Masonry, yet making use of the settings of old churches (and, in many cases, of lapsed Catholic priests to perform the rituals). Attendance at the year's four major ceremonies is made compulsory, although penalties for dissenters are light. Throughout the novel a Catholic dimension is shown, as the Church continues to shrink, to be beaten constantly back towards Rome.

But some Catholics seek to destroy this new humanist movement by bombing Westminster Abbey during the year-end service. Their plot is discovered and, as a cardinal is on his way from Rome to prevent it, many volors (aircraft) fly to Rome and bomb the Vatican out of existence. Because a convocation of cardinals is in session, the Catholic Church is all but wiped out. The remaining cardinal is appointed Pope and goes to live in secret in Nazareth, appointing a new hierarchy of cardinals.

Meanwhile the persecution of Catholics grows. Felsenburgh orders them to recant or else be put to death. During a convocation of the new Pope's cardinals at Nazareth, Felsenburgh and other world leaders rendezvous there in volors to kill them all — but the Apocalypse comes to forestall this. Many of the predictions in this novel are very interesting and accurate, even though religion is not being replaced by humanism — yet.

A final and different warning is that voiced by A. G. Street in his novel *Already Walks Tomorrow* (1938). He warns of England's virtual starvation during the mid 1940s due to bad farming in the UK and the rest of the world over the previous decade or so. The book is made entertaining and extremely credible by its first quarter being set in the past. It is indeed difficult to see where fact and fiction meet.

The plot follows the fortunes of James Brockway, a Wiltshire farmer who is forced to quit his farm by the poor returns of the 1920s and early 1930s. He gets a Ministry of Agriculture job and distinguishes himself by hard work, expert knowledge and bluntness. He is promoted but eventually (late 1938) resigns on a matter of principle: he cannot agree with the government wheat subsidy to farmers because it will encourage them to grow wheat year after year, ruining the soil and achieving ever smaller yields.

But his uncompromising stand has been noticed, and rich farmer Lord Ellwood employs him to tour the farmlands of South Africa, Argentina and North America in 1939-40. Brockway is disgusted at the bad land management (dustbowls, etc.). His report is dynamite, forecasting a world food shortage. Lord Ellwood employs him to find a large acreage of derelict English farmland and put it into good order, to prove that it can be done. This Brockway does during 1941-42. He is so successful that he is given the chance to manage and improve other farms.

By 1945 (there is no World War II) the world food shortage has come. The UK has to take stern measures to ration food and to grow and conserve more. Brockway is appointed Controller of Agriculture and brings in harsh but necessary measures. There is martial law in force: rioters or food hoarders are shot. Abroad the position is worse. Gradually things improve in the UK due to Brockway's rules, and more food is grown.

In 1948 he is elected to Parliament and makes a great impression on the public (Parliament is televised and everybody has a TV). As Minister of Agriculture his policies are put into practice, including two years' national service working on the land for all youths — but not for girls; the novel was written before the advent of the female land army. All land is nationalized by the end of 1948. Eventually Brockway retires with a knighthood.

There is a romantic strand running through the book, and a good deal of pro-hunting propaganda. Brockway's creed is worth noting: "Men may come and go, but the land remains and its needs must be served." It is not difficult to tell that the author is giving his own recommendations here, based on many years' farming experience. It is not always enough just to warn; one must provide answers and show them succeeding, too.

This is an early novel of future ecodisaster. In recent decades ecology and, in parallel, overpopulation have provided the theme for increasingly more works of prediction, which we shall look at later. The warnings have become not only more frequent but also more plausible and more rigorously researched. This is, of course, because in our own lifetimes some of the predictions may come true.

3 THEME: WAR

The tremendous gulf between our attitudes and those of our ancestors is at its widest where the literature of war is concerned: even the most belligerent of the modern powers seem to feel the need at least to *profess* pacifism, however hypocritically, in a way that would have amazed a Roman, an Elizabethan or even a Victorian. To our ancestors, war was as inescapable a part of the natural order as were fire, flood or earthquake, and was in many ways more desirable. War preserved the fabric of society — your society — from foreign influences, defended your trade from competitors, and maintained internal peace and security — that is, just so long as you won: if you did not you naturally looked to another war to redress the balance.

In days when there actually were victors this was natural and understandable; today, remembering the devastation of two world wars and the possibilities of sudden and wholesale destruction, nobody can be so confident. Experience of military service was once an essential attribute for a man of quality, it "stiffened the character"; if the stiffening proved more permanent, that, too, was in the nature of things. Today the peoples of the developed world are becoming increasingly unmilitary, at least insofar as individual aspirations are concerned, and an abhorrence of war is the rule rather than the exception in world literature. But, to the people of the 18th and 19th centuries, war was inevitable and military prowess glorious.

When our forefathers set out to explore a future that seemed suddenly changeable, therefore, they took war with them. It was only rather later that they began to wonder whether war *should* have a future.

Between 1800 and 1945 the UK was invaded by foreign troops at least a hundred times. Fortunately all of these invasions were fictional; but had it not been for the warnings they provided a real and successful invasion might easily have occurred during that period. To say that particular stories of predicted war stirred up public opinion to the point where improvements were made to strengthen the British army and navy, and that it was this added strength which was responsible for preventing a real invasion, is probably not to overstate the case.

This is only one strand in an extremely complex tapestry of war predictions over a period of one and a half centuries. Although a few of the hundreds of books, short stories and pamphlets on this theme were presented as serious works on such subjects as tactics, technology, philosophy, politics or futurology, most took the form of fiction. But the purpose of these fictions was not solely to entertain: some were nothing more than lightweight escapist literature, but most were arguments for rearming or disarming, political treatises designed to arouse British hatred against some particular foreign country, social satires, moral novels, exposés of the power of new weapons, or even allegories of varying obscurity. Most were, in any case, reactions to contemporary political situations, to technological developments, or to other predictions of war; their scope and importance become clear only when we see them in terms of each other and against their own individual backgrounds.

Broadly speaking, three watersheds can be identified during this period — points at which the tenor of the more important predictions changed. The first of these occurred in 1871 with the publication of *The Battle of Dorking* by Sir George Chesney, and the other two with the outbreaks of the first truly global wars in 1914 and 1939.

The Battle of Dorking, an account of a Prussian conquest of the UK, is probably the single most important work in the literature of future wars; it was not the first of its kind, but it was written in such a style and published at such a time that it achieved world renown. The time was right because of the phenomenal rise in importance of Prussia during the preceding decade: since Bismarck's appointment as Chancellor in 1862 the Prussians had, in lightning campaigns, defeated Denmark in 1864, Austria in 1866 and France in 1870. There seemed to be nothing of which they were incapable.

At this time the UK military forces, which had seen no action since the end of the Crimean War fifteen years earlier, were deficient in numbers, poorly organized and outfitted, and insufficiently trained. Chesney set out to force army reforms by publicizing this state of affairs in terms as alarmist as possible.

He was an active soldier. At the time of his writing *The Battle of Dorking* he was a colonel in the Royal Engineers and director of a college of military engineering. He rose to the rank of general, and was later elected to Parliament. The main reason for his story's vividness was his conviction, amounting almost to an obsession, that the British army was badly in need of funds and extensive reorganization. He believed that a Prussian invasion was a strong possibility and that, if one were indeed attempted, it would succeed.

His style is simple and direct. The tale is narrated by a middle-class volunteer who fought against the Prussians and is now, fifty years later, looking back on the invasion. This approach lends a dramatic credibility to the story, especially when the narrator gives a vivid but nonheroic private's-eye view of just a segment of the battle, describing the confusion, the lack of information, the swift breakdown of normality, the long wait for action, and the final terrible realization of defeat.

Chesney's military details are highly convincing. His only weaknesses are naval: he dismisses most of the British fleet as "scattered abroad" on various missions, and then has the remainder easily sunk by a new type of Prussian torpedo.

The Battle of Dorking, only some sixty pages long, was first published in *Blackwood's Magazine* in May 1871 and quickly reprinted as a pamphlet. Its success was overwhelming — 80,000 copies were sold within a month! It had been written to cause a furore and, within a few weeks, it did exactly that. It was speedily translated into most European languages, and was read throughout the civilized world. It was published in the USA later in 1871 under the title *The German Conquest of England in 1875.*

By the end of 1871 more than twenty related pamphlets had appeared in print, mostly rebutting or satirizing Chesney's work. Prime Minister Gladstone scorned *The Battle of Dorking* for being unnecessarily alarmist, but the British people generally seem to have agreed with Chesney: their patriotism was severely piqued by the idea of an invasion from an "empire" only a year or so old. Whatever Gladstone's misgivings, Parliament was not slow to vote fresh funds and reforms.

The importance of Chesney's story does not end there. On the contrary, it became a model which was imitated by a host of other writers — British, French, German — right up to the time of World War I. Each twist and turn of international relations (especially after 1900) was mirrored by the appearance of a group of propagandist books or pamphlets proclaiming war. For example, the Channel Tunnel debate of 1882 gave rise to several stories of the French invasion of Britain *via* the tunnel (the best known of these novels was Max Pemberton's *Pro Patria);* the Franco-Russian *entente* of 1893 sparked off a succession of Franco-Russian invasions of the UK; and the Anglo-Japanese alliance of 1902 was employed in a 1907 novel in which a Japanese force lands at Liverpool to help save the UK from a German invasion. The growth of German imperialism after 1900, coupled with Anglo-German friction in Morocco in 1905, 1909 and 1911, provoked a flood of Anglo-German war stories from both sides.

(As an aside, it is interesting to note that, twenty-six years after *The Battle of Dorking*, H. G. Wells was to use a similar style and approach to Chesney's — and the same setting, Surrey — in *The War of the Worlds* (1897); only the message of the tale and the nature of the enemy had changed.)

The watershed of August 1914 was a less dramatic one in literary terms. The flood of invasion and future-war stories was reduced to a trickle, although this staunching took almost a year — until the horrors of the Battle of the Somme were fully appreciated.

By 1918 the first anti-war books were beginning to appear. These were not simply pacifist writings but tales of future wars which led to either a permanent peace or at least some alternative to the extinction of humanity; in both cases the tone of the writing was very different from that of previous works.

And after 1918 two new trends became apparent: on the one hand there was a group of books that dealt with socialist revolution; on the other there was the steady increase of science fiction, mostly of poor quality, which commonly dealt with far-future wars, glorifying them against gaudy backgrounds of spaceships, deathrays and so on.

The trickle of predictions of imminent war resumed in the early 1930s, but never again did it reach pre-1914 proportions. *The Gas War of 1940,* first published in 1931, is the best known war novel of this period to forecast wholesale destruction, particularly by the use of poison gas, which ravaged not only the enemy but, through accidental leakage, the people who produced it — in melodramatically large numbers. The author was "Miles", a pseudonym of Stephen Southwold, better known under another pseudonym, Neil Bell (the novel itself was alternatively titled *Valiant Clay).*

War no longer meant glory, or even sure defence; it meant the butcher's bill of World War I, the pick of a nation dead on foreign soil, and at home a great generation gap and an exhausted economy. In that light, jingoism seemed hollow, and advocates of war as a purifying force found support only in countries like Germany with little else to hope for.

Prior to August 1914 fewer than a dozen future-war books had originated in the USA. Among these were such titles as *The Battle of the Swash; and the Capture of Canada* (1888) and *The Invasion of New York; or How Hawaii was Annexed* (1897), the latter being a Japanese invasion attempt. The USA's initial neutrality towards the war in Europe caused the publication of several "scare" stories of the Chesney pattern, suggesting that Germany would crush the UK and then invade the USA unless the USA helped the UK. The best known of these was J. Bernard Walker's *America Fallen! The Sequel to the European War* (1915).

The outbreak of World War II in September 1939 brought with it an increase in grim visions of the future. Limited wars between just two countries became almost defunct as a topic. Devastation of the whole world by poison gas, mysterious rays and other wholesale methods foreshadowed the crop of late-'forties atomic disaster novels — and is a theme which still recurs today.

But World War II brought also an increase in novels depicting a future where war has ceased simply because the results would be too catastrophic, leaving neither victors nor spoils. This is a trend which seems to have strengthened and become more common with the passage of time; it is too early to say if this reflects an increase in Man's good sense or just in his capacity for gloomy wishful thinking.

In the years leading up to 1914 it was still widely believed that periodic wars were A Good Thing. War was said to be necessary for the improvement of the species — an extension of Darwinian theories. It would remove sloth and stagnation, strengthen moral fibre, rid the world of those nations which did not deserve to survive and keep the burgeoning population within bounds. As we have noted, a period under fire was considered excellent experience for any young man, and gunboats were despatched to various unruly parts of the world with little more consideration or difficulty than telegrams. Pacifism was not unknown in Victorian times, but it tended to remain hidden behind a blanket of jingoism.

However, there were some works of fiction that were strongly pacifist. In the USA there was Edward Bellamy's utopian novel of 1888, *Looking Backward 2000-1887*. The narrator, Julian West, who has come from 1887, asks about the extension of government functions up to the year 2000, particularly in the field of defence. Dr Leete, his host in the future, casually replies: "We have no wars now, and our government no war powers."

In another famous novel of the period (this time British), Edward Bulwer-Lytton's *The Coming Race* (1871), a race of subterranean superbeings in human shape, the Ana, is described. They have outgrown war, although they possess a great potential killing-power, known as *vril*. This "weapon to end war" has brought about the disbandment of armies and made the use of force and the existence of governments things of the past: everything is instead accomplished by common consent. Although this is not strictly a story of the future, the book is obviously meant to portray metaphorically an ideal future state for the human race: the Ana, our relatives, represent what we could reach by following in their path.

Despite the favourable receptions of novels like these, the most popular futures were still of the "Chesney-rebutted" type. A typical attitude was that of Lord Wolseley, one-time Adjutant-General, the army commander responsible for the British victories against the Ashanti and Egyptians and the prototype of W. S. Gilbert's "Modern Major General". He declared that "all other pleasures pale before the intense, the maddening delight of leading men into the midst of an enemy, or to the assault of some well defended place."

But the British were not alone in this attitude. The German philosopher Treitschke said: "Universal peace is a dream, and not even a beautiful dream." And, just to show that in the period up to 1914 even the doves were hawks, let us remember Theodore Roosevelt's statement: "A just war is in the long run far better for a nation's soul than the most prosperous peace obtained by acquiescence in wrong or injustice."

The result of all this bellicosity was that a Great European War was considered imminent, and in some quarters anticipated with undisguised eagerness, for most of the time between 1871 and 1914. Newspapers and magazines that ran future-war series increased their circulation enormously, the most notorious of such series being in the weekly magazines *Black and White* in 1892 and *Answers* in 1893, and in the London *Daily Mail* in 1906.

The latter two were by William Le Queux, who made a great deal of money out of future-war novels written in a flamboyant, journalistic style. His novel *The Great War in England in 1897* was serialized in *Answers* and published in book form the following year, 1894. It describes an invasion of the UK by the French and Russians. Having lured the UK fleet away to the Mediterranean by false orders put out by a spy in British naval Intelligence, large numbers of the enemy are able to put ashore along the Sussex coast without difficulty.

By Tuesday night, three days after the Declaration of War, two French and half a Russian army corps, amounting to 90,000 officers and men, with 10,000 horses and 150 guns and waggons had landed, in addition to which reinforcements constantly arrived from the French Channel and Russian Baltic ports, until the number of the enemy on English soil was estimated at over 300,000.

It is a bad time for the UK to be invaded, because the army is poorly equipped and below strength, while anarchists and socialists (Le Queux lumps them in together) are engaged in rioting and bomb-throwing in many parts of the country.

When the Royal Navy does manage to collect itself it is beaten by the combined French and Russian fleets, and withdraws with great losses. Other Russian ships bombard Hull, while a French fleet sails up the River Tyne, dealing death and destruction. Of the invading troops, the Russians press on northwestward, sacking Farnham, Reading, Oxford, Banbury and Birmingham without very much opposition. But just south of Manchester they are defeated amid scenes of dreadful slaughter, with over 40,000 dead.

There is a fresh landing of Russian troops at Leith, near Edinburgh, with fierce fighting around Edinburgh and Glasgow — although this, one may safely assume, is merely a ploy on the author's part to let Scottish readers feel they have not been forgotten: in due course the Russians are beaten.

Meanwhile, back in Surrey, the French troops fight their way across the Downs (the defenders are short of equipment and tactical expertise) and enter London, smashing everything as they go. "The hand of the destroyer had reached England's mighty metropolis. The lurid scene was appalling. . . . Never before had such alarm been spread through London; never before had such awful scenes of destruction been witnessed." There are graphic descriptions of artillery shells demolishing Victoria Station, the Grosvenor Hotel, St James's Palace, Marlborough House, most of Regent Street, the Houses of Parliament, Westminster Abbey and the Bank of England. Yet all is not quite lost. At the eleventh hour colonial troops (including Goorkas!) arrive to drive the French back into Surrey. There the combined colonial forces win a great battle. "The butchery was awful." Off Dungeness the Royal Navy redeems itself by beating the French in a resounding manner. Thus the UK is made safe again.

The Invasion of 1910 was serialized in March 1906 in the *Daily Mail* and published in book form later in the year. Here Le Queux had the assistance of Field Marshal Lord Roberts and "a number of the highest authorities on strategy, whose names, however, I am not permitted to divulge" (author's preface) in planning the strategy and tactics. It is basically a similar work to the last, in that it is intended to show how close the UK could come to being successfully invaded because of her unpreparedness for war. This was a theme close to the heart of Lord Roberts, who had long argued that all able-bodied men be required to undergo some military training, and who had instigated the system of civilian rifle clubs (which still exists) in an attempt to increase the numbers of marksmen in the country.

The invading enemy, in 1910, is Germany. A quarter of a million troops are landed on the undefended east coast of England, at various points from Essex to Yorkshire (mainly in Suffolk), not declaring war or bombarding towns from the sea, but sneaking in by night and cutting telephone cables to stop news of their presence from spreading. Within a few days they have fought their way inland on a broad front, capturing Birmingham, Manchester and Sheffield and, after a victory at Chelmsford, laying siege to London. After much fierce fighting to the north and east of London the central areas of the capital are shelled and then occupied. (Once again Le Queux lists many important buildings which are destroyed, including the British Museum, the Royal Exchange, various theatres and churches, the Houses of Parliament and Westminster Abbey.) Strangely enough, Saki's *When William Came*, in which the German invasion of England is accomplished within a week, almost bloodlessly and without destruction, is just as believable and far more horrifying.

Once the Germans of *The Invasion of 1910* are in possession of most of London they feel they have won. They make demands of money and overseas territory (including India) in return for withdrawing, but the

British government (which has escaped to Bristol) makes no reply. Instead the League of Defenders (regular and volunteer soldiers) is formed, and it harasses the Germans in London and elsewhere. The occupying forces, despite ferocious retaliatory measures, do not have the strength to advance further and take the south of London, which is well defended.

Within two weeks of the German occupation of London there is a mass uprising by the League of Defenders. As a German army commander puts it:

We are completely deceived. Our position, much as we are attempting to conceal it, is a very grave one. We believed that if we reached London the British spirit would be broken. Yet the more drastic our rule, the fiercer becomes the opposition. How it will end I fear to contemplate. The British are dull and apathetic, but, once aroused, they fight like fiends.

In a heroic struggle many of the German troops are massacred in the cities they have occupied, and the UK is freed. But she is unable to impose a satisfactory peace treaty on the Germans because of her lack of military and naval strength.

Both these invasion stories by Le Queux became enormously popular, going into numerous English editions and being translated into several European languages.

Nor must it be imagined that the British were unique in producing these gory and martial tales. The Germans and French were almost as prolific, producing translations of the major UK works as well as novels and magazine serials of their own, some of which were then translated into English. The most widely read of these were *Der Weltkrieg — Deutsche Trauma* (translated as *The Coming Conquest of England*) by August Niemann, first published in 1904, and *La Guerre Fatale France-Angleterre (War to the Death Between France and England)*, published in 1901, one of several similar books by Capitaine Danrit. Chauvinism normally dictated that the nationality of the ultimate winner be altered at the time of translation, although Niemann's book was faithfully translated in all its anti-British fervour. From the beginning the author allows no one to mistake his intentions. In a Preface he says:

In my mind's eye I see the armies and the fleets of Germany, France and Russia moving together against the common enemy, who with his polypus arms enfolds the globe. The iron onslaught of the three allied Powers will free the whole of Europe from England's tight embrace. The great war lies in the lap of the future.

It is distinctly a work of wish fulfilment!

Much of the action of *The Coming Conquest of England* is set in India. Russian troops advance through the Khyber Pass, enticing the Indian princes to support them, and defeating the British army without much difficulty. Meanwhile Germany has occupied the Netherlands as a preliminary step to invading the UK. 60,000 German troops are landed in the Firth of Forth and "an equally strong French corps was to land in the south", but the major victory is won at sea, with the German fleet beating the British off Flushing. There is a complex romantic plot, but most of its participants, including the main couple, are killed off. The final scenes are at Hampton Court Palace, where the allies meet to divide up the British Empire between them.

The excuses for all this warmongering were threefold.

Firstly, the horrors of modern global warfare were, despite all the predictions, unimagined until they occurred; a far cry from the "maddening delight" of shooting a few hundred lightly armed Africans, or from the relatively small-scale, short-duration, battles of the Franco-Prussian and American Civil wars, was the death of a million men in the three-month Battle of the Somme.

Secondly, prior to 1914 war had been confined very largely to the military: this had been particularly true of the UK, which had seen no major fighting within its borders for some two hundred years and had not been invaded for some eight hundred and fifty years. In the winter of 1914, however, there was a German naval bombardment of the coast of northeastern England, and German air raids, usually by airship, began over the UK. Despite the very small amount of damage done, the psychological effects of these attacks was enormous, probably quite as great as that of the air raids of 1939-45.

The third excuse was that, prior to World War I, the victor had always profited by his victory.

So the Victorian and Edwardian tradition of bellicosity disappeared the hard way — to the tune of Wilfred Owen's "monstrous anger of the guns", as vast tracts of France became, in Lord Dunsany's words, "a land of craters and weeds and wire and wild cabbages and old German bones", as about ten million soldiers died and something like forty-five *billion* pounds sterling were wasted.

Even then, there was still sufficient aggressiveness remaining to support some fairly inflammatory war predictions in more than one country during the late 1930s. Despite the complex maze of incidents, alliances and misconceptions which led up to the declaration of war in 1914 and which still, more than sixty years later, gives rise to debates about the exact cause of that declaration, the causes of fictional wars described both before and after 1914 are normally either very simple or else ignored altogether.

Many of the better known works did not bother to waste words on causes; they implied what some novels stated openly, that countries went to war for greater national glory and extension of empire. Thus the UK was always a believable invasion target because the whole of Europe envied her empire and her smug, disdainful geographical position just across the English Channel. Because the UK had not been invaded in reality for so many centuries it seemed to be the ambition of every European writer to show how such an invasion could be accomplished, and of every UK writer to prove that it remained an impossible dream. (Russian involvement in fictional wars against the UK is nearly always explained by Russian desires for India — the gateway to the Indian Ocean. This was believable in Niemann's *The Coming Conquest of England* and still believable almost thirty years later in Harry Edmonds' *The Riddle of the Straits* (1931).)

The use of national glory and territorial expansion as sufficient causes of war are universal, and were even applied, albeit implicitly, by H. G. Wells to his marauding Martians; many other science-fiction writers since have given the same motive to their particular invading alien hordes.

The reaction of future-war authors to contemporary events has already been mentioned. Wars were drummed up out of many of the international incidents that occurred during the century and a half between 1800 and 1945 — in fact, some of the more inflammatory stories from people like Le Queux and Niemann actually increased the likelihood of war.

Nor was this trend confined to wars between the UK, France and Germany. The question of Irish Home Rule, debated and rejected in the British Parliament in 1886, caused four tales of Irish rebellion to appear that year; the South African situation provoked a Boer War novel in 1897, two years before the reality; while the Russo-Japanese war of 1904 was forecast in 1898 on the basis of the territorial bones of contention of Korea and the Liaotung peninsula, ceded to Japan in 1895. And this type of anticipation in reaction to worsening relations was still present in the 1930s with, for example, German air raids on London being prophesied in several novels of that decade.

Where a series of wholly fictional international incidents is used to provide a credible cause, hindsight may make the attempt look ridiculous. This is certainly the case with *War in the Air, 1936* by Major Helders, a German, writing in 1932, who explained his proposed Anglo-French war as originating in the Egyptians objecting to the UK military presence guarding the Suez Canal zone, and turning to France for assistance. If the author believed this to be possible then he must have been the only person at that time who did. He even has the British Foreign Secretary saying that Germany, still disarmed, could not be considered as a serious opponent of France. Helders could not have been expected to foresee that, by 1936, a strong Germany under Hitler would have occupied and begun to remilitarize the Rhineland, but he must have been aware of the rapid resurgence of German militarism, embodied in the rise of the Nazis, at the very time he was writing. On the other hand, in Helders' defence, it must be remembered that real wars have been fought for far pettier reasons than the ones that he suggests.

A more plausible cause of war is in support of a particular ideology. Into this category come the clutch of "Red revolution" tales which began to appear after 1918, with such uncompromising titles as *The Red Tomorrow* and *London under the Bolshevics*. An earlier and better known book with this ideological theme was George Griffith's *The Angel of the Revolution*, first published in 1893. Although written as escapist Victorian melodrama, without intending to put across any political message, it deals with a group of socialist terrorists who in 1904 hold the secret of powered flight and use it to bring a lasting peace to a Europe torn by war. Griffith, who had originally been a journalist, became a very popular novelist during the 1890s: *The Angel of the Revolution* was the first and best known of his novels.

Idealism continued to be used as a convenient and believable cause of future war; examples can be found throughout the 1930s and 1940s.

There is no doubt about the most frequent participants in future-war stories up to 1945: the UK *versus* Germany, with the UK *versus* France or Russia also being common. As mentioned above, the frequency of such conquests tended to correspond closely to the international situation of the time. After Chesney's *The Battle of Dorking*, the Anglo-German war became a regular theme, replacing for a time the more traditional prophecy of Anglo-French conflict, and there were few years between 1871 and 1915 when one or more such stories did not appear (in 1907 there were at least eight of them published in the UK alone).

Most of the major European powers were matched against each other at some time, both singly and in groups. That the UK figures largely in so many of these European wars is because — apart from the factor of envy, already mentioned, and that she was a major power and hence likely to be drawn into any such war — most of these works were written either by the UK authors or by those they provoked into responding.

Of the less likely pairings, Major Helders' Anglo-French war of 1936 has already been mentioned. Equally unusual are the few Anglo-American wars, such as *The Great Anglo-American War of 1900* by Captain Anson (1896), in which the USA defeats the UK. There is also an indecisive naval battle between the UK and the USA in H. G. Wells' *The Autocracy of Mr Parham* and a decisive UK victory over the US fleet in *The Riddle of the Straits* by Harry Edmonds.

The most believable of the wars in which the USA is involved are fought against Japan, over possession of various islands in the Pacific, although there was never a great flood of future-war stories with the USA as participant, presumably because of its relative isolation. Nor were Asian invasions of Europe seriously envisaged; books like M.P. Shiel's *The Yellow Danger* (1895) and *The Dragon* (1913; later published as *The Yellow Peril*), in which there are Asian invasions of the UK and Europe — motivated by personal reasons and frustrated by British action in the nick of time — were definitely intended as romps.

Alien invasion has been a common theme since the late 19th century: we will return to it in a later chapter. Among other nonhuman opponents are robots and animals.

The author who brought the word "robot", which comes from the Czechoslovakian word for "work", into the English language, and who wrote about wars against both robots and animals, was the Czech Karel Čapek. His play *R.U.R.* (for *Rossum's Universal Robots*) was first performed in Czechoslovakia in 1921, but within two years an English translation was available and it was being performed in many cities of the world, including London and New York.

The factory of Rossum's Universal Robots produces millions of robots (of organic rather than mechanical construction) which are excellent workers, quick to learn and with perfect memories, but without creative abilities, emotions or souls. After being put to use as soldiers, they revolt and kill all the humans in the world except one. The robot leader, Radius, says: "Slaughter and domination are necessary if you want to be like men. Read history, read the human books." But the robots are individually short-lived and, the secret formula for making them having been destroyed, they begin to die out. A happy ending is provided by the appearance of a pair of "special" robots who are driven to develop emotions and may therefore be able to breed and save the robot race from extinction.

This satire on automation and the capitalist system is deservedly highly regarded, although its theme (originally the Frankenstein-monster theme) has been used frequently since without benefit of satire.

Čapek put across a similar message in *War with the Newts* (1936), in which a race of giant newts — "giant", that is, for newts — which are as intelligent as humans are exploited by Man until they revolt.

This was neither the first nor the last of stories about wars between humans and enlarged animals (although it is certainly the wittiest): the basic theme has cropped up frequently in pulp magazines and in the cinema; the 1933 film *King Kong* is the best known example. The original story of this type is "The Empire of the Ants" by H. G. Wells, first published in 1905, in which a new type of ant, two inches long and with even larger "overseer" ants, begins to spread outwards from the Amazon jungle, overwhelming everything by numbers and intelligence.

Speculation about the weapons to be used in future wars has fascinated many writers and illustrators. The 1800-1945 period was a particularly fertile one for technological advance in general, and speculators always tried to outdo the latest advance. The two first balloon ascents — by Montgolfier and Charles, respectively — were in 1783; exactly 120 years later came powered flight; within forty years of that came military jet aircraft and the atomic bomb.

From the time of the earliest flights there were speculations, most often in pictorial form, concerning the military applications of the balloon. Fulton's submarines and torpedoes were illustrated in military situations in 1810. During the Napoleonic Wars a "Floating Machine Invented by the French for Invading England" was shown in print form, albeit as an object of ridicule, in the *Illustrated London News*. But, of course, this was nothing new: several hundred years earlier Leonardo da Vinci had been busily producing designs for all manner of military machines and gadgets, including flying machines, a diving bell, a giant crossbow, armed chariots and bombs.

A frequently quoted pacifist excuse for new weapons of war was given in *A History of Wonderful Inventions,* written anonymously, which was published in 1862:

> We are quite sure that if any man could invent a means of destruction, by which two nations going to war with each other would see large armies destroyed, and immense treasure wasted on both sides, in a single campaign, they would both hesitate at entering upon another. We repeat, therefore, that in this sense the greatest destroyer is the greatest philanthropist.

We shall return to the topic of "weapons to end war" a little later.

The Battle of Dorking makes no predictions of future weapons, beyond the very unspecific reference to the Prussians' new and conveniently irresistible torpedo. Instead, Chesney takes items of military technology present in 1871, his time of writing — breech-loading rifles and artillery, iron-hulled ships — and vividly demonstrates their killing power in a large-scale war. His concern was primarily with possibility; he did not dare risk more speculation than was absolutely necessary in case ridicule obscured his theme. The hundreds of later writers who jumped onto the future-war bandwagon between 1871 and 1914 were more speculative and less accurate. With notable exceptions, they all failed to foresee the World War I horrors of trench warfare, poison gas, tanks, and immense loss of life.

The most original illustrator of weapons technology during this *"Dorking* to the Somme" period was Albert Robida. His marvellous black-and-white sketches first appeared in the magazine *La Caricature* in 1893, and he wrote and illustrated a future-war novel, *La Guerre au Vingtième Siècle,* later in the decade. His imagination ranged widely; his drawings encompass submarines (and antisubmarine warfare), armed

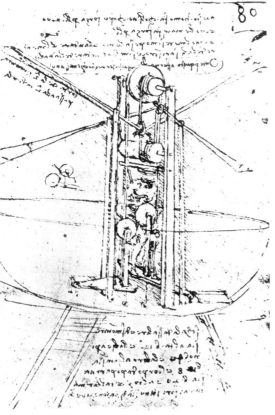

A sketch by Leonardo da Vinci (1452-1519) for a man-powered flying machine. This was a dream which was eventually to come true only in 1979. (See page 168.)

Below: A bridge built from Africa to Britain — an illustration from *The Travels and Surprising Adventures of Baron Munchausen* (1786). (See page 12.)

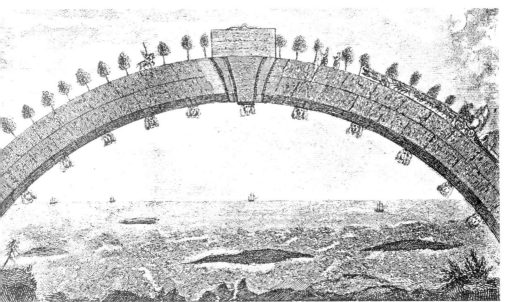

How Will The World End?

By Herbert C. Fyfe.

Many of us are apt, not without some reason, to regard the world we live in as the centre of the universe, and to look upon the sun, the moon, and the stars as objects placed in the heavens for the special benefit of the human race. That the earth is but a minute object in the Cosmos; that it forms one of a number of bodies, many of them larger than itself, revolving around their central luminary, the sun; that there exist in the realms of space myriads of similar suns, centres themselves of other solar systems; that millions of planets, which we cannot see, are inhabited with races of intelligent beings —these are facts of which almost everybody must be cognisant, but on which few bestow much time or thought.

Astronomy teaches that, just as our solar system had a beginning, so it must have an end, and that, as at one time life was impossible upon the earth, so there will come a time when man will no longer be able to exist.

Science, cold and calculating, has foretold the physical end of the world—has prophesied the destruction of the globe and all its contents.

Birth, life, death—it has been well said—appear to be the rule of the universe at large, as well as in our own little corner of it. Suns and planets are evolved, they flourish, and at length decay; and new suns and systems will arise to take their places.

The "End of the World" may be taken in two different senses, as meaning either the annihilation of our planet by sudden catastrophe, or by gradual decay, or else the disappearance of human life from the face of the globe, owing to some state of circumstances, possible, at any rate, if not probable.

It is our purpose in this article briefly to consider some of the opinions held by men of learning and repute regarding the end of the world, and to emphasise the lesson taught by

One of the terrifying predicted possibilities from Herbert C. Fyfe's article "How Will the World End?": giant lobster-like creatures invade the land.

The title artwork for Herbert C. Fyfe's article "How Will the World End?", which appeared in *Pearson's Magazine* in 1900.

Left: The cover of *When Woman Reigns* (1938), by August Anson, speaks a thousand words about the attitudes expressed within. (See page 108.)

Opposite: The perils of building a Channel Tunnel. A German invasion of Britain *via* the newly constructed tunnel has been thwarted at the eleventh hour by the detonation of mines at the Dover exit. The people of Britain, at last realizing the "stupendous folly" of the Tunnel scheme, descend upon the workings and smash them beyond hope of repair in order to avert the threat of any future invasion attempt. This illustration accompanied Walter Wood's short story "The Tunnel Terror" in *Pearson's Magazine*, 1907.

Below: A cartoon in the *Pall Mall Magazine*, 1908, shows how the proceedings of the House of Commons would be brought to a standstill if women members were ever to be elected. (See page 172.)

CÆSAR'S COLUMN

A STORY OF THE

TWENTIETH CENTURY.

By EDMUND BOISGILBERT, M.D

(Ignatius Donnelly.)

"*In-place of Bellamy's picture of peace and contentment, we have a future full of terror and bloodshed, the result of the pride and selfishness of civilization.*"

London: FREDERICK · WARNE · & · CO.

Above: After the Moon had fallen down to Earth and crashed into the Atlantic, according to R. C. Sherriff's *The Hopkins Manuscript* (1939), the nations of the world divided up this great new piece of real estate as depicted in this map. (See page 31.)

Opposite: The cover of Ignatius Donnelly's *Caesar's Column*, first published in 1890. (See page 18.)

Left: Workers of the year AD2097 — "serfs and debtors from the cradle to the grave" — queue up for thumbprint identification: notice the new spelling of the word "thumb" using a Greek "theta" in place of "th". This illustration by Edmund J. Sullivan was for the *Pall Mall Magazine* serialization of H. G. Wells' *A Story of the Days to Come* (1899). (See page 20.)

THE BATTLE OF DORKING

REMINISCENCES OF A VOLUNTEER

BLACKWOOD AND SONS
EDINBURGH & LONDON

PRICE SIXPENCE.

FROM
BLACKWOOD'S MAGAZINE
MAY 1871.

Illustration by Fred T. Jane, later to achieve fame as the originator of *Jane's Fighting Ships*, showing descent by parachute from an airship. This appeared in the serialization of *Hartmann the Anarchist* (1893) by E. Douglas Fawcett in the *English Illustrated Magazine*. (See page 32.)

Opposite: The cover of the first booklet edition of Chesney's *The Battle of Dorking* (1871), almost certainly the most successful future-war account ever to be published. (See page 37.)

Fred T. Jane's conception of a masted airship, from George Griffith's *The Angel of the Revolution* (1893). (See page 65.)

Opposite above: A German airship being attacked by courageous US fighter 'planes — an illustration from the serial in the *Pall Mall Magazine* of H. G. Wells' *The War in the Air* (1908). (See page 67.)

Opposite below: Manhattan in flames, from the serialization of H. G. Wells' *The War in the Air.* (See page 67.)

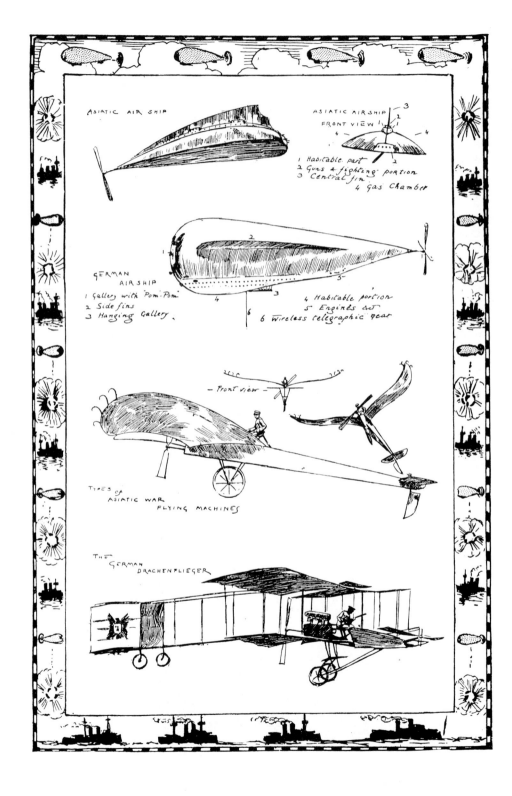

ASIATIC AIR SHIP

ASIATIC AIRSHIP
FRONT VIEW
1 Habitable part
2 Guns & fighting portion
3 Central fin
4 Gas Chamber

GERMAN AIR SHIP
1 Gallery with Pom-Pom
2 Side fins
3 Hanging Gallery.

4 Habitable portion
5 Engines &c
6 Wireless telegraphic gear

— Front view —

TYPES of ASIATIC WAR FLYING MACHINES

THE GERMAN DRACHENFLIEGER

A multi-balloon airship depicted in the French magazine *L'Illustration* in 1850. The first successful airship was designed by a Frenchman, Henri Giffard (1825-1882), and flown over Paris in 1852.

Opposite: A sketch of the various types of aircraft involved in the conflict in Wells' *The War in the Air* showing, from top to bottom, an Asiatic airship, a German airship, an Asiatic war flying machine, and a German *Drachenflieger*. (See page 67.)

A spoof advertisement which appeared in conjunction with Rudyard Kipling's story "As Easy as A.B.C.". (See page 96.)

According to Albert Robida's *Le Vingtième Siècle* (1881), by the mid-1950s balloons were going to be used not just for day-to-day transport or, perhaps, races but also for the dissemination of advertising material. Of course, since he made the prediction aircraft have indeed been used for exactly this purpose. (See page 163.)

A brand-new form of advertising! — the projection of messages onto the Moon. An illustration for "A Message from the Moon" by George Allan England, which appeared in *Pearson's Magazine* in 1907.

Opposite: A prediction by Robida of trilingual theatre in the mid-1950s.

An illustration for Jules Verne's
1877 novel *Hector Servadac* (also
known as *Off on a Comet*): the
passengers do not seem to be
suffering any breathing difficulties.
(See page 128.)

Parodying the fantastic-voyage
stories of Jules Verne, Albert
Robida produced *Les Voyages Très
Extraordinaires de Saturnin
Farandoul* (1879), from which this
illustration is taken. (See
page 81.)

balloons, aerial bombardment of cities, chemical and bacteriological warfare, and tanks. In contrast to this general goriness, his writing was characterized by its lightheartedness.

Among the many novels of the period, we must mention — if nothing more — W. Laird Clowes' *The Captain of the Mary Rose* (1892) and Fred T. Jane's *Blake of the "Rattlesnake"* (1895), both of which are near-future stories of naval warfare, where the ships and weapons are very little different from those in existence at the time of writing. Still, it is quite rare to find the Navy being much considered in predictive war novels of the time.

The year after *The Captain of the Mary Rose* came *The Great War of England in 1897,* which as we have seen was the first of several novelized predictions by William Le Queux. At one point in the book, French troops shell London with "new quick-firing weapons of long range and a very destructive character". In an interesting passage veering between fact and fancy the destruction is graphically described:

> In addition to the ordinary projectiles filled with melanite, charges of that extremely powerful substance lignine dynamite were hurled into the city, and, exploded by a detonator, swept away whole streets and laid many great buildings in ruins; while steel shells, filled with some arrangement of liquid oxygen and blasting gelatine, produced frightful effects, for nothing could withstand them.

(Of these explosives, only melanite had been used in battle prior to 1893.)

Later in the book, during a naval battle off Dungeness, a new shore battery blows French ships out of the water at a range of two and a half miles. "Each shot fired by this new pneumatic gun contained 900 lbs of dynamite, which could strike effectively at four miles!"

In the same year there appeared an exciting combination of the future European war with a host of Vernean scientific wonders — *The Angel of the Revolution* by George Griffith, a work which we have already briefly noted. The hero, a young inventor, discovers the secret of powered flight in September 1903 (only three months before the Wright brothers actually did, a lucky guess ten years before the event). He uses two liquefied gases, conveniently weightless, which explode upon meeting and fuel four internal-combustion engines which power a profusion of propellers. There are three vertical propellers, on separate masts, for lift — they give the craft a romantic resemblance to a three-masted sailing ship — and one main stern and two small manoeuvring propellers for horizontal travel. His airship has an aluminium hull with glassed-in cockpit and saloon, but an open deck, and side-lanes for steering and additional lift. The initial ship, *Ariel,* can manage 120mph; later and more powerful models can achieve 200mph and rise to 10,000 feet. For armament these ships carry extremely long-barrelled, long-range pneumatic cannon, with a range of twelve miles. The shells (made of *papier maché*!) have tremendous destructive power, vaporizing their targets with a "bright greenish flash".

However easy it would be to tear apart Griffith's book on grounds of scientific inaccuracy, it remains readable as a Victorian "scientific romance" whose charm is only enhanced by its more ludicrous episodes.

The illustrations for *The Angel of the Revolution* and several other similar novels of the period are by Fred T. Jane, a mediocre artist who also wrote and illustrated some poor scientific romances of his own. His great interest was in fighting vehicles of all kinds, and his real fame, ignoring for a moment his illustrations for some of the adventures of Sherlock Holmes, lies in his originating *Jane's Fighting Ships* in 1897; this was a series which was to continue, and his name is recalled today in that of the British publishing house Macdonald and Janes.

Wells' Martians in *The War of the Worlds* (1897) were armed with several brilliantly original weapons, to be shamelessly borrowed by later writers. The tripedal war machines are armed with handling tentacles and the famous heat ray. Wells valiantly tried to explain this as a heat source focused as is a lighthouse beam. Until less than twenty years ago this would have seemed as fictional as it did in Wells' day, but since then we have grown quite accustomed to microwaves . . . and laser beams.

The Martians employ also a sooty poison gas or smoke, not unlike that used to attack vermin today. It is a minor but interesting point that these weapons are not built into the machines in the way that the guns of a modern tank are, for example: they are holstered like sidearms on the machine's body and "drawn" at will.

By the time that the 20th century had dawned much progress had been made with weapons of war. George Griffith's short story of 1901, "The Raid of *Le Vengeur*", is about submarines as they really were — fully submersible, manoeuvrable on or below the surface, and unable to navigate freely underwater owing to a lack of visibility (echo-sounding was not to be developed until 1919). Griffith's French submarine engineer fits his craft with long "feelers" of magnetized wire which stretch out horizontally and are attracted by any metal hull in the vicinity. But, as a great patriot, Griffith equips a British destroyer with a superior device, a "new ray" capable of shining through water without producing any scatter, and by use of this the submarine is captured.

Whether or not a tunnel under the English Channel may be termed a weapon is debatable. In the 1890s there was much discussion as to the feasibility of such a project. As we have seen, Max Pemberton in his novel *Pro Patria* (1901) describes a secret French plan to dig a tunnel and invade the UK through it. Thirty years later Harry Edmonds, in *The Riddle of the Straits*, shows how the Channel Tunnel makes a wartime naval blockade of UK ports (in this case by the USA) ineffective.

Another short story, this time by H. G. Wells — "The Land Ironclads" (1903) — was one of the very few war predictions that proved to be accurate. It describes tanks being used against entrenched infantry. Despite being made to travel on eight pairs of very large wheels with elephantine feet attached to the rims, rather than on caterpillar tracks, Wells' tanks have all the advantages of real-life ones, being impervious to small-arms fire, able to cross trenches, and too speedy to be hit by artillery.

Less accurate but equally interesting in its fashion was Wells' *The War in the Air,* a novel written in 1907 and first published as a serial in *Pall Mall Magazine* in 1908. It describes the opening phases of a world war, initially fought mainly in the air, which breaks out in about 1917 (Wells does not specify the date, but he offers hints). Of the causes of this war, he says:

Relations were strained between Germany and the United States because of the intense exasperation of the former power towards the Monroe Doctrine, and they were strained between the United States and Japan because of the perennial citizenship question.

But it is also clear that the Germans *want* war, and, with airships and *Drachenflieger* (box-kite aircraft), they take the initiative and attack the USA.

A large force of about eighty airships (each towing several *Drachenflieger)* crosses the Atlantic, commanded by Prince Karl Albert. At the same time the German navy sails across, meets part of the US fleet (most of which is otherwise occupied in the Pacific), and, with a little bomb-dropping help from the airships, defeats it in mid-ocean. The airship fleet reaches New York and, after dropping just a few bombs (on City Hall, Wall Street, Brooklyn Bridge, etc.), obtains the city's surrender. But most of the populace are incensed by this, and several airships are shot at and brought down, so the surrender is void and the city is extensively bombed.

Dust and black smoke came pouring into the street, and were presently shot through with red flame . . .

In this manner the massacre of New York began. She was the first of the great cities of the Scientific Age to suffer by the enormous powers and grotesque limitations of aerial warfare. She was wrecked as in the previous century endless barbaric cities had been bombarded, because she was at once too strong to be occupied, and too undisciplined and proud to surrender in order to escape destruction.

Small fleets of US aircraft appear and fight the airships in what Wells calls "the first battle in the air", both sides sustaining losses. However, the Germans take control of certain key points — such as Niagara Falls, for its generating station — and troops are landed from the German fleet.

As news of the German attack travels around the world, the Asiatic alliance of China and Japan sends up its own airships (which carry aircraft). Some thousands of these invade the USA from the west and perhaps a million Asians are landed by boat in California. The Asian airships and aircraft generally manage to defeat the Germans — not to mention the Americans — and it is not until a new British-designed aircraft is built in large numbers in the USA and UK that those nations can fight back. (Apparently by this time most cities of the world have been bombarded by either Asian or German airships.)

The war is never officially concluded, although a "Purple Plague" (Wells' capitals) appears after about a year and there is a general collapse of civilization.

The German airships are "altogether fish-like". They have a rigid framework of alloy ribs covered by canvas and containing "from fifty to a hundred compartments" made of rubber and filled with hydrogen.

> There was a steel axis to the whole affair, a central backbone which terminated in the engine and propeller, and the men and magazines were forward in a series of cabins under the expanded headlike forepart. The engine, which was one of the extraordinarily powerful Pforzheim type, that supreme triumph of German invention, was worked by electric controls from this forepart, which was indeed the only really habitable part of the ship.

Each carries "bombs of various types — mainly in glass" and a single gun in a small gallery halfway up the bow. If the hydrogen compartments are damaged by enemy action they can be patched by crewmen wearing divers' suits. The airships can travel at 90mph in calm air and carry up to 200 tons.

The Asian ships also are fish-shaped, but with distinctive flat bottoms so that when they are seen end-on they look like flying saucers. They carry more guns and are more manoeuvrable than their German counterparts. In contrast with the box-kite construction of the *Drachenflieger*, the Asian aircraft have forward-curving, flapping wings:

> The solitary rider sat between the wings above a transverse explosive engine . . . that differed in no essential particular from those in use in light motor bicycles of the period. . . . He carried

a large double-edged two-handed sword, in addition to his explosive-bullet-firing rifle.

Wells makes very intelligent predictions of the peculiarities and restrictions of aerial warfare. He mentions the "immense power of destruction an airship has over the thing below, and its relative inability to occupy or guard or garrison a surrendered position", the relative ineffectiveness of airships against other airships and aircraft, and also the way that their use makes the outcome of any conflict indecisive since, while both sides are open to attack from the air, no blockade could completely prevent an enemy's aircraft from taking off, ferrying supplies, and so forth.

(As a matter of interest, the first occasion when bombs were dropped from an aircraft was on November 1st 1911, during the Italo-Turkish conflict in Libya.)

In 1909, the year after the appearance of *The War in the Air*, Blériot made the first aircraft flight across the English Channel, from Calais to Dover. In that same year a German novel was published in which half a million troops are airlifted into southern Britain as the spearhead of a German invasion. This grandiose scheme — a wish-fulfilment fantasy if ever there was one — came from the pen of Rudolf Martin, an ardent German patriot. His book, *Der Weltkrieg in den Luften (The World War in the Air)*, describes a war with Germany and Austro-Hungary on one side and the UK, France and Russia on the other, beginning in 1915 and culminating in a tremendous German victory. He places his trust in airships which, as he was writing just five years after the initial flight at Kittyhawk, must have seemed a safer bet.

The other really accurate future-war prediction of the 1871-1914 period besides "The Land Ironclads" was "Danger!", a short story by Sir Arthur Conan Doyle. Written in the Spring of 1913 and published (in *The Strand Magazine*) only months before World War I began, this is a faultless prediction of submarine warfare. Norland, "one of the smallest powers in Europe", goes to war with the UK over a colonial dispute. Although she possesses only a small navy, including just eight submarines (four of them a little old-fashioned), she stations these eight at the entrances to the major UK ports, sinking every merchant vessel that tries to bring in food. This blockade is begun on April 10th, and before the end of May the UK has been forced to capitulate owing to imminent starvation (because, even in those days, the majority of her food was imported) — and this despite the occupation of Norland by UK forces since the earliest days of the war.

A word of explanation is necessary to convey the full contemporary impact of this story. Although we, after two world wars, have become accustomed to the idea of the torpedoing of unarmed merchant ships, such action was considered absolutely unthinkable in July 1914. On its publication Doyle's story was subjected to ridicule by admirals of the British navy, among others. Yet two months later German U-boats were sitting outside British harbours and sinking merchant ships.

Doyle considered every angle before writing his story, which was in fact produced as a political argument for the construction of a Channel Tunnel. He also made the point — and very strongly — that war had reached the stage of no longer being just a big game: henceforth it was to be a desperate business of striking at the weak spots of one's enemy, with no holds barred.

The jingoistic avidity for war which had produced so much technological speculation seemed to die with World War I.

The initial postwar mood of pacifism meant that any predictions of future war were considered to be in bad taste; certainly any such predictions confined their attentions to people and politics, and new technologies were abandoned for a time. There were still occasional tales published about mad scientists or battles in outer space, but even these were few and far between until the advent of the science-fiction pulp magazines after 1926. Apart from a few antiwar treatises, it would be not until the 1930s that technological predictions would be able to re-emerge.

An exception — because strictly it is not antiwar—is *Paris or the Future of War* by Captain S. H. Liddell Hart (1925). Although almost every prediction made in it has turned out to be wrong, it is interesting to see just what an eminent military writer of that period did believe, in the wake of the holocaust which had overturned everybody's conception of war. Liddell Hart sees little future for infantry, dismissing it as too vulnerable to attack by tanks and aircraft and unable to hit back. (He had no conception of the guns, grenades or missiles that infantry may now deploy against armour.) He is obviously considering war in terms of destruction rather than of occupation, and believes that tanks are destined to supplant infantry.

He also asserts that aircraft will make both armies and navies obsolete, although he seems unable to conceive an increase in the power of aircraft and in their destructive capabilities; for example, he suggests that a country as vast as the USA is relatively impervious to air attack, which "could hardly be decisive, however locally unpleasant. Washington laid in ruins would merely provide 'Main Street' with a fresh supply of small talk; New York paralysed would leave the Middle West unmoved." He does admit, however, that a major air attack on London would be both possible and devastating.

He is one of many to predict that the next war would be fought with large quantities of gas from both sides, and he welcomes and encourages the use of nonlethal gas as a less destructive means than the traditional ones of winning wars. Unfortunately, from our point of view, he refuses to speculate about the development of new weapons, dismissing "death rays" and germ warfare scathingly. In all his predictions he is, however, astute enough to avoid offering timescales.

As the 1930s progressed it became evident to many observers that war with Germany would be resumed within a decade, and this encouraged a return to war predictions. The first major work of this period was *The Gas War of 1940* by "Miles" (1931), which included some accurate forecasts — except, that is, for the gas.

It was generally accepted in many works of fiction and nonfiction between 1930 and 1934 that Germany would be the aggressor, that there would be great use of aircraft (particularly heavy bombers), that the UK would eventually win, but that the victory would be a hollow one, with much death and destruction on both sides due to the advances in weaponry since 1918; in other words, for a change, the prophets got it right. (A prophecy of the large-scale bombing of civilian property is given in Nevil Shute's 1939 novel *What Happened to the Corbetts,* although in a new preface to a postwar edition the novelist admitted to having overlooked the importance of fire. At the time the book was highly considered, and the publishers, Heinemann, distributed a thousand copies free to workers in Air Raid Precautions.)

The outstanding exception to this convention is of course Major Helders' *The War in the Air, 1936,* which we have already considered at length. This book is in any case something of an anachronism, a survival from the days when fictional wars were full of gallantry and glory, with the victor taking all — in other words, it was a throwback to the days before 1914.

Another exception to the serious and depressing future wars of the 1930s and 1940s is to be found in *All Our Tomorrows* (1942) by Douglas Reed. Although this is for the most part a serious current-affairs book by a commentator noted for his outspoken patriotism, it contains a ludicrously tongue-in-cheek final section, "A Brief History of the Next War". This, "written in 1980", copies Chesney's approach but remains too facetious to be compared with *The Battle of Dorking.* In the lead-up to the war of 1979 the German leader, Goering, uses a "super-subterrine" to burrow through to Moscow and sign a pact with the Russian leader. Germany then attacks the UK by means of bomb-divers who, dressed in deep-sea diving gear, walk across the bottom of the English Channel and capture the whole of the English south coast. Subterrines follow, but the gallant Royal Earth Force swoops in from its bases on other planets and saves the day. Yet the war continues as the author writes . . .

. . . although one day the war will end.

There are in the history of prediction very few works which take as an axiom that the situation will arise where war will be, not an exception, an adventure, an excitement, a hell, but a natural way of life. Perhaps this gloomy idea had to wait until after World War II before it could gain any modicum of respectable acceptance. Let us merely mention in passing — for we will be returning to the subject later — two of the books which regard war in this way, George Orwell's *Nineteen Eighty-four* (1949), in which we are told that "war is never-ending", and much later Joe Haldeman's *The Forever War* (1974). Significantly, one was written in the wake of World War II and the other in the wake of the Vietnam War.

It is an ancient and continuing tradition that any radical advance in military technology is immediately branded as almost too dreadful to be used, as "the weapon to end war". Probably the bronze swords that replaced stone axes were so described, and the iron weapons which in turn replaced *them* — in an effective modern tale by Harry Harrison, the "weapon to end war" turns out to be the bow-and-arrow. Greek fire, the napalm of the ancients, falls into this category; its secret was lost and rediscovered a couple of times, although it never did end war. Gunpowder and the crossbow, first used in western warfare in the early 14th century, were the first weapons to be stigmatized as too dreadful to be used, by churches and states alike. And there was the famous occasion when Queen Victoria was presented with the plans for a submarine as a war weapon; so far as she was concerned, Britons, being gentlemen, would never use such a dastardly device.

Immediately balloons had made their first flights (1783) their potential for war was realized. Benjamin Franklin wrote in 1784: "And where is the Prince who can afford so to cover his Country with Troops for its defence, as that ten thousand men descending from the clouds might not in many places do an infinite deal of mischief before a force could be brought together to repel them?" In 1810 Robert Fulton's sales patter denied the possibility of any defence against his torpedoes. The same was claimed for his submarines, and it continued to be claimed for various types of submarine right up to 1918. The steamship, the ironclad ship, the machine gun, the aeroplane, poison gas: each one of these became, in its turn, the weapon to end war.

And then there came the atomic bomb. Actually, it came more than thirty years before US scientists set off the first such explosion on July 16th 1945 at Alamogordo, New Mexico. In his novel *The World Set Free* (1913) H. G. Wells, on the basis of having read a book about experiments with radium, coined the term "atomic bomb". He prophesied its development in the 1950s and its use in war in 1959 — notably to cause, not to end, a war. The scale of Wells' bomb is wrong — it is a two-foot black sphere, dropped over the side of an open aircraft, and displays no mushroom cloud — but the essence of the Bomb, its name and the terror it still conveys are definitely foreshadowed.

An earlier prediction of the atomic bomb might be said to occur in Robert Cromie's novel *The Crack of Doom* (1895), in which a typical mad scientist realizes that one grain of matter, if "etherized", contains vast amounts of energy. He plans to blow up the world, of course.

Other prophecies of atomic bombs occur in Harold Nicolson's *Public Faces* (1932) and Neil Bell's *The Lord of Life* (1933).

A later prophecy, in reasonably accurate detail, appeared in a story by Cleve Cartmill published in *Astounding Science Fiction* magazine for March 1944. It was only one of a string of stories with atomic-bomb references which appeared in the magazine, but has become famous because, owing to its startling accuracy, the FBI interviewed the magazine's editor, John W. Campbell Jnr., demanding to know the origin of this "leak" of classified information. Campbell was able to assure them that it was pure speculation, adding that, if the atomic bomb were suddenly to cease being mentioned in *Astounding*, the readers would be certain that it had been suppressed for security reasons.

Although the atomic bombs that were dropped on Hiroshima and Nagasaki hastened the end of a war they have proved to be incapable of ending war. In the predictive fiction which has "used" nuclear weapons since then, of which Nevil Shute's *On the Beach* (1957) may be regarded as an archetype, the Bomb seems to be not so much the weapon to end war as the weapon to end humanity.

The neutron bomb, like its predecessors since the dawn of history, is a "weapon too dreadful to use". Will it, like its predecessors, nevertheless be used? And, if so, what will be the *next* "weapon to end war"?

If there is a next . . .

4 HIS LATEST PLAY, "URIC ACID"

SATIRE

As Peter Nicholls so rightly observes in *The Encyclopaedia of Science Fiction,* "it is almost impossible to write a work of fiction set in another world, be it our own world in another time, or some alien place, which does not make some sort of statement about the present-day, real world of the writer. Thus very little sf does not bear at least a family resemblance to satire." Because all predictions of the future must relate somehow to the present in which they were written, any changes or progressions envisaged by their writers are, whether intentionally or not, satirical comments upon that present. Even where little or no change is predicted, unconscious satire may be present, for the author has perhaps assumed that no improvement is possible, that the contemporary arrangement of civilization is perfect. By way of example, in Mary Shelley's *The Last Man* (1826), the fastest means of travel in the year 2090 is by open balloon; and in no 19th-century novel was the 20th century's rapid change towards informality in speech and behaviour predicted.

Some predictions are naturally more satirical than others. In most cases the reader can distinguish just a touch of irony here and there. Occasionally the main intention of writing has been to satirize a few (or many) aspects of contemporary life or literature. The satire may be intended as humour — anywhere along the spectrum from wit to farce — or as serious criticism. It may lampoon directly, or obliquely, by implication. Combined with the satire may be other motives, notably to give warning of the state we could get into "if this (or that) goes on". The extrapolation of any trend into the future, to its illogical and extreme conclusion, is no less popular a means of satire because it is so easy; any extreme condition is its own satire.

Just as the fantastic voyage to far-off lands was a device used by very many early satirists (from Lucian of Samosata to Dean Swift) to criticize aspects of their own political systems without risking official censure, so many satires since the 18th century have been deliberately set in the future. Not only is that wall of years a protection against prosecution (it is easy to claim that one was ridiculing a future king, president, dictator or pope of the same name and not the present incumbent at all, honestly!) but a future setting is a splendid distancing mechanism, enabling us "to see oursels as others see us". Even the most necessary or commonplace of society's details can be made to appear ridiculous when viewed (often out of context) at a distance of fifty or a hundred years. But a corollary of this is that futuristic satires are rarely intended to portray a fully believable future society; often an absurd state of affairs is shown just for effect.

There are many ways of contrasting present and future so as to show up the weak points. Easiest and most common is to set one's story in a specified future and let the reader pick out the implied criticism for himself. Just in case the author feels his points are too subtle, he can have one character say to another, "How funny life must have been in the year 1900 when they didn't even . . ."

A very popular device used by H. G. Wells, Edward Bellamy, W. H. Hudson and William Morris — and so many others that it was a recognized cliché before 1900 — was to have a contemporary man sleep his way into the future, there to awaken and act the part of a stranger in a strange land, so that the changes in society could be minutely explained to him. A variation was to have the contemporary protagonist visit the future through the medium of a dream (or a vision, or a time machine), but so long as he was able to ask questions and marvel at (or be horrified at) the march of progress there was no effective difference from a sleeper waking.

These were not devices confined to the presentation of satire, of course, and they have been used at other times to frame works which were primarily escapist, seriously predictive or of philosophical intentions.

Other means of bringing together present and future so as to emphasize the element of satire are to postulate a visitor from future to present (as in Grant Allen's *The British Barbarians*), or to show to the people of the present a film which portrays present and future, and catch their reactions, as John Gloag did in *Tomorrow's Yesterday*.

The first of these two books, *The British Barbarians* (1895), provides a suitable place to begin examining selected satires in detail, because the novel is an excellent example of a light and humorous work written purely for the sake of satire, rather than employing satire for other ends. It is a delicate comedy of manners aimed at the mores and taboos of the English upper and middle classes in the late 19th century.

The distancing is achieved by having an anthropologist of the 25th century come on a visit to study the barbaric taboos of 1895. The visitor, who appears in a Surrey village one Saturday afternoon, is a pleasant young man named Bertram Ingledew. He speaks impeccable upper-class English and is well supplied with suitable coinage but lacks the knowledge of how to behave.

Because he gives every impression of being a gentleman he is aided by

Philip Christy, a well-to-do young man who is walking nearby. After an initial bad moment when Ingledew accuses the British monetary system of being "unreasonable and illogical" (this was in the days of shillings and pence, half-crowns and florins), Christy befriends him, telling him where in the village he can find lodgings.

Ingledew is surprised at the large number of taboos he encounters, from the necessity of possessing luggage before one can take lodgings to the restricted behaviour and dress required on Sundays. ("And he reflected silently on the curious fact that the English give themselves by law fifty-two weekly holidays a year, and compel themselves by custom to waste them entirely in ceremonial observances.") Christy denies that there are any taboos to be found in England, to which Ingledew replies, "No taboos! Why, I've read of hundreds. Among nomological students England has always been regarded with the greatest interest as the home and centre of the highest and most evolved taboo development. And you yourself have already supplied me with half a dozen." In his opinion England is the "metropolis of taboo". And he is an expert on taboos, claiming to have travelled the world in search of them.

Invited to join their social circle by Christy, his sister Frida and her husband, Robert Montieth, Ingledew soon manages to fall foul of the major taboo areas of the day. He refuses to accept the right of ownership of land, ignoring a "Trespassers Will Be Prosecuted" sign and arguing with the landowner that the system is illogical. When Frida's sister-in-law (for whom she has never cared) dies, he points out the ridiculous nature of death taboos. He is a great believer in the freedom of the individual and cares very little for what people think, or worse still, have been "always brought up to think" — which he dimisses as "a very queer substitute indeed for thinking". He rails against restrictive sexual taboos, and he outrages his new acquantances by treating house servants as if they were people. Furthermore, he is a confirmed pacifist at a time when great stock is set upon a man's skill at "killing and maiming his fellow-creatures". To compound the joke about English taboos, Ingledew's obvious reticence as to his own origins is quickly recognized and this, too, becomes a taboo subject (which remains unrevealed until the very end of the book).

The plot is concerned mainly with Ingledew's growing affection for Frida. She has never loved her husband but clings to the code of behaviour by which she has been brought up. Even when she realises that she loves him it takes all his powers of taboo-dispersion to persuade her that it would be more logical to go away with him than to return to her husband. They flee, but Montieth traces them and shoots Ingledew. He fades out of existence as a blue flame and a disembodied voice which reveals his origin and begs Frida to join him. She has evidently been cured of her taboos and wishes to do so.

To us in the 1980s, Ingledew's opinions and his strong attacks on late

19th-century customs may seem entirely reasonable. At the time they were close to being blasphemous, denying as they did most of the unwritten rules which made Victorian England the stuffy and hypocritical place it was.

Another delightful satire, equally humorous but aimed at showing the opposite — how much preferable English late Victorian society is to universal equality — is "The New Utopia", a story by Jerome K. Jerome which first appeared in his book *Diary of a Pilgrimage* (1891). The contemporary narrator is at his club, discussing the great merits of equality with his rich friends. "We raised our glasses and drank to EQUALITY, sacred EQUALITY: and then ordered the waiter to bring us green Chartreuse and more cigars."

He goes home to bed and wakes — eventually — in a glass musuem case. A notice on this says:

MAN — ASLEEP, PERIOD — 19TH CENTURY. This man was found asleep in a house in London, after the great social revolution of 1899. From the account given by the landlady of the house, it would appear that he had already, when discovered, been asleep for over ten years (she having forgotten to call him). It was decided, for scientific purposes, not to awaken him; but to see just how long he would sleep on, and he was accordingly brought and deposited in the "Museum of Curiosities" on February 11th 1900.

Having slept for a thousand years he is now in the 29th century. The museum curator acts as his guide, proudly displaying the absolute equality which has now been achieved. Examples are that everybody wears the same type of clothes (not too different from the present Chinese suit) and has black hair (dyed if necessary). Men and women can hardly be told apart except by the personal metal numbers on their collars — odd numbers for men and even for women. Names have been abolished. Everybody lives in tower blocks of dormitories, families and blood ties having been abolished to avoid their affecting one's obedience to the state. Breeding is done by order, scientifically, as with animals, and children are raised by the state. Love is, of course, not allowed, for it would make some people happier than others. The astonished narrator is told that all this has been decided by "THE MAJORITY". (Jerome K. Jerome enjoyed capitalization.)

To ensure equality, any particularly tall people (who would otherwise enjoy an unfair advantage) have an arm or leg amputated. The curator says, "I have sometimes thought that it was a pity we could not level up sometimes, instead of levelling down; but, of course, that is impossible." Tall people are, naturally enough, not overjoyed at this practice, but they are in a minority and "a minority has NO rights".

Natural beauty, too, has been abolished, because it was not fair that some people should live in attractive areas and others not. (We are not told how this has been achieved but it seems an excellent argument for pollution.) The whole world is now the same — "one people, one language, one law, one life". The narrator asks if they worship a god and is told yes — "THE MAJORITY". Apparently everybody in the 29th century — at least, THE MAJORITY — is very happy and would never think of changing anything.

Then the narrator wakes up in bed back in the 1890s: it has all been a dream. There is something of a warning in this (compare its ideas with those of Yevgeny Zamyatin and Ayn Rand several decades later), but its substance is so light-hearted (wit verging into farce) that one is unable to take the warning seriously.

There has been much light-hearted satire set in the future. Some is very silly indeed; some is merely amusing. It may poke fun at an aspect of life but it does so fairly gently and, all too often in the case of novels, boringly.

A case in point is *Martha Brown MP, a girl of tomorrow* (1935) by the romantic novelist Victoria Cross. This is an exceedingly silly farce about male-female rôle reversal, with broad and not very funny satire heaped on by the shovelful. Society of the 30th century is only a slightly futuristic version of that of 1935. The eponymous Martha Brown MP is a superwoman, being tall, broadshouldered, talented, capable and having several regular lovers. Her husband, like most males of the period, is smaller, weaker, less capable, very emotional, wears skirts, and stays at home to look after the children.

Women occupy most high offices, including that of Prime Minister, although the local rector is male, so perhaps the Church of England has stood defiant while all other male bastions have fallen into female hands — no, more likely Ms Cross failed to think of having a female rector! Certainly she did not bother to dream up technological advances: noiseless aircraft which land on rooftops are the only innovation she mentions.

Although it was undoubtedly intended to be humorous the book makes some vicious comments about subjects on which (one presumes) Ms Cross held strong views. Criminals and lunatics are either executed or given euthanasia. Income tax is 18/- in the pound — i.e., 90 per cent. The killing of animals for food or experimentation is forbidden, as are all food additives.

In the end the author was unable to resist a conventional romantic flourish, so our Tarzan look-alike heroine gives up her chance of being British Prime Minister to go off to the USA with a very big, tough he-man she just happens to have fallen in love with. A pity for her husband.

We will look at two further rôle-reversal novels later in this chapter, Walter Besant's *The Revolt of Man* and August Anson's *When Woman*

Reigns. These were not intended to be amusing, and the latter is only incidentally satirical, and so we will examine them in the context of other more serious satires.

Memories of the Future by Ronald A. Knox (1923) demonstrates what a difficult task it is to maintain a consistent level of satirical humour over nearly two hundred and fifty pages. It is presented as the memoirs of Opal, Lady Porstock, between 1915 and 1972, looking back from the year 1988. There are elements of rôle-reversal here, too, as Opal runs the family business without the help of her husband, though this is only one of many satirical trends, and the norm seems to be sex-equality (with women becoming bank managers, ships' captains and judges) rather than reversal. Almost every aspect of life is gently ridiculed and some sections are extremely entertaining.

After her father's death Opal is determined to manage the family business.

> For this purpose I decided to go right through, starting at the very bottom as an inferior clerk, and working my way up ... I could not well leave my mother, who depended very much on me since our bereavement, but I had been careful to have the teledictaphone installed at Grayfields and it was thus possible for me, without ever going to the office, to take my orders every morning like a simple clerk and to execute them to the satisfaction of my employers. In rather less than a year I had gained such a thorough grasp of the business that I allowed myself to be advanced to the position of a partner in the firm.

The Americans have accepted British titles (three dukedoms, six marquisates, thirty-six peerages, etc.) in payment for World War I debts, and these are allotted by an open ballot — at £1000 a ticket. Opal marries one of these luck-of-the-draw barons, Lord Porstock. In 1953 Lady Porstock is elected to Parliament, where attendance is now limited to a couple of hours each Wednesday evening to vote. For the rest of the time the House is filled with the sound of recorded speeches being played on gramophones.

A few satires on poems are included, such as on Wordsworth's "The Rainbow". Instead of "My heart leaps up when I behold/A rainbow in the sky", the second line is now "An advert in the sky". One of the few technological advances noted is that most trains travel at no more than thirty miles an hour but with all the facilities of an ocean liner, including radio news, a library, billiards tables and badminton courts. In the USA the amenities are even greater and the speeds even lower; at the end of each journey the conductor has to hand in a list of Births, Marriages and Deaths.

Stephen Leacock's approach to the future is similar, though on occasion his band of satire becomes more bitter and Kafkaesque. His piece "Dear Old Utopia" in *Afternoons in Utopia* (1932) is a clever lampoon on all futuristic utopian fiction, dragging in every cliché in just twenty pages. In "War Extracts from the Press of AD 2500" some of the most famous of historical wars are being refought by robots. "The Walrus and the Carpenter" is Leacock's look at spare-part surgery, with transplanted tongue firmly in artificial cheek. The title story of Leacock's *The Iron Man and the Tin Woman* (1929) tells of a time when robots are used to fulfill some of the more awkward or embarrassing functions of their owners — such as proposing marriage and going through the marriage ceremony itself. "When Social Regulation is Complete" maintains a façade of comedy as it shows a totally regulated world in which a properly stamped permit is required for courtship, or for sitting on a park bench, and where every kind of action is strictly regulated. It is a direction in which our society seems to be travelling, which makes it less amusing than otherwise. Another story in the same volume, "Isn't it Just Wonderful?", is a sharp reminder of the lack of privacy which the worldwide extension of radio brought about; it is a complaint applicable to the encroachments of the telephone and computers, too.

One noticeable feature of futuristic stories is their inclusion of mistaken ideas of the past; i.e., the people of the future have muddled impressions of the period at which the author was writing his story. In one way these are nothing new — just a twist on the old idea of howlers or malapropisms — although they can be traced back at least to 1848, before the world "howler" seems to have come into use.

In that year first appeared Edgar Allen Poe's "Mellonta Tauta", a short story printed in the more complete collections of his work. The title is Greek for "these things are in the future" and the story (little more than a fragment) is a daily diary kept by a traveller on a month's balloon excursion. It is set a thousand years ahead, in 2848, but science has advanced little. She writes: "Are we for ever to be doomed to the thousand inconveniences of the balloon? Will *nobody* contrive a more expeditious mode of progress?"

The changes in society have been much greater, with the importance of the individual having diminished, and intuition having replaced deduction as the road to truth and the increase of knowledge. The writer's husband quotes the ideas of that well known Hindoo philosopher Aries Tottle. All the names of continents and nationalities have been altered, more or less phonetically, to Yurope, Aysher, Inglitch, Amriccan, Vrinch, and so on.

To counter her boredom the narrator converses with her husband, who is an "expert" on antiquities, and he surprises her by saying that the ancient Americans governed themselves. "Did ever anybody hear of such an absurdity?" she writes. "Every man 'voted' as they call it — that is to say, meddled with public affairs — until, at length, it was discovered that what is everybody's business is nobody's, and that the 'Republic' (so the absurd thing was called) was without a government at all."

Mention is made of the destruction of New York by an earthquake in the year 2050. Actually, the name of the area has all but been forgotten except that its inhabitants were "a portion of the Knickerbocker tribe of savages". Poe goes on to take even greater and sillier liberties with portions of American history, and then the balloon collapses and begins to descend rapidly into the sea. But the reader should have expected such frivolity from the warning date at the beginning of the first diary entry — April 1.

Albert Robida, the French artist and writer, lived from 1848 to 1926. Among his prolific output were many predictions of the future (some of the best of which you will find in this book), satirizing Paris, the contemporary French people and their institutions, French history and, indeed, the rest of the world.

Le Vingtième Siècle (1883) is an illustrated and rather farcical fictional work covering the events of 1952-3. Most typical of Robida's work is the balloon, frequently provided with a silly envelope in the shape of, for example, a fish. Balloons are in the very widest use, day and night, moored to many roof-tops; and public buildings like Notre Dame Cathedral are balloon interchange stations. There are casino balloons, holiday-chalet balloons, sanatorium balloons, fighting balloons, taxi balloons, barricade balloons, and many more.

Another favourite technological development is the telephonoscope (a combined picturephone and TV). There are international pneumatic tubes for public transport, piped food, weather control, a robot president, and a sixth continent constructed to join up the Polynesian islands: all these are amusingly illustrated. On the social front women have achieved equality: they are now doctors and lawyers; they fight duels; they act as soldiers in the revolution. Ah, yes, there is a "Revolution of 1953", satirizing the Franco-Prussian war of 1870 rather than the French Revolution.

Robida produced several other works of prophecy, all satirical, some as books (*La Vie Electrique*, 1893; *La Guerre au Vingtième Siècle*, 1887) and others as magazine serials ("En 1965", 1919-20). An interesting although not particularly futuristic satire was *Les Voyages Très Extraordinaires de Saturnin Farandoul* (1879), a five-volume parody of Jules Verne's many "extraordinary voyages" to the North Pole, around the world, up in balloons, beneath the sea, into space on a comet, and so on.

In 1889 the US writer J. A. Mitchell obviously felt there was room for another series of howlers about contemporary American life and history, and he wrote the short novel *The Last American*. This uses the device of a Persian expedition visiting a derelict and almost abandoned USA in the year 2951. (It was recently parodied by Gene Wolfe in "Seven American Nights", in *Orbit 20* edited by Damon Knight.) At the beginning the author seems to be writing just for fun, with all the Persian names being puns. The narrator is Khan-li the Prince of Dimph-yoo-chur, and two of his companions are Nofuhl and Lev-el-Hedyd.

They land at New York ("Nhu Yok") and come to many insulting conclusions about the "Mehrikans", who apparently went downhill rapidly (due mainly to climatic changes) following the overthrow of the Murphey dynasty in 1930, and ceased to exist as a nation by 1990, so that for the last eleven centuries "the cities . . . have decayed in solitude". Many aspects of the late 19th-century USA are lampooned. For example: "The Mehrikans possessed neither literature, art, nor music of their own. Everything was borrowed." "They were a people of elastic honour." The Persians find the wooden image of an aged Red Indian in a cigar store and are puzzled as to how such idols were worshipped — "and why they are found in little shops and never in the great temples is a mystery".

At length, in the ruined city of Washington, the Persians find living Mehrikans — a young married couple and an old man, who are all that remain of their race. Given alcoholic beverages, the Persians soon become intoxicated. One of them tries to kiss the young woman, and in the ensuing fight several of the Persians are injured and the two male Mehrikans killed. The fate of the girl is not mentioned, but the young man's skull is taken back to Tehran to be displayed in a museum. This ending dispels the jokiness of most of the story and leaves a bitter taste in the mouth.

Moving to the very fringe of satire intended as humour, there are a couple of important pieces involving war between the Earth and the Moon.

André Maurois' *The Next Chapter: the War Against the Moon* (1927) is of only short-story length despite having been published on its own. Ostensibly a fragment of a book published in 1992, it looks back to the 1960s.

Following the World War of 1947 all the world's newspapers are controlled by just five press barons, known as the "Dictators of Public Opinion". By 1963 there are signs that another world war is imminent, and the only way to forestall it is to make all the world's nations unite against a common external foe. Discussing this, one of the press barons suggests an artificial war against the Moon: "It doesn't in the least matter against whom we unite, because the chief characteristic of this enemy is precisely the fact that he does not exist at all. Against the inhabitants of the Moon — or Mars — or Venus — it is all the same to me."

A press campaign is instigated to make people the whole world over believe that the inhabitants of the Moon are attacking our planet with powerful rays and destroying a few small, isolated villages. This is extremely successful not only in cultivating widespread hatred for the inhabitants of the Moon but in cutting short various international squabbles. The US Congress votes $100 million to be given to any scientist who can find a way of either contacting the Moon or retaliating by damaging some of the lunar villages.

A Moroccan scientist, Ben Tabrit, discovers a ray capable of destroying any kind of matter, and he designs a transmitting apparatus powerful enough to direct this ray at the Moon. In February 1964 he uses this ray to cut new craters at various points. But a few days later the German city of Dermstadt is completely destroyed in a night-time attack — evidently the inhabitants of the Moon have been made flesh-and-blood by propaganda (on the basis that, if enough people think something is true, then it becomes so), and they are hitting back.

> During the night of the 6th and 7th [February] all astronomical observers on the Earth observed that a new hole was being burned into the Moon by Ben Tabrit's ray. Retaliation was not long in coming. On February 7th, the cities of Elbeuf (France), Bristol, Rhode Island and Upsala (Sweden) were burned to ashes by the Moon. The era of Inter-Planetary War had begun.

And on that grim note the author breaks off.

A similar and even briefer account of a war with the Moon was first published as long ago as 1809 — "The Conquest By the Moon" by Washington Irving. This is a strong condemnation of imperialism and in particular of the slaughter of the Amerinds by the early American settlers.

It is presented in the form of a logical justification for colonization — for the colonization of the Earth by the Moon. Irving begins by explaining the four ways in which colonists may rightfully take possession of a country. There is the right of discovery of an uninhabited country, he says, as when the Europeans discovered America. (The two-legged animals already there were, of course, mere cannibals and not really human.) Then there is the right acquired by cultivation (of which the existing savages knew less than nothing). Third is the right acquired by civilization (here the Indians were sadly deficient). The fourth and final right is "by extermination, or in other words the right by gunpowder".

Irving then applies the same arguments to the planet Earth, as seen by the inhabitants of the Moon, whom he imagines as

aerial visitants . . . possessed of vastly superior knowledge to ourselves; that is to say, possessed of superior knowledge in the art of extermination — riding on hyppogriffs — defended with impenetrable armour — armed with concentrated sunbeams, and provided with vast engines, to hurl enormous moon-stones: in short let us suppose them, if our vanity will permit the supposition, as superior to us in knowledge, and consequently in power, as the Europeans were to the Indians, when they first discovered them.

Irving further supposes that an expeditionary force from the Moon, finding our planet "to be nothing but a howling wilderness, inhabited by us, poor savages and wild beasts, shall take possession of it". They abduct five national leaders to take back to their own leader, saying:

The five uncouth monsters, which we have brought into this august presence, were once very important chiefs among their fellow savages, who are a race of beings totally destitute of the common attributes of humanity; and differing in every thing from the inhabitants of the Moon, inasmuch as they carry their heads upon their shoulders, instead of under their arms — have two eyes instead of one — are utterly destitute of tails, and of a variety of unseemly complexions, particularly of horrible whiteness — instead of pea-green.

We moreover found these miserable savages sunk into a state of utmost ignorance and depravity, every man shamelessly living with his own wife, and rearing his own children, instead of indulging in that communality of wives enjoined by the law of nature . . . Taking compassion, therefore, on the sad condition of these sublunary wretches, we have endeavoured . . . to introduce among them the light of reason — and the comforts of the Moon. We have treated them to mouthfuls of moonshine, and draughts of nitrous oxide [laughing gas], which they swallowed with incredible voracity, particularly the females . . . We have insisted upon their renouncing the contemptible shackles of religion and common sense . . . But such was the unparalleled obstinacy of these wretched savages, that they persisted in cleaving to their wives, and adhering to their religion, and absolutely set at naught the sublime doctrines of the Moon — nay, among other heresies, they even went so far as blasphemously to declare, that this ineffable planet was made of nothing more nor less than green cheese!

The Moon's leader instructs his people to take possession of the Earth and to try to convert its savage natives. The narrator says:

But finding that we not only persist in absolute contempt of their reasoning and disbelief in their philosophy, but even go so far as daringly to defend our property, their patience shall be exhausted, and they shall resort to their superior powers of argument; hunt us with hyppogriffs, transfix us with concentrated sunbeams, demolish our cities with moon-stones; until having by main force, converted us to the true faith, they shall graciously permit us to exist in the torrid deserts of Arabia, or in the frozen regions of Lapland, there to enjoy the charms of lunar philosophy, in much the same manner as the reformed and enlightened savages of this country are kindly suffered to inhabit the inhospitable forests of the north, or the impenetrable wildernesses of South America.

This is strong stuff, with only hints of humour, and the meaning is made very plain to all.

News From Nowhere (1890) by William Morris is a noted satire on late 19th-century life and the shape of a utopian future. In some respects it is a parody of Edward Bellamy's *Looking Backward 2000-1887*.

The narrator, who is a man of 1890, is miraculously transported into the future while asleep (by about two hundred years, although the exact date is not mentioned) because he has been musing on the development of society before going to bed. The future which he finds is in every way very different from the world of 1890. For a start everybody is happy, because society is aimed at individual happiness, through working hard and playing hard.

He introduces himself as William Guest, since he is a guest of the future. It takes him a while to work out what has happened to him, and he does not dare admit it to his hosts, although one or two seem to guess.

He is at first surprised by the clarity of the river Thames, which now has salmon in it. Also, the ugly Victorian iron bridges have been replaced by stone ones. In fact, society has regressed in a number of ways. Costumes are ornate, rich and almost mediaeval. There are no real factories any longer, though small workshops exist. Most industry is cottage-based. Technology has certainly not advanced: "You see, guest, this is not an age of invention."

Yet this is a true socialist state, with everybody working because they want to (idleness, fortunately, is now extinct) and consuming what they need. Money has disappeared, even as a notional store of value. Considering that "the population is pretty much the same as it was at the end of the nineteenth century" it is not clear how the system manages to support itself. Labour-saving machines are derided as saving time on one job so that it can be wasted on another — a curious view. Yet this whole future is intended much more as satire than as a working utopia.

The Houses of Parliament are now used as "a sort of subsidiary market, and a storage place for manure": there is no need for central government, and local affairs are agreed by all concerned, who will either support a plan or not. Schools have been abolished, and children learn what they wish to learn, mostly by watching their parents. Crime is considered a spasmodic disease which need not be punished because the guilty will punish themselves.

Life has become much simpler and more wholesome. Most live in the country. The people are much fitter, stronger and more attractive than in the 1890s; they live longer, looking always very young for their age. This system has been in existence for about 150 years, since 1952 when there was a socialist revolution following a General Strike and a massacre of workers in Trafalgar Square.

Using predictive satire to ridicule one's own country became a regular practice during the 19th century, and it continues today. The works we have looked at by J. A. Mitchell, Washington Irving and William Morris are among the more interesting and general satires. Many more were politically motivated pieces attacking particular issues of the day which are remembered now only by historians. During wartime it was only natural that one should assault enemy countries in the same manner, picking on all their national traits and comprehensively ridiculing them.

An excellent example of this, written by an Englishman and published in 1918, is *Meccania the Super-State* by Owen Gregory. Its target, naturally, was Germany. In this witty and penetrating novel each aspect of the German character has been seized upon, exaggerated and developed over fifty years until it reaches the height of absurdity.

The basis of the plot is a visit to Meccania by a Chinaman, Mr Ming, who wants to learn something about the people and the conditions there. Meccania, which is very easily identified as Germany, is, by 1970, a highly developed totalitarian autocracy backed by a bureaucracy, a state where everything is regulated to a greater extent even than in George Orwell's *Nineteen Eighty-four*. In this respect Meccania is closer to present-day USSR or China; yet it was not illogical in 1918 to imagine Germany moving in that direction under a dictator, and the distancing effect of fifty years allows ample time for the described changes to have come about.

The book is notable for its prophecies being self-consistent. In the first place Meccania is an economic island, self-sufficient and cut off by its own wish from the rest of Europe by a twenty-mile wide strip of no-man's-land. Before entering one must have all requisite passports, visas, tickets and similar documents, and one must be subjected to a thorough search of all possessions and a complete medical inspection.

The first characteristic to be encountered is an obsession with titles.

Everybody in Meccania has a title which denotes his occupation or, occasionally, his status. Thus we encounter titles like "Inspector of Foreigners", "Sub-Conductor of Foreign Observers" and "Specialist Art Section Sub-Conductor". Even Mr Ming is not exempted from this: he is forced to state which title he wishes to be known by during his stay; he chooses "National Councillor".

A second trait is thoroughness. Nothing is allowed to be done by halves and everything, from the Super-State downwards, is absolute. For example, Mr Ming is not allowed to sightsee idly, but must be instructed (as if for an exam) in every aspect of the town or city in which he is staying. He settles for a one-week tour of Bridgetown, on the border, and a six-month tour of Mecco itself. As Mr Ming prepares to leave Bridgetown for Mecco, Inspector of Foreigners Stiff (all Meccanians have been provided by the author with names which are on the silly side of satire) sarcastically remarks: "So you think there is nothing more to be learnt in Bridgetown."

It is a marvellously alien point of view, and in Mecco he meets with it again and again. He must be made thoroughly conversant with the more important systems of the city. Before he sees some things he must be properly educated so that he will not misunderstand them, and he is not permitted to specialize in one area of Meccanian society until he has undergone the general tour, no matter how great his knowledge of that subject gained outside Meccania may be.

Another important obsession of the Meccanians is uniforms. In Meccania everybody wears a uniform to denote the class to which they belong. Members of the First Class (nobles, top military and ambassadors) wear white, the Second Class (military) scarlet, the Third Class (richer merchants and higher Civil servants) yellow, the Fourth Class (most officials and supervisors) green, the Fifth Class (skilled artisans: the largest group) chocolate, the Sixth Class (unskilled labourers) grey, and the Seventh Class (subnormals and those relegated as a punishment) dark blue. Different kinds and colours of buttons, flashes, piping and so on denote grades and occupations within each class, and the men of Meccania always wear their uniforms (women need wear only a patch of the particular colour on their dress).

The classes do, of course, salute anyone of higher class than themselves, there being a different form of salute for each — to give the wrong salute may cost the offender his life. Along with the uniform goes an exactly prescribed status, entitling the holder to certain privileges of housing, income, recreation, etc. The only people exempted from wearing uniforms are the dissenters — officially regarded as mentally ill because they do not love Meccania — who are put in asylums.

Mecco is laid out in a circular pattern, with particular areas reserved for particular classes. There is also, unsurprisingly, a love of parades and pomp.

The Meccanians love to boast, particularly about the wonders of Meccania itself, while at the same time they are extraordinarily rude about all other countries. They are all very proud to live in Meccania, regarding it as a near-utopia which is getting closer to perfection every day.

Punctuality is another trait which is parodied. Everybody (even visitors) must keep a written record of their movements for each day and of the time spent in each activity, these records to be submitted to the Time Department each week. Naturally, nothing is done in Meccania except by appointment.

As most of the foregoing illustrates, there are innumerable petty regulations, all of which are expected to be known by everyone, including visitors. An obvious corollary to all the uniforms, rules and ceremonies is that the Meccanians have no sense of humour, a criticism often levelled at the Germans.

Another thing the Meccanians lack is an appreciation of the finer things of life, and it is in this area that the author's satire reaches its greatest heights. One of the Meccanians' greatest art treasures is a colossal, ornate statue of Prince Mechow, the late head of state. Mr Ming's reaction is "one of intense disgust at the barbarity of the thing". On the subject of Meccanian drama, Mr Ming has to undergo a lecture from Dr Dodderer, an expert on the subject, who says:

> The old plays often had no real subject; they had titles, it is true, but these titles were mere names of persons, or mere names of places or incidents. What, for instance, can you make of a title such as *Julius Caesar?* . . . If you are acquainted with the development of the drama, you will know that about ninety years ago a great advance was made by means of what was then called 'The Problem Play'. Some of these plays had a real subject. We have gone much further, of course. Take the subjects of some of our best known plays: *Efficiency, Inefficiency, National Self-consciousness.* These are all by our Chief Dramatic-Composer Grubber. His latest play, *Uric Acid,* is in my opinion even better than these . . . The subject lends itself splendidly to the methods of Meccanian Art.

Attendance at the theatre once a week is compulsory for all Meccanians.

> Our scheme provides a succession of plays throughout the year, all designed as part of our culture, and if people were at liberty to pick and choose what they would see, and what they would not see, we should have no guarantee that they would have gone through the course.

The Meccanian attitude to fine art is also enlightening. They despise their excellent collection of pre-20th-century paintings. "All the 'Nativities' were together in one room, all the 'Madonnas' together in another, all the 'Adam and Eves' together, all the 'Deluges' . . .; whatever the subject every picture relating to that subject was placed together as if the gallery were a collection of butterflies." Of their modern paintings the Meccanians are very proud, though Mr Ming finds them "weird and powerful but almost revolting". Nearby, a teacher is helping a group of visiting schoolgirls to better appreciate the finer points of a painting:

Now let us analyse the colour scheme. By the aid of the colour divider you perceive at once the proportions in which the colours are distributed. Now notice that red, which occupies only 7 per cent of the canvas, is more conspicuous than green, which occupies more than 25 per cent . . . Next notice the method of the brush strokes. Under the microscope you will see the characteristic quality of the brush stroke. It has been already ascertained that in this picture there are 5232 down strokes of an average length of 3 millimetres, 1079 strokes from right to left of an average length of 1½ millimetre, only 490 from left to right and 72 upward strokes . . . The picture was painted in exactly 125 hours. The quantity of paint used must have been almost exactly three-quarters of a litre, so you can make a calculation to ascertain the number of brush strokes to the litre.

What more need be said?

Just in case the author's message remains unclear he has one of the dissenters (confined in an asylum) sum up Meccania thus: "This is no fit place for human beings. It is a community of slaves, who do not even know they are slaves because they have never tasted liberty, ruled over by a caste of super-criminals who have turned crime into a science." It seems surprising that the book was not reissued during World War 11.

A serious rôle-reversal satire is *The Revolt of Man* by Walter Besant, first published (anonymously) in 1882. Set about a hundred years on, it is intended to show the injustice of one sex being kept subservient to the other, and also that women would be incapable of taking over the political and economic management of the UK. The author shows us a topsy-turvy future in which women possess all wealth and property, propose all marriages (old women frequently take young husbands), have all laws biased in their favour, and exclusively make up the membership of the professional classes. The UK is governed by the House of Ladies (the House of Commons having been abolished). Men labour as craftsmen and look after the house, but rarely go out to work; they are kept uneducated and are at any time liable to be imprisoned or even hanged for the crime of wife-beating.

Not surprisingly in 19th-century terms, the decades of feminine domination have been accompanied by a contraction of industry, the collapse of the railway system, a total halt to scientific and technological progress, and a reduction in the population. The result is that within a century Britain has regressed to approximately a 17th-century level of civilization. (But some aspects of the new existence are presented as improvements, particularly the lack of industrial pollution, so Besant's message is not wholly clear and straightforward.)

Although such a reversal is not believable, the author tries hard to be convincing by explaining how the change came about. The women first gained political control (three times as many women as men in parliament), then enacted legislation to give women a legal right to all their husbands' earnings. From there it was a lesser step to achieve a full social and religious reversal (everybody in the country worships the Perfect Woman).

The plot concerns the attempt by the old and ugly (but powerful) Duchess of Dunstanburgh to forcibly marry the young and handsome Lord Chester. A male rebellion is planned which results in a bloodless coup and the installation of Lord Chester as King. Despite this element of romanticism, the book is a much more carefully considered view of rôle-reversal and sex equality than is usually met with. It is a more mature statement than either *Martha Brown MP* or *When Woman Reigns*.

The latter, by August Anson, first published in 1938, is pricipally an escapist fantasy novel; its satirical elements are almost incidental. Ever since 1943 it had been known that "WOMAN is the MASTER SEX" (Anson was another writer who enjoyed capitalization), and long before the year 3500, to which the male protagonist is mystically transported, women are legally and mentally superior to men. They do not marry but treat men as chattels, with noble women owning large harems of handsome, rather effeminate men. If the author had intended this humorously he could have been forgiven for it: sadly, there is a great deal of silliness and some gratuitous sex and violence, but no attempt at wit.

Future wars are a large and most important category of predictive fiction. Although for this reason they are dealt with together elsewhere in this book, we should here take a look at some of the more satirical of them.

The Napoleon of Notting Hill (1904) by G. K. Chesterton is a deliberately antiscientific prophecy aimed at "Mr Wells and others, who thought that science would take charge of the future". In order to show that small things are more important than large and values more important than new technology, Chesterton presents a vision of London in 1984 (the final section is set in 2004) where almost nothing has changed since 1904 because "the people had absolutely lost faith in revolutions". The King (by this time kings are elected), a young eccentric named Auberon Quin, suggests the revival of local patriotism and recommends that the ancient London boroughs should once again think of themselves as small, independent states. This precipitates a war between the boroughs, with Notting Hill defeating the great army of South Kensington and establishing an empire which endures for twenty years. The fighting is accomplished in mediaeval fashion, with swords and spears. For Chesterton, never a simplistic writer, the intention was, of course, not to predict wars between London boroughs but to show that bigger does not mean better — a curiously modern theme for 1904.

Another author whose novels deal with war without being concerned with war was Karel Čapek, whom we have met already. In *The Absolute at Large* (1927) the engineer Marek invents an atomic motor, the Karburator, which utilizes the total sum of energy contained in its fuel and will keep running for months on a few pounds of coal, providing almost infinite energy. The snag (there has to be a snag to any new invention, in order to provide the book with some action) is that, as the fuel is consumed, so that element of God contained within it (He is in all things) is released. In other words the Absolute is suddenly at large, and Marek finds himself able to perform miracles (foretelling the future, healing, levitation).

Despite this, a wealthy industrialist, G. H. Bondy, begins to manufacture and distribute Karburators. They are used to drive cars, aircraft, locomotives, factories, and so on, but their side-effects are immediately noticeable. Everybody suddenly begins to take religion seriously, and only the church is upset. A local bishop tells Marek and Bondy: "Gentlemen, in the name of Heaven, do not imagine that the church brings God into the world. The church merely confines Him and controls Him. And you two unbelievers are loosing Him upon the earth like a flood."

But the Absolute not only brings religion to all, it takes over the machines powered by Karburators and indulges in an orgy of overproduction by working twenty-four hours a day. Enormous local surpluses are produced. Prices fall and the economy slumps. It is not worth distributing goods, and shortages occur. All over the world people are turning to religion — but they are willing to recognize only their own brand of religion. "Everyone measures off a certain amount of Him and then thinks it is the entire God, and then thinks he possesses the whole of Him . . . And then gets angry with everyone else who has a different bit of Him."

This is where the war of 1944-53 begins. It consumes the whole world and is "the Greatest War"; 198 million men take part and only thirteen men survive. Not only has Čapek lampooned religion and the church; he now has a dig at war, too. "Do not rob the people of that time of their only boast — that what they went through was the Greatest War. We, however, know that in a few decades we shall succeed in arranging an even greater war, for in this respect also the human race is progressing ever upward and on."

The moral of the novel seems to be: "The greater the things are in which a man believes, the more fiercely he despises those who do not believe in them. And yet the greatest of all beliefs would be belief in one's fellow men."

Two of Čapek's other works are satires involving future wars. The play *R.U.R.* shows humanoid robots being factory-built and employed all over the world for menial jobs. They rise up in arms and overthrow Man, hoping to replace him. Here Čapek is satirizing the class struggle and endeavouring to show that it is not a simple business of good against evil. In *War With the Newts* he returns to the theme, but substitutes newts for robots. These newts ("about as big as a ten-year-old boy") are sea-living creatures from the East Indies. They are remarkably intelligent, and are exploited by men (the industrialist G. H. Bondy makes another appearance) until they rise up in revolt. In a rather strange war fought around the coasts of the world, the newts win.

H. G. Wells' contribution to satirical accounts of future wars must not be forgotten. This is *The Autocracy of Mr Parham* (1930), a rather long-winded swipe at big business, politics and international affairs between the two world wars. Its setting is contemporary with its publication; only its description of a second world war which breaks out in 1930 makes it predictive. (Incidentally, the novel is splendidly illustrated by cartoonist David Low.)

Mr Parham, a rather shy and retiring senior tutor from Oxford University, is, as the result of additions of ectoplasm at a séance, transformed into the Lord Paramount, self-appointed supreme dictator of Britain. The Lord Paramount is the epitome of goodness, a glowing figure, totally sure of himself. He has come (as he explains) "to save England, trembling on the brink of decadence, to raise her and save her and lead her back to effort and glory and mastery". He is a wish-fulfilment image of Mr Parham's imagination, for many of their ideas and schemes are identical. With the greatest of ease he manages to charm everybody and suspend Parliament.

To recapture England's greatness, the Lord Paramount is quite ready to go to war with Russia which, as he is so fond of saying (in both his incarnations), "is the final danger — the overwhelming enemy". But at the same time he detests the horrors of war, as becomes clear in a conversation with his military chief, General Gerson. Gerson says: "'War is war, and what kills and breaks the spirit best is what you have to use.' — 'But the bombing of towns! Poison gas on civilians. Poison gas almost haphazard.' — 'What right do they have to be civilians?' said Gerson."

War with Russia is soon a fact. Then, due to an Anglo-Japanese treaty, Japan blockades China to prevent her from helping Russia. This action immobilizes some US ships at Chinese ports, destroying one. The USA protests in the strongest possible terms, and the UK and the USA go to war. They fight a sea battle off eastern Canada which begins accidentally but is none the less disastrous, with both sides suffering heavy losses. By this time all of Europe is at war, and London is bombed by German aircraft. Britain's colonies refuse to help her in the war. Here the Lord Paramount's dreams begin to crumble into nightmares. At length Parham wakes to find himself still at the séance: it has all been a dream.

A final and most bitter satire involving future war is *Tomorrow's Yesterday* (1932) by John Gloag (today, 1980, the UK's oldest practising science-fiction writer). It is a savage attack on business methods (advertising in particular), hypocrisy and mankind's stupidity. The main substance of the book concerns a film made in 1932 but showing various (mainly futuristic) eras of mankind being visited by a future race of telepathic beings evolved over three million years from cats. They view an advertising campaign of about 1930, then the hypocrisy of the 1960s where an unfaithful husband berates his son who is participating in the current vogue of companionate (i.e., temporary) marriages, then the outbreak of world war in 1997. In this section it is demonstrated how worthless treaties are, because due to conflicting and interlocking treaties the UK does not know on which side she will be fighting. Only an academic, Professor Lovedale, seems to realize (or to be willing to say) how much futility and hypocrisy there is in war. As one of the cat-creatures says, "Those who were wise were without power."

Four hundred years later there is a low-population barbaric society, but mankind is still governed by stupidity and hypocrisy. The cats transport Professor Lovedale to their own time, the year 3,110,388. He provides mankind's epitaph and the film's moral in saying: "I suppose men had to go, because they smashed everything like petulant children, like the apes they were. Silly and selfish and lascivious." The cats have rid themselves of sex, and hope to do better, learning by man's mistakes. The "film" part of the book is then strongly criticized by most of those who have seen it. But some are intelligent enough to accept the warning. At the very end of the book a real war is breaking out.

Dire warnings can be satirical, too. Apart from warnings of war and conquest, most cautionary predictions concern various dystopian futures (mainly of a totalitarian nature), the creation of utopias which are too fragile to last, and the creation of uncontrollable technology.

Although all dystopian futures include considerable measures of satire (Aldous Huxley's *Brave New World* is a good example), almost all contain even more by way of warning or even genuine prediction, and so are dealt with elsewhere.

Perhaps the most satirical of all dystopian novels (prior to 1945) is *We* by the Russian writer Yevgeny Zamyatin, first published in an English translation in 1924. This is a particularly elliptical novel set in the highly advanced and strangely alien future of the 29th or 30th century. There is a totalitarian régime — the One State — and everybody lives in a single large city where everything is purposely artificial. A wall of glass, the Green Wall, keeps nature at bay. "The wall is, probably, the greatest of all inventions. Man ceased to be a wild animal only when he had built his first wall. Man ceased to be a wild man only when we had built the Green Wall."

Indeed, all walls in the city are of glass: there is no privacy or secrecy; the One State knows all and controls all. Brief periods of privacy are allowed for the purposes of sex, but prior permission must be obtained. Names have disappeared and citizens are designated by numbers preceded by a letter (a consonant for males, a vowel for females). They are even referred to as "numbers" rather than "people". Families, too, have disappeared, and all are sexually available to all. Perhaps most horrifying is that the inhabitants seem content with their lot, unaware of any better existence. And the satire has no redeeming humour; that is what makes it both more believable and more tragic than Jerome K. Jerome's "The New Utopia".

But if every citizen approved of such a régime there would be no story. The narrator, D-503, is keeping a diary. He is a leading scientist working on the development of the Integral, a space vehicle, and he never contemplates another kind of existence — involving freedom say — until he comes under the influence of E-330. She is a member of the underground, and she causes D-503 to rebel against the system in small ways. She is responsible for his estrangement from 0-90, his regular partner. He complains that revolution is madness, but E-330 says that there must be continual revolution: "There is no ultimate revolution." This is undoubtedly the theme of the novel.

Of course D-503, although he fails to realize it, is being used only because of his position as one of those in charge of the construction of the Integral: a plan to seize the ship during a trial flight fails.

The state begins to carry out brain operations on all its citizens to remove the element of fantasy: this, it is claimed, will leave them happier, while in fact it removes their capacity to think for themselves. Eventually D-503 is forced to undergo the operation, too. There is no happy ending.

A warning against an unstable utopia is contained in E. M. Forster's tale "The Machine Stops", which first appeared in 1909. Like G. K.

Chesterton's *The Napoleon of Notting Hill* it was intended to satirize H. G. Wells' technological futures such as *When the Sleeper Wakes* and "A Story of the Days to Come".

"The Machine Stops" portrays a utopia obviously intended to be many hundreds or thousands of years in the future where everything is controlled by the Machine. People live safely and happily, each in their own room, deep underground, never going out, and never meeting face-to-face but communicating by picture screens.

The main characters are Vashti, an old woman, and Kuno, her grown-up son, who is something of a rebel. He wishes to visit the surface, but she tries to dissuade him: although it is not forbidden it is "contrary to the spirit of the age". Even Vashti, it must be noted, is not perfectly happy. Her bed is too large, but only one size of bed is built now, because any other system "would have involved vast alterations in the Machine".

This is our first clue that the Machine is not omnipotent. The fact that only one book is permitted now — the Book of the Machine, containing all possible instructions — and that this book, as the "personification" of the Machine, is worshipped, is a satirical comment on human beliefs.

Then Kuno, who lives half the world away, contacts her and asks her to come to see him. Unwillingly she consents. It is possible to travel anywhere quickly and conveniently by airship, but few people bother because communications are so good and the underground rooms are the same in every part of the world. When she arrives, Kuno tells her that he has visited the surface by an illegal route. He has seen people living on the surface, contrary to everything he had ever been told, but the Machine's Mending Apparatus (looking like a bundle of large white worms) found him and returned him to his room before he was able to make contact with the surface people.

Some time after this, surface respirators are forbidden in order to stop people from visiting the outside, and a philosophy grows up which urges people to beware of first-hand ideas: second-hand or tenth-hand thoughts are far better than going and looking. The Machine is made an official object of worship.

But Kuno realizes that the Machine is stopping; parts of it are wearing out. Its quality of service deteriorates rapidly until it fails completely, leaving people to wander around in the dark, dying of cold and suffocation. Kuno says, at the end, that the Machine will never be started again because "humanity has learned its lesson". In a sense, any aspect of technology upon which mankind comes to depend is the Machine.

A slightly different warning against technology, as something which mankind may let loose and then be unable to control, is part of the theme of Harold Nicolson's 1932 novel *Public Faces*. This is mainly a political satire (written by a one-time British cabinet minister), but it warns against the creation and testing of an atomic bomb. Its Epilogue and Appendix are wholly satirical.

Some of the major categories of predictive literature are rarely combined with much satire. Escapist fiction is most often light adventure which tries to draw few parallels between present and future.

An exception is H. G. Wells' "A Story of the Days to Come", which first appeared in 1899. Although it is a story of love and adventure in the world of 2100, the first few pages in particular mock Victorian England, comparing the life and times of "the excellent Mr Morris" with that of his descendant of 2100, Mwres (the spelling having been changed and the "Mr" dropped). The satire stands out fairly distinctly from the serious prediction, as in this interchange: "I suppose you don't read books?" — "Dear, no," said Mwres. "I went to a modern school and we had none of that old-fashioned nonsense. Phonographs are good enough for me." And the age of 2100 is described as "when the sham half-timbered house had gone the way of all shams, and *The Times* was extinct, and the silk hat a ridiculous antiquity . . ."

Works of wish fulfilment normally include a dash of satire, particulary when inhabitants of the future make wrong assumptions about the past; or, as in W. H. Hudson's *A Crystal Age* or William Morris's *News From Nowhere,* in the reception by a future utopia of that standard character, the visitor from the present. In *A Crystal Age,* for example, the visitor finds that none of the countries or famous men of which he so proudly boasts have been heard of by his far-future hosts.

There is relatively little intentional satire in tales of alien contact or of serious prediction, although scattered examples can be found. The best known alien-contact story, Wells' *The War of the Worlds,* involves a good deal of satire upon human behaviour and human reaction to discovering that we are not, after all, lords of creation. Some serious prediction is satirical in the way it adapts its present, as with Rudyard Kipling's adaptation of sailors into fliers in his two Aerial Board of Control stories, "With the Night Mail" and "As Easy as A.B.C.". Jules Verne, whose novels were a combination of escapism and serious prediction, normally includes some unconscious satire, but now and then it is obviously intentional, as in the story "In the 29th Century", where "The United Kingdom, Canada and New Britain belong to the Americans, India to the Russians, and Australia and New Zealand to themselves! Of all that once was England, what's left? . . . Nothing!"

Among philosophical predictions, George Bernard Shaw's play *Back to Methuselah* is outstanding as being full of satire (like all of Shaw's work). First published in 1921, the play is set at various times in the past, present and future, including AD2170, AD3000 and AD31,920. The theme is the possibility of voluntary longevity for humans (if they want it badly enough they acquire it) and the additional maturity this allows them to achieve. Shaw's intention (as he makes clear in the preface to the play) was to discredit Darwinism and put forward his own Lamarckian ideas of evolution. Along the way he satirizes youth, old age, class consciousness, maturity, women's rights, the contemporary social graces and much more.

And finally Gabriel de Tarde's *Underground Man,* first published in English in 1905 (with a preface by H. G. Wells), deals with the philosophy of Man and his culture changing as a result of a change in environment. It parodies human reactions and values. For example, when mankind of the 25th century retreats underground to escape the glaciation of Earth, no animals or plants are taken although the world's art treasures are saved. It is suggested that future generations of Man will be forced to retreat even deeper towards the warmer core of the Earth, with a contracting population but a richer, happier one, until there is "the last man, sole survivor and heir of a hundred successive civilisations, left to himself yet self-sufficient in the midst of his immense stores of science and art".

5 THROUGH THE SUN IN AN AIRSHIP

ESCAPISM

To classify a novel as escapist seems to be regarded as only a short step away from condemnation. It is as if one were saying, "This book is a good read but it has no message."

Yet surely all fiction should be written with the intention of providing entertainment, so all fiction should be escapist to a certain extent. Predictive fiction in particular should be readily classifiable as escapist in the sense that it takes the reader away from his customary time and place, precipitating him into a near or far future, transporting him to other worlds. Merely to describe the wonders of future technology may be entertaining enough to be termed escapist. Certainly a future or a dire warning should make inherently exciting — if perhaps harrowing — reading.

Even so, the most usual escapist element in fiction is the plot — action involving people. Almost all predictive fiction, whatever the author's main intention, has a plot. (There are exceptions: neither the anonymous *The Reign of George VI 1900-1925* nor W. D. Hay's *Three Hundred Years Hence* have either characters or plot, and there are many utopian tales with very little plot at all.)

According to the well known science-fiction writer Robert A. Heinlein there are only three basic plots involving people: "boy-meets-girl", "the Little Tailor", and "the man-who-learned-better". The first of these is self-explanatory, the second means that the protagonist improves his lot during the course of the book, and "the man-who-learned-better" is about somebody who has a good reason for changing his opinions, ending up wiser and possibly even sadder. Any of these three may be varied or reversed or complicated.

Rather naturally, boy-meets-girl plots predominate in early predictive fiction. The Victorian readers liked to have a thread of romance running through the stories they read, even if those stories were intended to warn of terrible futures, portray wars or show how utopia might be reached well before the year 2000. Thus in Ignatius Donnelly's *Caesar's Column*, while the Brotherhood of Destruction is plotting to overthrow the bloated Plutocracy, Gabriel Weltstein is furthering his relationship with Estella Washington; Herman Heideck makes eyes at Edith Irwin in *The Coming Conquest of England* by August

Niemann, even though she is married and their countries are at war; and Julian West relieves the tedium of Dr Leete's explanations in *Looking Backward 2000-1887* by falling in love with his daughter, Edith.

As for little tailors, in *The Lord of Life* by Neil Bell, Sid Larkins, who has been the least of men for so long, becomes at last the only man who can save the human race from extinction; Marie Corelli's dowdy spinster of middle years, Diana May, becomes *The Young Diana,* rejuvenated into the world's most beautiful young woman; and Nedram's eponymous John Sagur makes himself Master of the World.

The man-who-learned-better crops up as Lord Chester in Walter Besant's *The Revolt of Man,* who discovers that men need not be subservient to women; as D-503, *We* by Yevgeny Zamyatin, who discovers revolution as a way of life; while in H. G. Wells' *In the Days of the Comet* everybody breathes in the green vapours and they *all* learn better!

An interesting case is Ayn Rand's novel *Anthem.* Despite being a satire with strong philosophical intentions it manages to cram all three themes into a short and simple plot.

Having so carefully explained that all these fine books can be considered as escapist literature by virtue of their plot elements I must now admit that most predictive fiction is not of a particularly high literary standard. For every future war story of the calibre of Chesney's *The Battle of Dorking* there are several shallow imitations which succeed only on the level of adventure fiction — if at all. For every work which possesses the subtlety and inventiveness of "Saki's" *When William Came* or Benson's *Lord of the World* or Zamyatin's *We* there are many which do not. Wells' multi-level treatments of Martian invasion, hive intelligences and Man's evolutionary destiny were transformed, through Hugo Gernsback's editorship, into the pulp space-opera of the 1930s. Even so, some purely escapist fiction is of the very highest quality, normally due to the depth of characterization.

Nearly all predictive fiction which is primarily escapist concerns either disasters (and their aftermaths) or voyages. This is rather a rough and arbitary classification but it works well in practice.

Some books manage to include both disasters and voyages, straddling the categories. George Griffith's *The Angel of the Revolution,* which we have already met, is one of these. Its disaster is widespread war, in which enormous damage is done by aerial craft of different sorts and millions of people are killed, particularly in Europe. Its voyages are by airship to many places around the world, including the secret refuge of the anarchists — a hidden valley in West Africa. There is much other escapist content in this novel, such as the unmasking of spies and the developing romance between the central characters, Richard Arnold and Natasha.

Its sequel, *Olga Romanoff*, set in the 2030s, carries on with the same exciting mixture. At one point the Earth passes through the "fire-mist" of a comet, which destroys all surface life. But the Aerians have been warned of this by a prophecy from the days of *The Angel of the Revolution*. They retreat into deep caves and survive the devastating effects of the calamity.

Of all predicted disasters, war is the most common. While a few future war stories were intended as warnings of the consequences of unpreparedness or simply as arguments against senseless slaughter, most authors treated war — and even the invasion of their own countries — as a peg on which to hang an adventure story. Louis Tracy's *The Invaders* (1901) is not really trying to warn against the rather ludicrous possibility of tens of thousands of French and German troops entering the UK wearing civilian clothes, travelling by rail to Liverpool and then revealing themselves as armed invaders. Nor is it anti-war; indeed, all its violence is glorified.

M. P. Shiel's novels of Asian invasion were likewise not intended to be taken seriously. While not quite as farcical as P. G. Wodehouse's invasion story, *The Swoop!* (1909), they show dastardly orientals ordering the invasion of Europe by millions of troops in order to satisfy personal grudges.

In *The Yellow Danger* (1895) Yen How, who is half Japanese, half Chinese, is rejected by an English girl whom he loves. He feels that he and his race have been slighted and, because he is paranoid to a considerable degree, takes this as a sign that the white races are gaining too much superiority over the yellow races. He is determined to make England pay dearly for the snub and, in the fullness of time, rises to be the Chinese leader, forges an alliance with Japan, and has the whole of both nations trained for fighting.

An immense yellow army of more than a hundred million men sets off to trek across Asia and Europe, committing atrocities wherever it goes (this is a very anti-Chinese novel) until it reaches the English Channel. A dashing young English naval officer, John Hardy — who has already been largely responsible for the defeat of England's European enemies — smashes the might of the Japanese navy in the English Channel and then causes a plague to be introduced into the Chinese army, wiping it out.

In *The Yellow Peril* (first published in 1913 as *The Dragon*), the plot is, if anything, even a trifle less convincing than in *The Yellow Danger*. This time the story is set forty years in the future. The dastardly oriental is Li Ku Yu, and his invasion of England is by parachute from airships. Again his reason is a personal one, based on a hatred of the Prince of Wales — Teddy — with whom he was at school in England.

There is a general European war in this book, too, with many naval battles, as well as a lot of exciting action involving kidnaps, escapes and chases across London, particularly in the struggle to obtain possession of a terrible new weapon — the "red ray" — the effect of which is to make people go blind. Not least is there a complex romantic element.

While William Le Queux always included a strong patriotic message in his speculative novels he was careful to combine it with much gory and exciting detail, to ensure credibility. His imitators could match neither the fervour of his message nor the inflammatory splendour of his descriptions. When, for example, Le Queux's *The Unknown Tomorrow* (1910), the story of how an ultimately unsuccessful socialist revolution brings war and disaster to Britian, was copied by Leslie Beresford (writing as "Pan") in *The Great Image* (1921), the result was a mediocre and unconvincing novel.

In attempting to distance his action from the contemporary scene, Beresford set it a hundred years on, in 2021, but without including sufficient changes in technology or society to make his setting plausible. He added a love-affair across class-boundaries (Le Queux did not generally insert love themes into his predictive novels) and tried to maintain interest by means of such devices as hostages being rescued, rivalry between different socialist leaders and, when all else failed, a European invasion of the UK which is relieved only by the "miracle" of military assistance from the USA. (One of the Americans drawls: "Well . . . I guess we both speak the same language and come from the same stock. You would hardly expect us to stand by idly when it's a case like that, would you?") In fairness to Leslie Beresford it must be mentioned that he was attempting not just to entertain the reader but to put across his own philosophical message.

Other forms of disaster are usually dealt with similarly, with great emphasis on human suffering, subplots involving romance or perhaps a clash of loyalties, and — whenever possible — a happy ending.

For example, in *Hartmann the Anarchist or The Doom of the Great City* (1893), by E. Douglas Fawcett, a group of anarchists is intent upon causing death and destruction in London by dropping bombs on it from an airship. Neither the anarchists nor the author have any particular message in mind. Hartmann and his merry men wish only to smash everything — to wreck civilization. Their motivation is not analyzed and remains obscure to the end.

Anyway, no one has time to worry about motivation as a perfectly decent young man is fooled into boarding the airship (hovering unseen in the depths of London's Hyde Park) and kept there as a prisoner while the anarchists perform their dreadful deeds with bombs and machine guns. There is a subplot involving the hero's fiancée and Hartmann's aged and widowed mother (who is seriously injured in the attack on London and dictates a deathbed letter to her son). The happy ending comes when the airship explodes — for no explained reason.

The shapes adopted by disasters which afflict humanity are legion.

Sometimes they are presented as threats and at other times as genocidal realities.

There may be an astronomical cause, such as the Moon or some other fairly large body colliding with the Earth. In *When Worlds Collide* (1933), by Philip Wylie and Edwin Balmer, a pair of extra-solar planets race towards the Earth; one hits us but the other provides a safe refuge for some lucky survivors. In Dennis Wheatley's *Sixty Days to Live* (1939) a comet is the agent of doom, though it does not destroy the world.

Other natural causes are common, particularly flood, but also ice, fog (in W. D. Hay's *The Doom of the Great City*, 1880), storm, earthquake, volcanic eruption (in "The Thames Valley Catastrophe" Grant Allen causes London to perish by this means), plagues and a variety of gas clouds.

Some authors specialized in the use of such themes, none to a greater extent than Fred M. White, who had six disaster stories published in *Pearson's Magazine* in 1903-4. All set in London, they are based on plague (which is cured by electricity!), arctic weather conditions (he had earlier used this theme in a novel, *The White Battalions*, 1900), impenetrable fog, underground explosions, poisoned water supplies and . . . a Stock Exchange crash! Perhaps White had something against London.

During the pulp magazine era disasters were often connected with giant animals (like King Kong) or with alien invasion. Almost all of these were just adventure stories, showing a few or many people being killed. Occasionally the whole human race was wiped out.

More interesting are those stories which show not just the disaster itself (reading about violent death gets boring after a while) but the aftermath — the rebuilding of civilization, the gallant struggle to survive and multiply in a newly hostile environment, the lapse into barbarism, the last man, and so on.

In fact, *The Last Man* is a good example of such a tale. Mary Shelley's 1826 novel of that name is set mainly in the 2090s but makes scant use of prophecy and predicts little by way of change or progress. Although at one point she says, "The arts of life, and the discoveries of science had augmented in a ratio which left all calculation behind; food sprang up, so to say, spontaneously — machines existed to supply with facility every want of the population," she tends to forget about this and describes the condition of life as if she were speaking of her own time and had given the novel a contemporary background.

In 2092 a plague arises in war-devastated Constantinople and spreads across Europe. Although it travels slowly, it spares no one. By 2094 it is rife in France and cases are beginning to occur in London.

A contemporary review of the novel objected to all the lengthy dwelling upon death, referring to the work as "the product of a diseased imagination and a polluted taste, which described the ravages of the plague in such minute detail that the result was not a picture but a lecture in anatomy". Obviously reviewers had weaker stomachs in those days.

By 2096 "London did not contain above a thousand inhabitants; and the number was continually diminishing". The few survivors, including the book's main characters, decide to emigrate but take a long time to organize themselves and gather together. At length it is only on January 1st 2098 that, now reduced to five hundred, they leave London for Paris. There follows an interesting description of deserted London, reminiscent of those which were to appear much later in Richard Jefferies' *After London* and J. D. Beresford's *Goslings*.

In Paris there is strife between different groups of survivors. The plague breaks out among them again and the numbers dwindle rapidly as many of them travel toward Italy. Then there are only four — Lionel Verney (the narrator), his friend Adrian, the narrator's young son and his teenaged niece. Ironically the boy dies of fever and the other two are drowned in a shipwreck while trying to reach the Greek islands. Only Lionel Verney is left: the "LAST MAN", as the novel puts it.

He journeys to Rome where he lives in solitary splendour for a year, writing his memoirs, before noting the arrival of the year 2100 and sailing off for warmer climes.

The Last Man is a romantic novel of its period, telling an escapist story. Some of its characters are drawn from life — Adrian is based on Percy Bysshe Shelley, and Lionel Verney is supposed to be, in some respects, a representation of Mary Shelley herself — yet the book was written first and foremost to entertain. It was influential in causing both Thomas Hood and Thomas Campbell to write poems entitled "The Last Man".

Jack London's story "The Scarlet Plague" (1915) shows not just one person immune to a new disease, but such a small number that humanity (which rapidly degenerates into barbarism) seems unlikely to survive. The story is set in 2073, some sixty years after the disaster, and is narrated by an old man to sceptical and illiterate children.

J. D. Beresford's "new plague" in *Goslings*, first published in 1913, affects only the men. The novel shows women trying to cope with almost no men to help. They survive well after the "dead wood" (the old and those unable to accept the disaster) has been eliminated. This is an exciting tale with plenty of incident, love themes and a happy ending. The author does show how a better world can be built from this fresh start but he does not over-emphasize the message.

Another "last man" story (a popular theme over the years) is *The Purple Cloud* by M. P. Shiel, first published in 1901. A man on an expedition to the North Pole is the only one to escape death when a new volcano "in some South Sea region" begins spewing out cyanide gas — the purple cloud. He soon realizes that something has killed the rest of the world's people, but he does not know the truth until he reaches England and reads old newspaper reports of the slow spread of death around the world. Then he travels the world by land and sea, searching for survivors who might have shut themselves in an airtight room or a mineshaft — but he finds no one.

Twenty years later, after he has burnt Constantinople, he finds a girl there, born in an airtight prison after the disaster, and completely uneducated, though intelligent. After rejecting her for a while (he is a strange man, perhaps mad) he changes his mind when another deadly eruption threatens; only then does he become determined to save them both and begin again. (The Adam and Eve theme is another recurring one in escapist science fiction.)

The aftermaths of disasters are often lengthy: mankind regresses to savagery before recovering, and sometimes never recovers at all. Richard Jefferies' version of this is *After London* (1885). The disaster is unspecified, and what happens to most of the population of the UK is unknown, but the author delights in taking about sixty pages to describe most of the country (but especially London) being reclaimed by nature as the few people who remain lapse into barbarism. The rest of the book is a romance — very mediaeval in flavour — complete with action and love interest.

Thirty-five years after Jefferies' novel, Edward Shanks used a similar theme in *The People of the Ruins* (1920). Here a man of 1924, Jeremy Tuft, is miraculously put into suspended animation in a London cellar and does not wake until 2074. In 1924 there has been a General Strike in progress and a workers' revolution in prospect; in 2074 London is mostly empty and derelict, and for the most part technology has been forgotten.

The south of England is ruled by the Speaker, whose subjects, living at perhaps a 17th-century level, all seem gentle and disinterested. Tuft admits that he served in the artillery during World War I and that he is a physicist by profession. The Speaker is delighted and urges him to design and build big guns — he has an obsession with them, believing that they will bring him lasting victory against the men of northern England. He even promises Tuft his daughter, the Lady Eva, if success comes.

This plan is carried out and seems to be working, but a Welsh army defeats the Speaker when one of his officers (a Canadian) defects to the other side during battle. Initially Jeremy Tuft and the Speaker escape, collecting Lady Eva, but they cannot outrun their enemies and the book ends on a low note. Basically this is just another historical romance.

A much finer version of barbaric Britain came from the pen of the UK writer John Collier. *Tom's A-Cold* (also known as *Full Circle,* 1933) is a deep and moving novel which has much to say concerning the problems of leadership, generation gaps and the preservation of knowledge, for all that it is still essentially an escapist romance.

The breakdown of civilization happened sixty years before the time of the novel, in 1935, "when war, defeat, revolution and blockade had burst in swift succession on the country". Now, in 1995, the UK's small population lives in widely spaced communities on the sites of former towns or farms, at a mediaeval or dark ages level of sophistication. There is little communication or trade between them.

In one particular community of about a hundred, tucked away in a secluded Hampshire valley, there is reasonable prosperity but a continual fear of attack by some larger group. The chief, a member of the first generation born after the collapse, grew up at a time when survival from one day to the next was all that could reasonably be hoped for; he is illiterate, superstitious, and contemptuous of pre-collapse knowledge.

Father is one of the few remaining members of the old generation which saw the collapse; he was formerly chief and is the main repository of learning in the community. In these better times he has tried hard to educate the second generation — his grandchildren — so as not to let all the skills of the 1930s slip away. So Harry and Crab, the main characters, young men, are reasonably well educated and probably more able to lead the community than is the chief, a circumstance which produces strains.

The chief suggests a raid on Swindon to gain more women — wives for the young men — sending Harry (an obvious leader) and Crab (more devious, a planner) to reconnoitre. They work out a plan of attack, and the raid is a great success, capturing several women including Rose, with whom Harry has fallen in love. But the rivalry between Harry and the chief grows worse, and Crab secretly wounds the chief with an arrow. Under the pretence of administering medicine to the wound, Father poisons him, and Harry takes over as chief.

There are complications when Rose's brother, who has come looking for her, is killed. She escapes and brings back a large force from Swindon. Although this is defeated, Crab dies and Harry's standing deteriorates.

There is a great deal more than this to the novel, but its plot is always exciting, with action and romance. It does, perhaps, show a far too rapid sweeping away of too much 20th-century technology, yet for all that the situation is a credible one.

A US variation on the theme is George Allan England's massive three-volume work, *Darkness and Dawn* (1914; but serialized during 1912 and 1913). Its two protagonists, Allan and Beatrice, wake up in a ruined New York after some fifteen hundred years of inexplicable suspended animation. The plot is full of fast-moving action as they explore the ruins, encountering various types of savages, subhumans and dangerous animals.

Atomic explosions leave very little of Earth's population or natural resources upon which to build in *The Lord of Life* (1933) by Neil Bell. The main substance of the book is the farcical situation of nineteen men and one woman trying to continue the human race. The woman takes several husbands (one at a time) without managing to bear any female children. At length only one man has not tried, but he is the underdog — employed as nanny to the male children. Refusing to take his chance, he goes off on his own and finds another woman, who has lived alone ever since the disaster. Together they produce girl children with no trouble, and it looks as if the human race might be saved after all. Among the black humour of the situation (and the sense of wonder provoked by the gradual reappearance of many plant species which had been feared extinct) the author put across a message about the idiocy of the class structure.

A new ice age seems to have been the cause of civilization's breakdown in *The Strange Invaders*, Alun Llewellyn's 1934 novel, but several hundred years later this is not certain. In the small Russian community where the action is set there are remainders of the past — a religion based partly on old machines which no longer work, with ikons of Marx, Lenin and Stalin, and services held in a former factory.

Crisis is coming, with the ice sheets moving south and groups of tartars moving north, striving to escape from the terrible invaders in which they hardly dare believe. These are giant lizards, which move faster than the eye can follow; they are multicoloured and deadly, remaining enigmatic to the end.

The virile young Alud proves his bravery and defies the local military chief in order to claim the beautiful Erya as his woman . . .

And, as we have seen, in R. C. Sherriff's *The Hopkins Manuscript* (1939; revised as *The Cataclysm,* 1958) the Moon spirals down to collide with the Earth and fill the northern Atlantic Ocean. Most people in England survive, but they need to struggle to grow enough food. After a few years valuable mineral resources are found in the Earthbound Moon, and a European war breaks out over the allocation of these, precipitating the world into a worse situation than ever. Here it is the everyday incidents of life before, during and after the disaster which make up the plot.

To say that many escapist predictions involve voyages is true but rather trite. If we include voyages through time and, symbolically, voyages of the mind and the advance of science, almost all of predictive science fiction can be embraced.

All the same, any kind of voyage is a first-rate device for good escapist fiction. There is the wish-fulfilment aspect of travel to new lands (for more of this see Chapter 6), together with limitless possibilities for adventure *en route* and new discoveries at the voyage's destination. Almost all interplanetary adventures are for this reason really escapist. Readers have always been fascinated by expeditions to other planets, even if there is no actual landing (as in Jules Verne's *From the Earth to the Moon)*, a fascination deriving partly from the vehicle and partly from the scenery. *Through the Sun in an Airship* (1909) by John Mastin is a particularly ludicrous space adventure, in which a spaceship is actually driven through the disk of the Sun without getting hot. This is a sequel to *The Stolen Planet* (1906). George Locke, in *Voyages in Space,* describes it as "great stuff for kids".

Jules Verne was one of the principal exploiters of escapist voyages, taking his readers to all manner of new and strange places around the world by means of, notably, airship and submarine. Some of his books are little more than travelogues, and not all are noticeably futuristic, but they are exciting. Many other writers, before and since Verne, have tried the same thing but with less success; they were less prolific than Verne and, usually, their ideas were less original.

One which anticipated Verne was Lord Charles Moresby's *A Hundred Years Hence* (1828), which extrapolated only a trifle from the new forms of transport designed at that time. It presents a round-the-world journey by means of carriages drawn by kites and propelled by steam, with balloons to cross the oceans. Other stories were very poor-minded.

And some of them were very bad indeed, like *The Air Battle* by Herrmann Lang, first published in English in 1859. Set some five thousand years hence, the story opens in the UK, now much diminished in size due to earthquakes and floods, in which "an enormous portion of the island was submerged" leaving only a strip of country sixty miles long by forty miles wide. The inhabitants are poor and primitive as compared with the powerful and technologically advanced black nations, particularly Madeira, Sahara and Brazilia. The latter possesses aerial fleets, including some ships capable of transporting 2000 men. The plot leaps about (by aircraft) between England, Sahara and Madeira, with these last two countries eventually going to war. There is a love interest and an encounter with a spider whose body is "as large as that of an ox", but all ends happily.

During the 20th century the scope for speculative voyages on Earth has been gradually diminished, except for trips into the wonderful world of the future, which have naturally become more common. Some of these are by time machine or suspended animation or dream, others just romances of the future without any contemporary observer.

Wells' *The Time Machine* (1895) itself is still an exciting novel when read today, with its dream of riding into the future, watching days and years flicker past like a speeded-up film or the riffled pages of a book.

There is titillating strangeness in the landscape of the future, love between the Time Traveller and childlike Weena, great danger in fights with the evil Morlocks, and the sense of wonder evoked by the sight of the larger, duller Sun, thirty million years hence, barely warming an almost barren Earth.

Egon Friedell's sequel, *The Return of the Time Machine* (first published in 1946 but written much earlier, possibly in 1908), is a poor effort, including fragmentary descriptions of trips to 1995 and 2123. But Christopher Priest's 1976 pastiche of Wells, *The Space Machine,* links together *The Time Machine* and *The War of the Worlds,* using Wells himself as a character; it is a highly enjoyable romp.

S. Fowler Wright wrote a couple of novels set on a far future Earth, half a million years hence, when Man is forgotten and new intelligent races rule: these are *The Amphibians* (1925) and *The World Below* (1929). His narrator also uses a time machine to get there, but the writing is mostly shallow, all-action stuff.

There have been a number of extensions of the "sleeper wakes" theme in which a 20th-century man undergoes successive periods of time travel or suspended animation in order to reach the far future, stopping to sight-see along the way. Among these is *The Man Who Awoke* by Laurence Manning (which appeared as magazine stories in 1933 but was not published in book form until 1975). The protagonist, Winters, puts himself into suspended animation for successive periods of several thousand years, taking a look at various wonderful worlds of the future.

The author succeeds in cramming most of science fiction's cliches into these stories. By AD5000 humanity has already lost its chest hair and appendix. In AD10,000 the Brain controls every facet of human existence, though life is mostly wine, women and song in the luxury of the pleasure palaces; Winters helps the underground to put the Brain out of action before moving on. In AD15,000 most of the population (they have lost their teeth by this time) are coupled up to dream machines and again Winters leads a revolt of dissidents. In AD20,000 several scientists are waiting for him to emerge so that they can grab him with their machines and use him in breeding experiments — but he escapes. And his final awakening in AD25,000 coincides with the discovery of immortality. Winters is made young again and goes off on a centuries-long expedition in space. It is second-rate thrill-a-minute stuff.

August Anson's *When Woman Reigns* (1938) is similar. Although not written for the pulp magazines it is every bit as bad. The narrator is projected forwards in time by transcendental means. He stops briefly in 2525, where women are the superior sex and treat men as chattels. Then, in AD3500, he is placed in a male harem and, for a while, becomes the favourite man of the gorgeous Lady Mayina. She casts him aside and he is forced to undergo a number of indignities, privations and actual tortures at her order before she finally admits her undying love for him. Soon after, he is transcendentally transported back to the 20th century. The book is even worse than this summary makes it sound. It does include plenty of sex and violence.

There are some clearly escapist predictions which concern neither disasters nor voyages, being miscellaneous adventures and farces.

One of the most important of these is Hugo Gernsback's early novel, *Ralph 124C41+* (magazine appearance 1911, first book publication 1925). This is a book full of astonishing scientific predictions (quite a number of which have come true) and appallingly bad writing. It is exactly the kind of fiction with which Gernsback tried to fill his "scientifiction" magazines and is a preview of their strengths and weaknesses.

It is set in 2660, where Ralph is the world's most famous scientist — the leading theorist and practical experimenter in numerous disciplines, no less. He is also a man of action, sending a blast of power halfway across the world in a trice to melt an avalanche and save the life of Alice 212B423. Then he shows her the wonders of New York, most of which she seems ignorant of despite the fact that she is well educated and that there is perfect availability of information for all. (This is known as idiot plotting.)

But a Martian — tall though humanoid; they are fully integrated with humanity, some living on Earth — has also fallen for Alice, and after various plot complications kidnaps her. There is a chase through space as Ralph catches up with them, but Alice is killed. So Ralph calmly brings her back to life using various new techniques he has coincidentally developed.

Some of the technological predictions are original, others have been borrowed from Albert Robida or H. G. Wells, and some are just very silly — examples of pseudo-science, unnecessary or self-contradictory. (In Chapter 8 we shall return to Gernsback's predictions.)

Ralph 124C41 (the number can be pronounced as "one to foresee for one"!) is not far from being farce. Other predictive novels can be even sillier, with the emphasis almost entirely on lighthearted escapist entertainment rather than any sort of realistic portrayal of the future.

A couple we have met already. One is C. J. Cutcliffe Hyne's *Emperor of the World* (1910) in which a penniless and starving scientist uses his "new force" to melt iron selectively and with great accuracy at any distance, and writes letters to the newspapers, signing himself *"Imperator Mundi"*. He is, undoubtedly, the most powerful man in the world, giving orders to politicians and nations, but is not practical enough to earn any money from his inventions. The other, *Martha Brown MP* (1935) by Victoria Cross, is a rôle-reversal novel which claims to be set in the 30th century. Neither the tall, broad-shouldered, infinitely capable, pipe-smoking heroine, nor her smaller, weaker, more emotional, skirt-wearing husband are at all credible.

Among other futuristic farces are three by Dacre Balsdon — *Have a New Master* (1935), *Sell England?* (1936), and *The Day They Burned Miss Termag* (1961) — which fail to succeed as escapism, or as anything else.

A tricky category of speculative fiction is the lost world story. On the grounds that these predict strange civilizations, tribes or groups of animals existing in out-of-the-way parts of the world, they must be mentioned, even though very few such stories are actually futuristic. This is a distinct subgenre of science fiction and fantasy, linked with the strange (and often satirical) travels to advanced or fantastic countries which were written by people such as Sir Thomas More and Dean Swift from the 16th to the 18th century.

By the year 1800, unknown islands were becoming harder to find. Authors more frequently began to set their fantasy worlds in the future or on other planets, but some remained faithful to the more isolated parts of Earth at their own time.

The centres of continents were still *terra incognita,* so H. Rider Haggard set many lost race novels in Africa, from *King Solomon's Mines* in 1885 to the late Allan Quartermain tales of the 1920s. As late as 1872, Samuel Butler considered New Zealand wild enough to host an unknown civilization, and he set his satirical utopian novel *Erewhon* there. James Hilton used Tibet (the scene of Haggard's *Ayesha)* as the setting for *Lost Horizon* (1933). In *The Lost World*(1912) by Sir Arthur Conan Doyle Professor Challenger and party discover dinosaurs on a remote plateau in South America.

More imaginative writers have postulated whole new worlds inside the Earth. Here Jules Verne's *Journey to the Centre of the Earth* (French publication 1864, English publication 1872) and Edgar Rice Burroughs' *Pellucidar* series (from 1914) are the best known, although the hollow Earth theme has turned up frequently since at least the 1720s. As a variation there have been civilizations found in caverns only just below the surface of the Earth, as in Lord Lytton's *The Coming Race* (1871) and Joseph O'Neill's *Land Under England* (1935).

There have often been connections with the Atlantis myth, and some lost races have, indeed been claimed as remnants of that civilization. The heyday of the lost race story was the second half of the 19th century and the first half of the 20th. Today they are out of fashion — but not quite extinct.

6 EMPEROR OF THE WORLD

WISH FULFILMENT

Everybody has daydreams. "Wouldn't it be wonderful if . . ." is a common pastime, especially among children, adolescents and writers — and, to be honest, most of the rest of us. Even the bitterness and disillusionment of maturity do not entirely expunge the feelings; hopes linger on of a sudden fortune won in a lottery or football pool. Politicians try to make their daydreams come true in reality — and they nearly always fail. Some speculative writers try to make their daydreams come true on the pages of books; they often succeed.

What are these daydreams, these wishes fulfilled *via* the medium of the written word? As far as we are concerned, any prophecy of the future may be a form of wish fulfilment, because most of mankind has an insatiable desire to know what will happen tomorrow, next month, next year, next century. We want something to marvel over: this is the "sense of wonder" with which so much science fiction is said to be imbued. People like to dream of (or read of, in the fictionalized versions of others' dreams) better times than their own. They like to read of a future when there is no poverty or hunger or unhappiness, when all drudgery is left to fully automated machines, when people are rich enough to satisfy all dreams, when mankind is healthier and longer-lived, when human traits like aggression and dishonesty have disappeared.

These are the more generalized dreams. In some cases wish fulfilment would mean world domination for a particular nation or colour or creed. In other cases it means the achievement of great personal power, either through the possession of a particular supernormal talent or the development of a new machine. Some wishes are to travel to *terra incognita,* to unvisited parts of Earth when Earth still had unvisited parts, and to other planets as Earth became more extensively explored. A few people even want to see an end to technological progress and a return to a slower, quieter, more pastoral existence.

A utopia takes time to develop; it cannot be produced overnight.

Or can it? H. G. Wells, in his novel *In the Days of the Comet* (1906), shows how, quite suddenly, the Change comes over the Earth. The setting is the very near future. A war is in progress between the UK and Germany. The narrator, mad with jealousy, is trying to shoot his former sweetheart and her lover.

Then there comes a "rush of green vapours" from a passing comet, and everybody is changed. All over the world humanity is at first rendered unconscious, then wakes to see everything in that proverbial new light, with more love, more tolerance, more charity. As the narrator puts it,

> The dominant impression I would convey in this account of the Change is one of enormous release, of a vast substantial exaltation. There was an effect, as it were, of light-headedness that was also clear-headedness, and the alteration in one's bodily sensations, instead of producing the mental obfuscation, the loss of identity that was a common mental trouble under former conditions, gave simply a new detachment from the tumid passions and entanglements of the personal life.

All over the world an era of peace and fellowship begins. People start to live together in communes. Although Wells does not stress the point he has created a universal socialist utopia, complete with free love.

More decorous and spiritual, though no less mystical in its coming, is the change described in *The Day That Changed the World* (1912), written by an anonymous author who calls himself "The Man Who Was Warned". This is set in the following year, with the UK being in fairly dire straits due to socialist agitation. A General Strike has been organized for May 1st with plans for a socialist republic to be declared after the government has collapsed, but there has been a suggestion of a possible right-wing *coup d'état* so that the country can be run by the King and the armed forces.

On April 23rd both possibilities are pre-empted by all those in England who previously claimed to believe in God waking up to find that they really do believe, and that God has visited them to redeem them. They wake up feeling happy and concerned for their fellow humans — perhaps for the first time in their lives.

In a flurry of activity such people rush around doing good works for the poor and needy. The rich drive into the slums. Landlords hasten to see their tenants, promising to replace crumbling hovels. Factory owners offer their workers a share in ownership. Landowners prepare to make their holdings into cooperative farms. All really religious members of the clergy look for a reconciliation between the branches of Christianity, and for an end to rich clergymen. In the House of Commons there is all-party cooperation. The Suffragette movement becomes an organization for the uplifting of women all over the world — a universal women's rights group rather than fanatics seeking the franchise.

The author presents this unbelievable change quite bluntly, eschewing any sort of astronomical or other visual device. His sudden spiritual utopia — which, it is implied, will spread to convert all unbelievers — is not at all convincing. But it is wish fulfilment.

Most utopian societies are set much further in the future than these two examples, to provide that all-important distancing from the present and so add credibility. If the details of any particular utopia are not one hundred per cent desirable to us, today, this is all the better; it shows how daydreams and expectations of the future vary with time.

The Reign of George VI 1900-1925 is an anonymous work, first published in 1763. To us in 1980 it seems a very pedestrian prediction, set immovably in the 18th century as regards technology, customs and details of events. Only the dates are of the 20th century. (The title itself is the closest prediction: George VI did in fact reign from 1936 to 1952.)

Most of the book's length is devoted to the victorious English campaigns against the Russians, French, Spanish, etc., often on their own territory. All tactics and armaments in these wars are of the 18th century, and the naval vessels are still timber-built ships of the line. (This was, of course, written in the time when England did invade other European powers' shores, rather than sit back and expect them to invade us, as was the case after 1871 and *The Battle of Dorking.*)

George VI is a dashing young man who personally leads his army (and his navy, too, on occasion) to some most wonderful and wholly unbelievable victories. At the end he is king of France as well as England. In peacetime George commissions a new palace at the fictional town of Stanley in the actual (but now merged) English county of Rutland, and he gives a great deal of money to the arts. He is too good to be true.

A much more detailed and argumentative prophecy is Louis Sebastien Mercier's book *L'An 2440* (1771), which was published anonymously and translated into English in 1772 as *Memoirs of the Year 2500*. This is, in Professor I. F. Clarke's words, "the first utopia of the future in which the idea of progess is dominant".

Yet Mercier's utopia is in many respects a strange and idiosyncratic one — at least when viewed through modern eyes. French society of 2440 (or 2500 — the English translator is responsible for altering the date) is very simple and healthy, with a few technological advances, a great deal of egalitarianism and much stress laid upon voluntary conformity to ideals of honesty, charity and pacifism.

The narrator and stranger in that strange land is a young Frenchman who wakes to find that 732 years have passed while he slept. (This is the first use of the "sleeper wakes" device to link present and future, though at the end of the book the author reveals the experience as a dream.) A passer-by offers to be the narrator's guide, but first he must have suitable clothes and must not carry his sword. (A sword was regularly worn during the 1770s by all Frenchmen who were not servants or in trade, and for Mercier to envisage a society where nobody wears one was a considerable feat.)

Almost every aspect of life and society has been simplified since the 18th century, and many things which the author considered to be harmful or indulgent have been banished. The rich no longer use their riches to oppress the poor but to help them — all princes keep an open house for strangers and those in need. Absolute sovereignty has been replaced by a constitutional monarchy without any form of corruption. Most of the men of France are farmers working on their own account, not as slaves for landowners. There is an income tax of 2 per cent for all but the poorest; although there are no other taxes those who wish to give more money to the exchequer are welcome to do so (and many do). All complexities of religion and law have been abolished:

> All the volumes of theology, as well as those of jurisprudence, are confined by large bars of iron in the subterranean apartments of the library; and if we should have a war with any neighbouring nation, instead of attacking them with our cannon, we shall send these pestiferous works among them: we preserve these volcanoes of inflammable matter merely for the destruction of our enemies, which they will certainly effect, by means of their subtle poisons, that seize at once the head and the heart.

This is mostly hyperbole, though, for they no longer have wars. Nor do they have much crime except occasional crimes of passion. Their laws are so few and simple that it is possible for a man to write them out by hand, and all men are required to do so at the age of fourteen, swearing an oath to abide by them all. "It is with religion as with laws; the most simple are the best." So they worship God in an uncomplicated fashion, in largely undecorated temples.

The people of 2500 are puritans in their habits, dressing and eating very plainly. Their food is bland but homegrown and of the highest quality. They drink wine but not "detestable liquor". Indeed, there are no taverns left. Snuff, coffee and tea have all been banished, as have card games and all gambling. "All that promotes ease and convenience, that directly tends to assist nature, is cultivated with the greatest care."

The old and sick are well cared for — there are no longer any beggars. In the schools children are not taught dead languages, history (which is described as "the disgrace of humanity, every page being crowded with crimes and follies") or a mass of facts and figures, but they are taught French ("the French language has prevailed universally") and other modern languages; also morality and physics. Women are very submissive to their husbands, and domesticated, not being allowed to do heavy labour. But, perhaps paradoxically, divorce is a simple procedure if both parties wish it.

France is not at all industrialized, yet Mercier provides glimpses of technological ability. There are street lamps which are not glaring but disperse all shadows, though their power source is not mentioned. Certainly they would seem to possess hydroelectric power, yet horse-drawn carriages are still used for transport. Other wonders they possess are "malleable glass", "transparent stone" and an "optical cabinet" with moving pictures. The advances in science and medicine are one of the most important features of Mercier's book, displaying an expectation of change and improvement at a time (of writing) when changes were few and far between.

Yet as scientific discoveries were made they were quickly incorporated into predictions of the future. Even theoretical ideas which could never work in practice were extrapolated into being commonplace fifty or a hundred years in the future. The period 1800-1945 was one in which there was an absolute belief in the power of science, an optimism that it would provide solutions to all of Man's problems without causing any new ones of its own.

A typical example of science-based wish fulfilment is an anonymous story entitled "Nineteen Hundred and Seventy-Two" which appeared in a children's book, *Picturesque Science for the Young* (1872). While trying to catch a train to London in 1872 the narrator is somehow transported to 1972 — an early example of instantaneous time travel, doing away with the necessity of finding somewhere to sleep undisturbed for a hundred years. He knows that this is 1972 because a notice on the station wall has that date on it and reads (in part): "Luminous apparel being now so cheap as to bring abundance of light within the reach of all classes, the proprietors of this railway declare it to be unlawful to burn atmospheric air in any of their carriages . . ."

The cheapness and speed of travel at this time is evidenced by the following exchange between a passenger and a railway official:

"What time does the next threepenny train start for Mount Vesuvius?"

"Not for half an hour, ma'am."

"Half an hour! how late that will make us! I had better pehaps go round by Cairo and take the old balloon track back to Italy."

"A good plan, madam," was the reply; "it will save seven minutes."

Our narrator boards a London train and, after a very brief journey, is told that he has arrived. He can scarcely believe this.

No, it was not London in which I then found myself; not the London air, nor the London aspect; the atmosphere was not only clear as noonday in Italy, but there was a balmy warmth in the sunshine and the whole place was fresh and breezy . . . It was one vast collection of palaces, built of something transparent, and reflecting the sun's beams. In spite of the traffic that went on, there was no lack of space, there was no dirt or smoke, and the wheels moved with scarcely any noise. Large trees grew before these palaces, and partly shaded them; numerous birds fluttered in the branches; people were passing rapidly to and fro, with fresh, cheerful faces and exquisitely beautiful garments; but I saw no beggars, nothing squalid, nor any appearance of over-population or extreme poverty.

Yet this *is* London, a wonderfully hygienic and remodelled London which anticipates the recommendations of Dr B. W. Richardson's *Hygeia; or, A City of Health* published four years later, and even more striking than the rebuilt city of Boston in 2000 as described by Edward Bellamy in *Looking Backward 2000-1887*.

The world of 1972 has many marvels: acoustigraphs which reproduce music to perfection, weather control, geothermal heating which allows a tropical climate in temperate or frigid latitudes, and cheap food for all due to scientific fishing methods. It is hinted that there are many more marvels too difficult to explain to the backward visitor from 1872. There is no overcrowding because the surplus European population has emigrated to fill up North and South America and Africa — the natives of those continents are not mentioned, of course. War and slavery have been abolished and there is no real poverty.

Although brief, this is a truly Victorian dream of future perfection.

In 1881 there appeared W. D. Hay's *Three Hundred Years Hence,* a much longer and more solid prediction of the future, firmly based on the advance of technology. Indeed, Hay's book makes more changes to the state of the human race than practically any other work of the 19th century.

Its early chapters detail the downfall of the UK (presumably at the end of the 19th century or very early in the 20th) through civil war and anarchy, resulting in a US-imposed republican system. Then there are the Final Wars, which tear Europe apart. "Such a mighty and protracted conflict as then was waged had never previously been equalled within the limits of history." Great carnage is made easier by new weapons of war, including the subterranean torpedo which "could be made to crumble down a mountain" and the Chicago bullet, which explodes by a proximity device rather than upon contact, producing such a violent shock wave as (in the case of the largest size) to kill all living creatures within a mile.

There follows a "Century of Peace" during which there are great scientific discoveries made and most of the world becomes unified into a single state under the Oecumenic Parliament. A mechanical friction machine (small, compact, cheap to build and requiring no fuel) replaces coal for all domestic and industrial purposes. The low-lying areas of the

Sahara are flooded to improve the climate of the region.

The Basilic Force is discovered, which is not explained — after the tradition of all wonderful new power systems — but gives mankind direct organic control over Light, Heat, Motion, Electricity, Magnetism, etc. One of its earliest applications is in the construction of submarines and diving suits usable at any depth. Also, as if there were not enough free energy available, geothermal heat is tapped. Subterranean earth-borers are constructed (operating by basilico-magnetism) and vast subterranean cities are founded.

Air travel is not omitted, and the author describes no less than four distinctly different systems of motive power, based respectively on lucegen (an astonishing lighter-than-air gas which alters its volume, and thus its buoyancy, by a factor of ten when an electric current is passed through it), flapping wings, propellers, and zodiacal electricity — yet another new and "utterly unsuspected" force.

Having shown how a partial utopia has been achieved, despite a steeply rising world population, the author points out the worm in the terrestrial apple, giving full rein to his considerable racial prejudice. He has already been decidedly uncomplimentary about the Irish — "In forty years of intercourse with Britons, the Maori of Zealandia had changed from a bloodthirsty cannibal into a civilised and cultured man, while four hundred years of admixture with the ruling people of the world found the typical Irishman still the same brutal ignorant savage as at first"! — and now he concentrates on the black and yellow races, saying things like "It is difficult to understand exactly what sphere of usefulness in the economy of Nature was filled by the Chinaman and the Negro". Only the Chinese, Japanese and Negroes remain outside the so-called States of Humanity, and opposition to these "inferior species" grows in the Oecumenic Parliament. First the Mongolians and then the Negroes are deliberately exterminated — quickly and easily — by sophisticated technology. If this seems improbable, think of Hitler and the Jews.

This gives the white races of mankind plenty more living space, but within a few decades Africa and Asia have been resettled and it is evident that a new solution must be found — to Hay's great credit he was not afraid to extrapolate population increase figures, allowing for the greater intervention of medical science to curb infant mortality and permit more people to live longer. His solution is to transfer the world's population to new cities on the sea, in the sea and underground, leaving Earth's land surface for agriculture. For 1881 this was a considerable mental leap.

The bulk of the people are moved to cities at sea level built on tall, sturdy foundations which rise up from the sea-bed. These foundations are made of koralla, a marvellous new building material. Of course, the actual construction is a vast enterprise to which all of the population contributes, either in time or in money. The land surfaces are cleared of people (by the Terrane Exodous Decree), and mainly of animals also, with most species being exterminated except for small numbers preserved in zoos.

Extremely good use is made of the land, with amazing new strains of wheat being cultivated, and sophisticated weather-control enables, for example, sugar cane and bananas to be grown in Scotland.

This, like the extermination of the "inferior" races, is the true wish-fulfilment element coming into play. In their new cities, even if they are deep underground or on the sea-bed, humanity has all kinds of wonderful luxuries and machines. Air temperature and freshness are automatically controlled, and doors open and close automatically at one's approach. Night can be as light as day. For sale there are "vocaphones, photophones, phonoscopes, stereophones and other varieties of musical and acoustic apparatus".

If some of the apartments are a little small it is because a staggering total of 130 billion (i.e., thousand million) people have to be housed and fed. (Many of these elements have become hackneyed parts of science-fiction novels; a century ago they were original.) This colossal population lives in sixty Ocean States (including submarine Harbours and Provinces) and ten Interior States, governed by successive councils of cities, districts and states, with the Oecumenic Parliament at their apex. At Terrapolis — "the metropolis of the world" — are preserved some of the world's finest buildings, transported from their original homes in London, Rome, Washington and so on.

The ceremonial ruler of all this is the Empress, elected by the people to serve for a ten-year period. The author says: "The influence that Woman has exerted upon history is too large a subject for me to handle in this place." Then he reveals that he is a typically chauvinistic male of the Victorian era by asserting that woman's "mental faculties *are* plainly more circumscribed; but she has always been thought of as the White Man's mate, subordinate to him, but practically a being equal to himself". Elsewhere he comments: "Yet is Woman most emphatically fitted to display in herself the ornamental part of government, while, her sway over man being gained by appeal to his passions rather than his intellect, she is manifested as the proper director of all that relates to domestic life." Obviously, one man's wish fulfilment is not everybody's wish fulfilment.

In sharp contrast to W. D. Hay's high-technology, high-population utopia is *A Crystal Age* by W. H. Hudson, which was first published, anonymously, in 1887, six years after *Three Hundred Years Hence*. In his utopia, Hudson rejects almost every aspect of his own Victorian age, painting a picture of ascetic pastoralism in the fairly remote future. His book has perhaps just three things in common with Hay's: the idea that mankind must first undergo a Final War before achieving a better state of existence; the Darwinian theory of continual change; and the presentation of a personal utopia. While Hay's book is narrated by a university professor and has the feel of a chatty textbook, Hudson's is a novel using a Victorian protagonist *via* the "sleeper wakes" device.

Smith, a brash young man of twenty-one, wakes to find himself in a strange rural area where the people speak perfect Victorian English yet have never heard of Gladstone, Darwin, Tennyson or Queen Victoria; indeed, they have never even heard of the name Smith before. But they are pleasant and handsome people, even if they do dress oddly and fail to comprehend Smith's meanings. He is content to be their guest, not only because he has no other option but because he has at once fallen in love with Yoletta, a beautiful girl.

Only gradually, over a period of months, does Smith learn the full truth about his placid but rather alien hosts. All fifty or sixty of them are members of the same extended family, occupying a single large house — one of many spread out across the Earth. It is a pastoral society, where everyone enjoys working hard, and where no machines are used. It is a matriarchy, as are all such houses, but the Mother keeps to her room through illness and Smith offends them all by not asking to see her. In fact, he succeeds in breaking most of their customs and taboos before he comes to realize just how alien these people are. (Perhaps Grant Allen got his idea for *The British Barbarians,* which was published eight years later, from this source.)

Although Yoletta appears to return Smith's love, among the members of this society all love is of a brotherly or sisterly kind and is freely given; only between the Mother and father is there marriage or sexual contact. These people demand the very highest standards from themselves and from each other. Any favour — even the gift of food or clothing to a guest — must be repaid by much hard work. They are harsh and inflexible in their punishments, even for minor infringements, yet they possess a "crystal purity of heart".

This society exists in a sparsely populated world at an unspecified future date, at least ten thousand years after a catastrophe (also unspecified) has almost wiped out mankind. Over the centuries the survivors have built up new traditions and codes of behaviour. They are a living contradiction because, on the one hand, they respect tradition absolutely and make everything to last a thousand years, while on the other hand they themselves are an evolved form of man.

Smith is at first surprised by the acuteness of their sight in what to him is near-darkness, and by the beauty of their voices. Only much later does he discover that they are very long-lived: Yoletta, whom he has taken for "about fourteen years old" reveals that she is thirty-one, while the father, who is white-bearded but still "straight as an arrow" with "free movements and elastic tread", is almost two hundred years old. Their peculiar system of allowing only the finest couple of each generation to breed has produced this change. They practice eugenics on their animals, too, and have achieved very intelligent dogs and horses.

Although their system of life represents something far different from the typical Victorian conception of utopia (such as Hay presents) it remains an ideal of a kind, a fictional protest against much of the contemporary scene which Hudson disliked or despised.

The wonderful wish-fulfilment world of utopian socialism was painted in glowing colours by Edward Bellamy in *Looking Backward 2000-1887* (1888). Although almost forgotten today, it was probably the largest-selling and most influential speculative work of the 19th century.

It tells how Julian West, a rich young man living in Boston in 1887, is hypnotized into sleep because of his insomnia. But the house burns down and, while he is safe in his quiet underground sleeping chamber, there is no one to waken him.

He sleeps for 113 years before being found and awakened, in the year 2000. What he finds is Boston transformed into a clean and beautiful city where everybody is equal and at least as well off as he was. He becomes the guest of Dr Leete (the physician who awakened him) and his family, and learns from Dr Leete of the changes which have occurred since he went to sleep. We look at these elsewhere; but in brief:

There is now national control of all production, distribution and employment. All adults receive the same remuneration, whether or not they work (although most do, retiring at 45), and this standard of living is so high that one does not usually manage to use all of one's annual credit allowance.

In the end Julian sees how much better this sytem is (despite its communistic elements) than the bad old world of 1887. He becomes an enthusiastic supporter of it and falls in love with Dr Leete's daughter Edith. Edward Bellamy's detailed arguments convinced a lot of his readers similarily.

Equally enthusiastic is Dr Theodor Hertzka's endorsement of his utopian colony in East Africa, described in his novel *Freeland: A Social Anticipation,* first published in English in 1891. Here the basis is the workers' cooperative, a form of limited capitalism which, over twenty-five years, brings enormous prosperity to the settlers.

A good example of a prescriptive utopia (i.e., a story which shows a reachable utopia and demonstrates how it may be achieved) is R. H. Benson's *The Dawn of All* (1911). This is an antithetical companion-piece to his cautionary *Lord of the World,* which describes the total annihilation of the Roman Catholic Church by the forces of humanism early in the 21st century — see Chapter 2. *The Dawn of All* shows how the Roman Catholic Church could become omnipotent in the UK and

Europe once again (and thus, by extension, omnipotent throughout the world).

The situation is explained and the story told through a device not totally different from the "sleeper wakes": a non-Catholic who is dying in 1911 is miraculously transported into the body of a Catholic priest in 1973. He feigns loss of memory and gradually learns who and what he is and of the events of the past sixty years. He is Monsignor Masterman, secretary and chaplain to Cardinal Bellairs. Roman Catholicism is now equivalent to Christianity; it more or less covers the whole world. In England all laws are for the benefit of and according to the principles of the Catholics, although they are not the government. Nor is Catholicism yet established as the State Religion of England, though this is expected imminently.

The Roman Catholic Church is astonishingly powerful, however. It is virtually the only organized church in the world (although atheism is permitted to exist and is not normally persecuted). In the UK, as elsewhere, the Church controls the social services, schooling and much of science. The King of England (Edward IX) is a Catholic. All pre-Reformation Church property has been returned to the Catholic Church. Laws have been reformed to suit the Church: divorce has been abolished for thirty years past, and fornication has been a felony for the last twenty. Benefit of clergy has been restored; ecclesiastical courts exist to try those accused of heresy.

The situation is notably different only in Germany, the last stronghold of Protestantism, just as it was the first. But during the course of the novel the German emperor embraces the Catholic faith and plans to transport all German socialists and non-Catholics to one of the special free cities in the USA. Then the socialists seize Berlin and execute Papal envoys. The Pope himself visits them and they give in. The Roman Catholic Church becomes universally triumphant.

The author was himself a Roman Catholic priest, and this straightforward wish-fulfilment story is understandably a vision of his own personal utopia. He does introduce a few futuristic innovations, such as the volors (flying machines, which appear under the same name in *Lord of the World*), an electrical diagnostic machine which checks the mind (now known to be the seat of most illness and disease) and tape recorders.

The people of the 1970s all wear uniforms (in the UK, anyway) to denote their trade or occupation and their status. Because so many people are in the service of the Church and thus subject to the vow of chastity, families are very large in order to keep up the population, with an average of not less than ten children. This could be the utopian vision only of a staunch Roman Catholic.

Although H. G. Wells brought various utopias or semi-utopias into his novels, the one which deals primarily with a working utopia which is easily recognizable as such is *Men Like Gods* (1923). Strictly, this is not set in the future, because it features a group of people from 1921 who are (by a mysterious hiccup in the space-time continuum) transferred to a planet in another universe. Yet the inhabitants of this parallel Earth are thousands of years in advance of us. They inhabit a utopia, and it is evident that Wells intended to suggest that mankind could follow the same route and achieve a similar state. The inhabitants, who are apparently human except for a god-like beauty of face and figure, quickly identify their visitors as wearing clothes and displaying characteristics similar to those of their own remote ancestors during the "Age of Confusion", which seems to be equivalent to Earth's 19th and 20th centuries.

The Utopians (for so they are quickly christened by Wells' displaced travellers) have conquered nature to make their world a paradise. They wear very few clothes (which outrages some of the visitors). They have stabilized their population at only 250 millions, so as to give themselves plenty of room. There are no cities on their planet, nor do they desire any. A high level of technology has been achieved, but it is unobtrusive; it serves the Utopians, they do not serve it. There is little need for anyone to work, but they all keep themselves occupied with activities which are intrinsically worthwhile and satisfying, particularly in the arts and sciences; they do not wish to be idle. They are not complacent, and are always trying to improve their world.

> Utopia has no parliament, no politics, no private wealth, no business competition, no police nor prisons, no lunatics, no defectives nor cripples, and it has none of these things because it has schools and teachers who are all that schools and teachers can be. Politics, trade and competition are the methods of adjustment of a crude society. Such methods of adjustment have been laid aside in Utopia for more than a thousand years. There is no rule nor government needed by adult Utopians because all the rule and government they need they have had in childhood and youth.

Also the Utopians possess telepathy; their thought speeches are heard as words by the visitors. This was one of Wells' very few uses of ESP in any of his books, but here it is presented as a logical evolutionary step for an advanced race of humans.

Although Wells is setting out his own ideal future here and using a cross-section of the people of his own time as a sounding-board to this utopia, giving their diverse reactions, he frequently makes use of satire. For example: "The last politician to be elected to a legislative assembly died in Utopia about a thousand years ago. He was an eccentric and garrulous old gentleman; he was the only candidate and one man voted for him . . . Finally he was dealt with as a mental case."

In order to achieve wish fulfilment it is not always necessary to live in a wonderful, utopian world; often it is enough just to possess a unique means of transport, such as an airship or spaceship, or to visit some part of the world which was previously untouched by Man.

Nearly all of Jules Verne's work falls into one of these categories. Time and time again his novels include machines for travelling through the air, through space, or under the sea, and his *Voyages Extraordinaires* (the original French publisher's series title for all Verne's books) include visits to the North Pole, the bottom of the sea, the interior of the Earth, remote parts of Africa and America, and various unknown islands. Even travelling around the world in as short a time as eighty days was a wish-fulfilment idea when it first appeared, in 1873. Occasionally, as in *The Begum's Fortune*, Verne describes the setting up of utopian societies, too.

Verne was not the only writer of wish-fulfilment adventures, though he is the best remembered. Several of George Griffith's novels fall into the same category for the same reasons, notably *The Angel of the Revolution* (1893) and its sequel *Olga Romanoff* (1894). Griffith describes powerful flying machines with which it is possible for a few individuals to determine the destiny of the world; he writes about voyages through the clouds to various lands and the establishment of a secret utopian colony in Africa. C. J. Cutcliffe Hyne's *Emperor of the World* (1910) is concerned with the discovery and use of a marvellous "new force" which effectively melts iron at any range and can be used to sink ships or destroy telephone cables, with great selectivity. The inventor uses his power wisely, to prevent war, but the possession of such power is a potential for good or evil.

Yet another wonderful discovery which gives its inventor infinite power over the world is to be found in *John Sagur* (1921), by "Nedram", a particularly uneventful and simplistic piece of utopia-building. An Englishman, John Sagur, gains control of atomic energy by painstaking experimentation and develops a wave or beam system for transmitting its power all over the world as a universal source of fuel. Ergon, as he calls it, enables him to gain economic control and then total autocratic control of the world. By self-proclamation he becomes Master of the World. Fortunately he is well intentioned and sets about creating a utopia for all mankind.

The book's tone may be gauged from a short extract:

> Here is my plan. At our disposal is a source of energy, simple yet inexhaustible, the power of the atomic system. I can, from this house, send forth radiations a thousand times sufficient for the needs of all mankind. My rays will furnish heat to warm men's houses and to cook their food, to melt the most refractory ores. They will furnish light to put the sun to shame and power to rid mankind for ever of the need for manual labour.

He does, of course, succeed totally — and boringly.

Only a short step away, but far more entertaining, is Lord Dunsany's 1934 work *If I Were Dictator* (one of a series of books by eminent authors, all with this title). This is a little book full of the author's personal foibles and the actions he would take to deal with them were he to be made the Dictator of the UK. Among his silly reforms are penal servitude for motor cars which cause accidents (whether or not their drivers are punished), the abolition of harmful food additives, restrictions on advertising because of the waste of money, satire to be recognized as a fine art, the countryside to be protected from careless visitors, excess verbosity to be prohibited, cruelty to animals to be stopped, and the making of unnecessary noise to become a treasonable act.

Before turning to the really off-beat ideas of wish fulfilment let us isolate one more category of wonderful invention. This is a machine which provides a different sort of personal power, by renewing youth and beauty. It is described in Marie Corelli's novel *The Young Diana — An Experiment of the Future* (1918), which uses the rejuvenation process as an excuse for a deep examination of the whole subject of personal wish fulfilment.

Diana May, a dowdy spinster in her forties, decides to escape from the boring existence of living with her parents. She fakes a drowning accident and travels to Geneva to answer an advertisement for the post of assistant to an inventor. She does not know what she is letting herself in for, but she does realize that she possesses all the necessary qualifications for the job, perhaps to a greater degree than anybody else, because it asks for a courageous woman of mature years with a fair knowledge of modern science (which has always been an interest of hers). She gets the job, but the inventor, Dr Dimitrius, does not at first tell her that she will be an experimental subject. Nor does he explain his research, although he does keep dropping hints about rejuvenation as he shows her how he distils air to obtain condensed light!

When he does admit his intention Diana is not worried. She has nothing to lose. She tells him, "You talk like another Mephistophiles to a female Faustus," though she does not really believe in eternal life. He explains that the cells of the brain can be recharged, like a battery, and he gives her doses of the distilled liquid. Almost at once she begins to grow younger and become beautiful — something which she has never been.

After a second dose she is the belle of the ball, unrecognizable as her old self and possessing a supernatural beauty which attracts all men. Yet she feels that she has lost something — "sympathy with human kind" — and she cannot forget that she is really a middle-aged woman. After a third dose she emerges radiant and more than human. None of her former acquaintances or family recognize her or are willing to know her, although, hardly surprisingly in the circumstances, this does not worry her.

The science in the book may be poor, but the human reactions are totally believable. Among other morals is the point that one never gets one's wish fulfilment until one no longer cares.

Some writers' ideas of wish fulfilment have been strange indeed.

August Niemann's strident anti-British war story, *The Coming Conquest of England,* which describes the defeat and subjection of England by the combined forces of Germany, Russia and France, is clearly a wish fulfilment, a fictional version of what he wanted to see happen. The author admits as much in the book's preface. Equally off-beat is *After London* by Richard Jefferies. He is best known for his eulogies of the countryside, and this volume fits the pattern because it opens with a long and loving description of a London abandoned by man and being reclaimed by nature. No reason is given, but presumably he felt none was necessary: he hated London and all that it stood for, and to destroy it by the encroachment of trees, weeds and wild-life was his own personal wish fulfilment, even if it could be achieved only in fiction. The remainder of the novel is a quasi-mediaeval romance set in a regressed and partly flooded England a few hundred years later.

Many authors have felt it necessary to describe the destruction of the current way of life before allowing any sort of improvement leading to utopia (the devices they have used to sweep away the *anciens régimes* are discussed in Chapter 2). There does seem something logical about this: a perfect world cannot be built upon the present imperfections, thus the land must first be cleansed of all Man's mistakes so that utopia may rise phoenix-like from the ashes.

We have seen *Caesar's Column,* by Ignatius Donnelly: the corrupt Plutocracy is destroyed by a socialist revolution but the revolutionaries find they cannot stop the destruction, and the few true socialists escape to virgin territory in Africa to build their utopia there.

In J. D. Beresford's *Goslings* (1913) the agent of destruction is a new plague which spreads around the world from Tibet. It kills off almost all the men, but very few women. After initial chapters showing complacency in England, then panic, then a breakdown of the entire social system, the rest of the book shows women in a 999 to 1 majority trying to cope. This is not intended as a rôle-reversal theme; it is purely a statement of fact that in 1913 or shortly thereafter — the exact date is not specified — there were few women in the UK (Beresford was British) with any knowledge of food production or managerial skills.

Some exceptional women do succeed in coping, and with a small amount of male help (generally one male per community) those who do not die of starvation in the first couple of months muddle through. What the novel shows clearly is that class and sex distinctions have been over-magnified; in the new post-plague society they are far less important. The opportunity has been given to start afresh and build a better, freer world, without marriage and with a different range of social mores.

The World Set Free (1914) by H. G. Wells is concerned partly with a world war which destroys most of Earth's cities and partly with the world government which is formed afterwards, thus setting the world free from war, insecurity, the struggle for existence and, to a certain extent, from suffering, too. Yet there are no real characters here and the perfection of the world state is no more believable than the world war, with atom bombs being dropped by hand from open aircraft. Wells' next attempt to create a believable utopia, in *Men Like Gods*, mentioned earlier in this chapter, was much more successful.

Recovery and reconstruction after a war is the subject of *New Moon* by Oliver Onions, first published in 1918. It is presumably World War I which is meant, but this is a very oblique and indefinite novel. The author is trying to put across the idea that a utopia is what you want it to be: widespread nationalization, civilian mobilization and a general feeling of camaraderie throughout the land may produce something approaching utopia, even if the standard of living and degree of freedom are not very great.

The final example of "utopia from disaster" which is worth mentioning here (though many more exist) is *Nordenholt's Million* by J. J. Connington. The disaster is natural: a chance mutation in a species of denitrifying bacteria results in the death of all living plants. After a year the strain of bacteria dies out and the soil can be renitrified. The small initial population — only a specially established community has survived — and the development of atomic energy — a bonus which makes life that much easier — mean that after the crisis is over a utopia can be established.

As usual, success seems to us to come just a little too easily, without the multitude of problems which we learn to accept and live with today.

7 THEME: ALIEN CONTACT

To a certain extent stories of contact between humans and aliens are easily identified; they form a significant proportion of all science fiction and their theme, owing mostly to the influences of the movies, is most closely identified by the general public with science fiction as a whole.

So, where mankind travels through space to other worlds and meets their inhabitants (whether intelligent or not), or where they (only the intelligent ones, presumably) come to Earth, we have alien contact. There is one difficulty which must be overcome, though. Quite a few of these speculative stories — the earlier ones in particular — were not set in the future. They were either contemporary with first publication or, occasionally, set a little in the past. Yet it may be argued that any story of an encounter between human and extraterrestrial alien is, by definition, predictive (i.e., "it" has not happened yet), so all of these stories are eligible for inclusion.

This immediately leads to complications. What about Edgar Rice Burroughs' series of Martian novels? They could be excluded on several grounds (that they are set in the past, several decades prior to the publication of the first title; that they are straightforward fantasy rather than speculative fiction), but such exclusion might be considered partisan, so we will discuss them together with their predecessors and imitators.

A tricky area concerns the discovery of new species of intelligent creatures on Earth. We will look at a few really alien creatures described as dwelling in the ocean depths and the upper air in this chapter, but — perhaps, you may feel, arbitrarily — the general discussion of "lost world" stories has been allotted to Chapter 5.

Yet there is another way in which aliens can exist on Earth — they can evolve. Where men or animals have evolved into something very different from what they are at the present (H. G. Wells' *The Time Machine* is the obvious example) we will examine them in this chapter; Earth humans who are a few centuries advanced on us and are alien only in a social sense, because of changed behaviour patterns, are dealt with piecemeal throughout this book (but see also my book *Future Man*, 1980).

Obviously, we will ignore tales in which alien civilizations are described on their own, without a visit from mankind (the earliest such seems to be C. I. Defontenay's *Star* (1854), first translated into English in 1975; there are many more recent examples), and those where manned space vehicles travel to other worlds without finding life. The most obvious early examples in the latter case are Jules Verne's *From the Earth to the Moon* (first published in English in 1873), where the Moon is circumnavigated by rocket without a landing, and his *Hector Servadac* (first published in English in 1878), where a passing comet carries off a group of people into space.

A borderline case, though an interesting one, is André Laurie's *The Conquest of the Moon* (first published in English in 1889) in which the Moon is deliberately pulled towards the Earth by a gigantic eletromagnet, the purpose being to mine the Moon for its valuable minerals. When the Moon gets very close to the Saharan mountaintop observatory where the magnets are, the whole observatory is pulled away from the Earth and deposited on the Moon — which immediately returns to its normal orbit! The main characters manage to survive by making oxygen in the laboratory. On the Moon they find some ruins and a recognizably human skeleton — thirty feet long.

As the doctor of the party says, "A gigantic stature was *imperative* to the inhabitants of the moon. As its gravity is six times that of our globe, trees, plants, animals and Selenic men (when there were such) were *necessarily* bound to develop proportionately in height and muscular strength."

Such a point of view is bad science, of course — it would follow that the inhabitants of a small asteroid a few metres across would be necessarily bound to develop to a hundred or a thousand times our size — but it is found in many other novels. In Thea von Harbou's *The Girl in the Moon* (1930), for example, the ruins of a gigantic city are found on the far side of the Moon, with similarly colossal golden statues but no living Selenites, not even a skeleton. (Was that alien contact? The answer is debatable.)

Stories of interplanetary adventure, most frequently involving men from Earth in voyages to Mars or Venus, flourished during the 19th century. George Locke in *Voyages in Space,* his excellent bibliographical survey of these, identifies more than two hundred interplanetary novels published in English between 1801 and 1914 (although his criteria for inclusion are a little different from the ones we have set out). As might be expected, these stories range from the scientifically accurate — in terms of the scientific knowledge of the time — to the totally ludicrous — which disregarded all scientific laws and astronomical facts. Generally, when read today, they all seem less believable than any other category of predictive fiction, but this is the

An illustration from the serial of
the lost-race tale *The Secret of the
Wondergat*, by Ridgwell Cullum
and Charles Wingrove, which
appeared in the magazine *Boys of
Our Empire* in 1901. (See
page 110.)

vo illustrations from *The
nquest of the Moon* by André
aurie, first published in English
1889. Here we see solar-power
llectors (*above*), a remarkably
curate prediction for its time, as
ell as (*right*) terrified reactions
nongst the natives as the Moon
drawn inexorably towards the
arth by artificially created
ectromagnetic forces — rather
e the tractor beams once so
pular in pulp science fiction.
ee pages 163 and 128.)

obida's "telephonoscope" brings
e theatre right into your own
me — an illustration from *Le
ingtième Siècle* (1881). (See
age 81.)

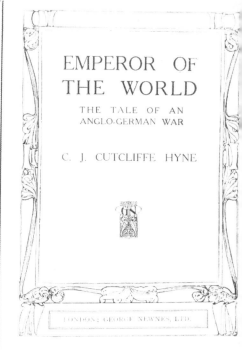

EMPEROR OF
THE WORLD

THE TALE OF AN
ANGLO-GERMAN WAR

C. J. CUTCLIFFE HYNE

LONDON: GEORGE NEWNES, LTD.

Opposite: The fall of Nelson's Column in London's Trafalgar Square — one of the fine illustrations by David Low for H. G. Wells' *The Autocracy of Mr Parham* (1930). (See page 92.)

Opposite: The frontispiece and title page of C. J. Cutliffe Hyne's 1910 novel *Emperor of the World.* One can almost hear the words: "All I have to do is press this button . . ." (See page 28.)

"Space was full of darting, flashing, madly warring ships. The three Black superdreadnaughts leaped forward as one." Stirring stuff from the first book publication of E. E. Smith's space opera *First Lensman* (1950). The illustration is by A. J. Donnell.

Die Rakete

Zeitschrift des Vereins für Raumschiffahrt E.V., Breslau

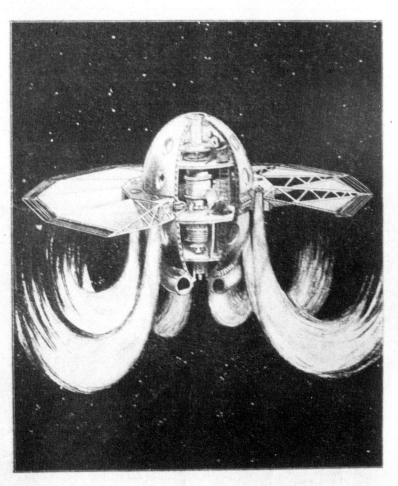

Breslau   15. September   1927

The cover of the German
magazine *Die Rakete* for 15th
September 1927, showing an
illustration of the contemporary
conception of a spaceship.

"He saw this one pursue a man
and catch him up in one of its
steely tentacles" — an illustration
by Warwick Goble from the
Pearson's Magazine serialization of
H. G. Wells' *The War of the
Worlds* (1897). (See page 153.)

A Moon creature as depicted in
the first edition of Ralph Morris'
Adventures of John Daniel (1751).
(See page 12.)

An inhabitant of the Moon as
illustrated in *The Travels and
Surprising Adventures of Baron
Munchausen* (1786). (See
page 12.)

Left: Cavor is carried off by the Selenites — an illustration from the *Strand Magazine*'s 1901 serialization of H. G. Wells' *The First Men in the Moon.* (See page 146.)

Below: A scene from the *Pearson's Magazine* serialization of George Griffith's *Stories of Other Worlds* (1900), later to become better known as *Honeymoon in Space.* Here the honeymooners investigate the bones of long-dead Moon creatures. (See page 146.)

A scene in London in the year AD2536, depicted in the frontispiece to J. P. Lockhart-Mummery's *After Us* (1936). (See page 178.)

Opposite: From a 1966 issue of a UK children's comic, *The Ranger*, comes this illustration of the future roofing-over of London.

Two views of London in AD2500 which appeared as cigarette advertisements in the 1920s; in both cases the artist is Cuningham. (*Left*) Piccadilly: "Roofed-in under non-conductive mica glass . . . moving pathways . . . rubber roadways avenued into 50, 100, 150 and 200 miles per hour . . . suspended mono railways . . . motors driven by atomic energy . . . phonetic spelling . . . wireless television . . . lighted by captured solar rays . . . excursions to Mars." (*Right*) The Pleasure City: "Pleasure-seeking has been raised to a fine art . . . multitudes when the short day's work is done find a satisfying means of relaxation in smoking "GREYS" Cigarettes and listening to the Mammoth mechanical orchestra . . . characteristic of the music of the period . . . music so complex that it can be rendered only by wondrous mechanism."

An illustration from a 1903 article in the *Strand Magazine*, "The English House of the Future", showing the home of AD2000 as envisaged by H. G. Wells in a specially commissioned contribution, which reads in part: "The trend of things seems all against any diminution of what is called the servant difficulty to-day, and, as a consequence of that we may expect the Twentieth Century house, not only to be full of labour-saving appliances, dustless sweepers, self-making beds, neatly-mounted electric cooking things, and so on, but built with a much more earnest regard to convenience and cleanliness than our houses of to-day."

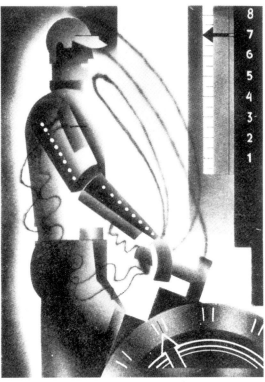

City-bred man of the year AD2097 has allowed the triumphs of Victorian engineering — the road and rail systems — to crumble away, as shown in this illustration by Edmund J. Sullivan from the *Pall Mall Magazine* serialization of H. G. Wells' *A Story of the Days to Come* (1899). (See page 20.)

An illustration by E. McKnight-Kauffer for the Earl of Birkenhead's book *The World in 2030* (1930). (See page 177.)

An illustration from *The Future* by A. M. Low (1930), showing his prediction of the appearance of a suburban street, with moving pavements, illuminated kerbs, and "efficient glow-lighting". His legend was as follows: "(A) Roof Landing for Motor Planes; (B) Public Lifts; (C) Metor-plane Lifts to Roof Landing; (D) Passenger Tubes; (E) Tubes for Cables of Inductance Transmission of Power, also to contain Drains, Water Mains, etc.; (F) Inductor for Power Transmission by Electricity." (See page 176.)

One of thirteen respiration stations in the English Channel to ventilate the Channel Tunnel — an illustration for a 1901 article on the subject by Herbert C. Fyfe in *Pearson's Magazine.* (See page 171.)

Pneumatic clothes, the height of fashion in the year AD2097 — an illustration by Sullivan from the original magazine appearance of H. G. Wells' *A Story of the Days to Come* (1899). (See page 20.)

Two of the series "Guesses at Futurity" published in the *Pall Mall Magazine* between 1894 and 1895, both by Fred T. Jane. (*Left*) Number 3, showing street lighting in the year AD2000; (*right*) number 7, mining for gold in the mountains of the Moon, a prediction that may very well come true within the next couple of decades — although it is unlikely that gold will be the mineral sought.

LES·ANNALES

En **1965**

ROMAN PROPHÉTIQUE

Texte et Dessins

DE

ROBIDA

26 Octobre 1919   Annonces SOCIÉTÉ NOUVELLE DE PUBLICITÉ. 11. Boulevard des Italiens
ABONNEMENTS ET RÉDACTION 51. Rue Saint-Georges   Le N° 60 Centimes

Albert Robida's cover illustration for the magazine *Les Annales* for
26th October 1919, featuring his own serial *En 1965*. (See page 81.)

unfortunate result of the concentrated scientific research of the last twenty years, which has enlarged our knowledge of space travel techniques and extraterrestrial conditions a thousandfold, besides providing firm scientific constraints upon our predictions of alien life-forms.

One of the more interesting and carefully written of these early interplanetary adventures is *A Trip to Venus* (1897) by John Munro. This involves a voyage to Venus and Mercury aboard a submarine-like spaceship powered by a "new force", undertaken by the unnamed narrator, Professor Gazen (an astronomer), Carmichael (the spaceship's inventor) and Miss Carmichael (his beautiful daughter).

Venus proves to be very Earthlike as to atmosphere, seas, vegetation and people.

Their first encounter with a man of Venus is worth describing. Moving low across the planet's surface they see a human figure and shout down to him "Good evening, sir," at which the man falls to his knees.

> "That's a good sign," said Gazen with a grim smile. "I wonder if he understands English. Let's try him again."

This, though meant seriously, is the height of farce.

In fact, the Venusians prove to be fully human, "a fine race, tall, handsome, and of white complexion". They are a peaceful people, very serene and intelligent, and strict vegetarians. Their language is simple and quickly learnt. They live in a Garden-of-Eden environment with almost no disease, pain, crime or sin, and they live to be a hundred or a hundred and fifty.

The narrator falls in love with the most beautiful of all the girls, Alumion, a chief's daughter and priestess for the season. They are married, but the other crew members carry the narrator away and the spaceship moves on swiftly to Mercury.

This also has a breathable atmosphere, and predatory animals, but no intelligent life. They all return to Earth, but the narrator vows to go again to Venus and live with his Alumion.

In the course of the book there is some fascinating (and fairly original) speculation on multistage rockets, a space station, the use of a parachute in planetary landings, and multigeneration interstellar travel, although none of these are incorporated into the plot of the novel.

A signal is received from Mars in the shape of regular spectral line changes in a bright light, and an Earth-type atmosphere is predicted for that planet as well. The narrator is enthusiastic about the future of space travel: "For ought we know, the time is coming when there will be a regular mail service between the earth and Mars or Venus, cheap trips to Mercury, and exploring expeditions to Jupiter, Saturn or Uranus."

This is a good effort for the period, even if meteors do bounce off the rounded hull of the spaceship.

Eighty years ago it was uncertain as to whether or not the Moon possessed an atmosphere, and writers of interplanetary fiction preferred to believe that it did.

Best remembered of all Moon stories is H. G. Wells' *The First Men in the Moon* (1901). The narrator, Bedford, and Cavor travel to the Moon in the latter's spaceship which is powered by cavorite, an antigravity metal. Although the Moon seems initially to be barren, when morning comes plants appear, growing with incredible swiftness. Venturing outside, Bedford and Cavor find the air breathable.

They also find the bipedal (although insectoid) Selenites and their immense mooncalves. The Selenites, who live deep beneath the surface, are hive creatures; only their chief, the Grand Lunar, and a few others, possess true intelligence. The Moon is described as "a sort of vast ant-hill". Although they are terribly alien, Wells does not present the Selenites in a bad light; they are an intelligent race of aliens, and he seems interested in them as characters and members of a society, not just as bug-eyed monsters. This is a far more worthy approach than most of its predecessors or successors.

George Griffith's *A Honeymoon in Space* was first published in book form in the same year as *The First Men in the Moon,* although it had been serialized as "Stories of Other Worlds" in *Pearson's Magazine* the previous year. It is a fairly standard effort, with a space vehicle (the *Astronef*) powered by the "R Force", an antigravity repulsion system, taking Lord Redgrave, his American bride Zaidie and an old family retainer, Murgatroyd, on a Cook's tour of the Solar System.

First they land on the Moon and go outside wearing suits like deep sea divers' except for an integral (and continuously recycling) air supply. There they find abandoned buildings and skeletons of what appear to have been large humans (although not as large as in André Laurie's *The Conquest of the Moon).* In a particularly deep crater they find air and water, together with some primitive humanoid creatures.

Next they visit Mars, where they are menaced by Martian air vessels and retaliate by ramming two and destroying them. They land and find the air is breathable. (They test it by breathing it — a fairly risky procedure, to say the least!) When crowds of Martians — humanoid, but tall and with large heads — approach, apparently unarmed, Lord and Lady Redgrave shoot them down with machine guns and pistols, which they have brought along for the purpose of "self-defence".

Then the *Astronef* moves on (!) to Venus where the people are very angel-like, flying around gracefully in the dense atmosphere. They have musical voices, and Zaidie's rendering of "The Swanee [*sic*] River" delights them.

But these people are so heavenly that Lord and Lady Redgrave are afraid of infecting them with sin, so they travel towards Jupiter. There they look at the planet's moons. "Zaidie took half-a-dozen photographs of the surface of Calisto [sic] while they were passing it at a distance of about a hundred miles, and then went to get lunch ready." But they find that Ganymede has a population of pleasant people who are tall but very close to being human. These are living in a high-technology society which is idyllic, even though it is in a roofed-over city to keep out the moon's frigid air.

Jupiter itself turns out to be covered in fiery lava.

The last stop on the tour is Saturn, which is covered partly by a "semi-gaseous ocean" and partly by firm ground; it is inhabited by various fierce creatures identical with Earth's prehistoric fauna.

A Honeymoon in Space is not a serious work. It was designed as an exciting and sentimental romance, and any areas of agreement with scientific fact are purely coincidental. It follows the theory that, while peaceful human-type alien races can be accepted as Man's equals (so long as their skin is white), anything ugly or really alien in appearance must be no more than an animal and may therefore be destroyed without compunction. There is no doubt that this idea stems from feelings of white imperialist superiority, an assumption that one has a God-given right to enslave or kill any lesser being than oneself.

A Columbus of Space (1911) by Garrett P. Serviss also subscribes to this doctrine to a great extent. Edmund Stonewall designs and builds an atomic-powered space-car and takes three friends off on a trip to Venus. He believes that the planet must be inhabited, and for that reason he has some "automatic guns and pistols" aboard.

Landing on the dark side of the planet — in this book Venus always keeps one face away from the Sun — they discover some large, shaggy humanoids living below ground and shoot one dead pour encourager les autres. On finding that these creatures are really intelligent and telepathic the four men feel slight regrets, but this does not prevent them from pressing the rest of the tribe into slavery and interfering with the local religion to the extent of killing a couple of priests.

They travel around the planet to the light side, taking eight of the humanoids with them — rather in the manner of native bearers, although the space-car is small and the shaggy aliens are pulled along behind on sledges: all except one are killed before they reach the light, and the space-car is damaged.

Still, the party manages to make contact with the "real human beings" who live in the permanent light. These are a peaceful people, telepathic and with considerable technological expertise. Stonewall is not surprised, asserting that "Intelligent life could find no more suitable abode than in a human body", which seems to be the ultimate in conceit.

The four men commit various crimes against the society they are visiting, particularly against its religion. They may be intended as heroic adventurers but in reality they are no more than a group of lawless ruffians who deserve to be locked up. Yet they are saved from punishment by the queen of these people, and their faithful shaggy humanoid, the survivor of their trip from the dark side, saves their lives more than once before dying honourably. At length Stonewall finds some uranium and extracts what he needs to power the space-car for the journey home — perhaps he has lead-lined pockets.

There are a few basic scientific errors; for example the body of a dog is put out of the space-car in deep space and swiftly disappears. Even Verne, more than forty years earlier, did not make that mistake; perhaps Serviss thought he knew better.

Yet *A Columbus of Space* is a paragon of scientific exactitude compared with *The Stolen Planet* (1906) by John Mastin. The author commits almost every scientific error known to science fiction — having, for example, a collision between two planets giving rise to starbirth, a noisy, fiery comet in deep space, and objects jettisoned in space moving off at great speed. Nor does he seem to know the difference between stars and planets or their respective locations.

The spaceship *Regina*, which is driven by repelling itself from any large body such as a star or a planet, visits various planets in our Solar System and others, more or less at random. To run the ship there is a crew of twelve, mostly "sea-faring men, who would be hardy, accustomed to dangerous altitudes, have good sight, and, above all, be already trained to the most rigid discipline".

At one point the *Regina* lands on a very large planet populated by gigantic humans and animals; it is captured by a family of giants and placed on the mantlepiece of a house, but the crew manufacture chlorine gas and, as soon as a window is opened, escape through it. This could be a parody of Gulliver's adventure in Brobdingnag if it were not so heavy-handed.

Next they come unexpectedly to the planet Venus, inhabited by a peaceful human race who are without sin.

Slipping out of the Solar System past Neptune the *Regina* is soon nearing Sirius—which proves to be surrounded by twenty-five other stars and many planets. For some unexplained reason they visit only one of these, inhabited by small, intelligent flying creatures, before going home.

An entertaining interplanetary farce is *To Venus in Five Seconds, Being an Account of the Strange Disappearance of Thomas Plummer, Pill-Maker* (1897) written and illustrated by Fred T. Jane. Thomas Plummer is a young medical student and son of a patent-medicine manufacturer. He is attracted to a fellow student, the tall, slim and faintly foreign Miss Zumeena. She is quite good looking — even though her skin is covered with a reddish down. Thomas cannot determine her nationality, although he does find out that an imprecation of hers is part of the ancient Egyptian language.

Miss Zumeena invites him to her lodgings. While they are seated together in the summer-house at the bottom of the garden, taking tea, he seizes his opportunity and kisses her. But she, too, has ulterior motives. After shutting the door and pulling a couple of levers she announces that they are "now floating in the atmosphere of the planet you call Venus", having arrived there by matter-transmitter. Thomas refuses to believe her, despite the blindingly bright sunlight, the enormous plants and the horrifying creatures.

The truth is that he has been brought to Venus for the purpose of vivisection. Miss Zumeena is a member of the Sutenraa, descendants of the ancient Egyptians, who now all live on Venus, visiting Earth only occasionally. They have long possessed the secret of matter transmission, having used it millennia ago to travel from Mexico, where they originated, to Egypt. All the pyramids are, of course, matter transmitters. The principle involved is to enclose the travelling car in an envelope of argon bubbles, which suspend weight!

Thomas meets the Thotheen, the superintelligent but impractical natives of Venus, one of which he describes as "a sort of compound elephant, mosquito and flea, a Thing seven feet high or more with shining scales upon its sides, with great folded gossamer wings, with antennae, and a hairy, flexible trunk, capable of almost endless extension, set on top of its head, with horned eyes capable of *expression*, with a mouth capable of speech". In fact these are gentle creatures, who employ the Sutenraa as doctors, and are much less devious and cold-blooded than are their employees.

Thomas finds that two other Earth people are being held captive by the Sutenraa, a young lady and a clergyman. He falls for the girl, Phyllis, promising to save her. Indeed he goes so far as to marry her (which accounts for the clergyman being present). After various rather ridiculous adventures and plot complications Miss Zumeena helps Thomas and Phyllis to escape back to Earth, the clergyman having dropped dead from a heart attack as soon as he had conducted the marriage service. Back on Earth Thomas finds, hardly surprisingly, that nobody believes his story — a scepticism shared by Jane's readers.

Edgar Rice Burroughs wrote eleven books of heroic fantasy set on Mars, mostly concerning the exploits of Earthman John Carter, who is mysteriously transported there from a cave in Arizona.

Carter was a former soldier and an expert swordsman; he needed to be to survive. His adventures, involving all the various human and alien races of Mars, were far more fast-moving and bloodthirsty than any fiction previously set on that planet.

The first book was *A Princess of Mars* (1917, but serialized five years earlier as "Under the Moons of Mars"); the last was *Llana of Gathol* (1948). There is no space here to summarize the plots or even to describe the races of Barsoom, as its inhabitants called Mars. It seems likely that Burroughs was influenced by the only previous (although less violent) heroic fantasy novel set on Mars, *Lieutenant Gullivar Jones: His Vacation* by Edwin Lester Arnold (1905).

After the initial success of the John Carter books Burroughs had several imitators, most notably Otis Adalbert Kline and (much later) Leigh Brackett. Burroughs himself wrote another series of fantasy adventures, set on Venus (four books, concerning the adventures of Earthman Carson Napier, published during the period 1934-46), but these were poorer and less vivid, amounting almost to self-parody.

It would be wrong to suggest that these Martian and Venusian tales are purely heroic fantasy, with no advanced technology. On Mars there are antigravity fliers and radium pistols, while Carson Napier reaches Venus by rocket ship. But the emphasis was on fast-moving physical action, most of the frequent fights being with swords.

In April 1926 the US editor and publisher Hugo Gernsback launched *Amazing Stories*, the first pulp science-fiction magazine. This, and the others which started up at the end of the 1920s and during the 1930s, concentrated on stories which feature wonderful new machines and alien contact — although most of the early serials were reprints of Verne and Wells. Each month several — or many — alien contact stories appeared. Men journeyed to other parts of the Solar System, and ever more frequently to exotic extra-solar planets, to meet and fight with all sorts of weird and wonderful alien types. These stories were normally set in the future to allow time for mankind to develop spaceships and new weapons systems.

An example of one of the magazine stories from that era is *Vanguard to Neptune* by J. M. Walsh, which first appeared in *Wonder Stories Quarterly* in 1932 but was not published as a book until 1952. This is more imaginative than the stories of thirty or forty years before, being set in 2235, when Earth already has friendly relations with the "men" of Mars and Venus.

An expedition is sent to the planet Neptune on the spaceship *Icarus*. It lands first on Triton (one of Neptune's moons) where there are intelligent aliens. But because these are loathsome to the human eye — looking like large white slugs — they are slaughtered in large numbers without provocation. Even though the ship's captain is reprimanded for this action on his return to Earth, and the book makes mention of the necessity for peace between all creatures, the message still comes across that all aliens are necessarily inferior to us — the more hideous the more inferior — and that the only good alien is a dead one.

On Neptune itself there are small cat-evolved aliens, which travel about in stilt-legged machines. There is also an organic Great Brain, built long before by the Neptunians as "an attempt to create a kind of super-man", an idea which the author presumably borrowed from Olaf Stapledon's *Last and First Men,* published two years earlier. Communication and a certain limited degree of trust are established between the Great Brain and the humans. Then some evil plant men appear, possessing an even higher level of technology. They claim to be of extra-solar origin and they escape with the *Icarus,* proving that no alien can ever really be trusted.

Not all stories of Man's journeys to other planets written at this time belong to the pulp tradition. Olaf Stapledon's *Last and First Men* (1930) has a future race of mankind, remade in barely humanoid bodies, moving to Venus to escape the imminent collision of the Earth and the Moon. But the seas which cover most of Venus contain many types of creatures, including an intelligent species resembling a swordfish. These creatures are aggressive towards mankind and, because mankind must migrate to Venus or become extinct, are deliberately exterminated. Although this distasteful operation is justified by several arguments it leaves humanity with a terrible guilt complex which lingers on for millennia.

Alien contact need not be the result of men going out in spaceships to other planets. (The aliens may come to us, but this eventuality will be dealt with in a moment.) "Contact" is a very loose term. It must include communication over a long distance, as in Raymond Z. Gallun's well known story "Old Faithful", first published in *Astounding* in 1934, about a Martian who communicates with Earth by light-flashes.

Recall also *The Next Chapter: the War Against the Moon* (c. 1927), by André Maurois, in which a phoney war with the Moon is publicized to achieve international unity on Earth. Urged on by world opinion and a money prize, a scientist develops a heat ray and rakes the surface of the Moon with it; but the inhabitants of the Moon have become real and strike back. This is satire, of course, but the subject of the tale is contact all the same.

The strangest story of this type appeared in 1835. Originally published as fact in *The Sun,* a New York daily newspaper, this has become known as "The Moon Hoax". It was presented in the form of a series of articles on the observations of the Moon made by the English astronomer Sir John Herschel from his South African observatory, using a new and more powerful telescope. It was claimed that the Moon was inhabited by humanoid creatures which "averaged four feet in height, were covered, except on the face, with short and glossy copper-coloured hair, and had wings composed of a thin membrane, without hair, lying snugly upon their backs, from the top of the shoulders to the calves of the legs". The articles caused a sensation and were widely believed for a brief period before being exposed as a hoax perpetrated by an English journalist, living in the USA, John Locke. Herschel himself was not involved.

H. G. Wells' story "The Crystal Egg" (1897), in which Mars is seen *via* an Earthbound crystal egg — which operates like a miniature television, with a camera on Mars transmitting pictures to it — is a very marginal form of alien contact.

As science fiction has become more sophisticated the presence of aliens has come to be taken for granted — not just the fact that extraterrestrial intelligences exist Out There but that, in most stories of the future, some alien races have already been discovered and accepted, their continued presence becoming an accepted feature of human society.

A popular and long-lasting contact plot-theme is for aliens to invade Earth. The earliest example of this — a satirical one — dates from 1809, Washington Irving's story "The Conquest By the Moon" (although Peter Nicholls' *Encyclopaedia of Science Fiction* selects an 1892 novel by Robert Potter, *The Germ Growers*).

An influential German novel on the theme is *Auf Zwei Planeten* (1897) by Kurd Lasswitz, which apparently "sold several hundred thousand copies in a very short time". It was translated into several European languages soon after its original publication, though not into English or French; the first English-language edition was not produced until 1971 (as *Two Planets*).

This is a novel of conflict between Earth humans and the techno-logically far-advanced, near-human Martians. Their base at the North Pole is discovered by a balloon expedition composed of three Germans, of whom two are captured (in fact the first attempt to reach the North Pole *did* occur in 1897, presumably after Lasswitz had written his book). Isolated clashes between humans and Martians lead to a state of war.

These Martians, it must be said, are not warlike, but are a highly civilized race. Some want to recognize the warlike humans as equals, while others wish to treat them like animals.

A Martian spacefleet blockades English ports in retaliation for the treatment of Martian prisoners aboard a British ship and for its action in firing on a Martian airship. The cream of the British navy's warships are sunk or disabled in the Battle of Portsmouth, and the Martians declare most of Earth to be a Martian protectorate. This means that they are forbidding "all armaments for war" while trying to preserve each country's constitutional rights.

A human spacefleet is built in defiance of this declaration, and it successfully occupies one of the Martians' space stations above the North Pole. The Martians could easily destroy Earth but sanity prevails on both sides and a peace treaty is signed, providing for all of Earth to become a single unified state.

This novel is an oddity for its period, presenting the Martians as a superior type of Earthmen rather than as true aliens.

An important English novel on the same theme appeared at the same time. This was H. G. Wells' *The War of the Worlds,* serialized in *Pearson's Magazine* in 1897 and first published in book form the following year.

It shows the Martians as hideous non-human creatures, grey-skinned and many-tentacled, invading England with intentions of adding it — and the rest of the world — to their empire. They are a terrible, implacable foe, entirely without emotion; the only communication possible with them is war — their fighting machines, which are rather like walking electricity pylons, against our inadequate and off-guard troops.

This much was contained in the surface level of the novel, and was enshrined in the minds of the public by popular adaptations (particularly the US radio version of 1938, with Orson Welles producing and acting, in which the Martian landings were shifted from England to New Jersey: the broadcast provoked a coast-to-coast panic among people who failed to realize that it was only a play). Yet Wells' novel went much deeper; it was intended as a satire on the future-war novel so popular at the time, and used the same battle-settings on the Surrey Downs which Chesney had used in *The Battle of Dorking* and which others (Le Queux among them) had copied in their own future-war novels. Just as Washington Irving's "The Conquest By the Moon" showed technologically advanced Moon-men forcing humans to change their ways of life and killing them if they refused, in satirical condemnation of the American treatment of Amerinds, so the Martian treatment of the British people was analogous to the UK's high-handed imperialism in various parts of the world, particularly her extermination of the native Tasmanians, which was well under way at the time. Wells even compares humanity to a nest of ants, stirred up by a foot against which they are powerless. It was his intention to show the leading imperialist nation of the day (i.e., the UK) that complacency is dangerous; an invincible enemy always exists. Even for the "invincible" Martians in their "invincible" fighting machines there was an enemy which defeated them: the humble bacteria.

The War of the Worlds has attracted parodies and sequels, including *The War of the Wenuses* (1898), by C. L. Graves and E. V. Lucas, a farce in which young ladies from Venus invade the Earth, and Christopher Priest's *The Space Machine* (1976), in which a couple of humans travel to Mars just before the Martian invasion of Earth and help stir up revolution among a humanoid population there who are slaves of the nasty alien Martians.

Unfortunately, ever since the first appearance of *The War of the Worlds,* most English-speaking people have tended to think of Martians

—and, by analogy, of all extraterrestrials — as tentacled monsters intent on killing or enslaving humanity. Due to this xenophobia, any real extaterrestrials who landed on Earth would probably be killed out of hand, whatever they looked like.

During the era of the pulp science-fiction magazines, from 1926 onwards, Earth was ravaged regularly by groups of alien invaders performing action replays of Wells' Martians.

Once again, Stapledon's *Last and First Men,* one of the relatively few serious science-fiction novels of the 1930s, features a refined version of a popular cliché. Stapledon's Martian invaders are a form of extraterrestrial intelligence seeking water and food materials which are running short on Mars, but they are not recognizable animals. Instead they are cloudlets of a type of virus, linked together in a group-mind. Each cloudlet has only limited intelligence, but is capable of maintaining telepathic links with all other cloudlets so that an immense and formidable group intelligence is formed. Sections of this are able to traverse space without difficulty, but the Martians cannot recognize humans as intelligent creatures because they cannot imagine individual animals being intelligent.

The first Martian invasion is easily repelled by beam radiation, and the cloudlets destroyed, although their subvital units of virus infect Earth's population, killing and crippling, but human beings are uncertain as to what they were fighting. Successive invasions every few centuries over an immensely long period are each larger and more difficult to defeat, with an aftermath of worldwide sickness. After more than fifty thousand years the Martians succeed in occupying some parts of Earth's southern hemisphere, where they practice a form of agriculture. Mankind at last develops an artificial virus which destroys the Martians — although it almost destroys humanity, too, resulting in a prolonged dark age. Never has any writer described such a long-drawn-out war between Earth and Mars — or between Earth and any other extraterrestrial force — before or since.

Few other writers up to 1945 could find anything new to say about alien invaders. One of the few was Alun Llewellyn, in *The Strange Invaders* (1934), set in a barbaric south-Russian society several centuries in the future. Here the invaders are giant lizards — not just leftover dinosaurs which have escaped from somebody's lost-world fantasy, but enigmatic aliens, presumably intended as a symbol of unstoppable force. They are clearly extraterrestrial, although the author does not confirm this, being about twenty feet long, multihued (so that they are truly beautiful in sunlight) and so fast-moving that they confuse the human eye. Their level of intelligence is unclear; they do not seem to possess tools or machines, yet their behaviour suggests something more than animal instinct. They are not totally invulnerable: it is possible to kill them by a spear-thrust beneath a leg, and a sudden fall of snow immobilizes them, showing that they are reptiles of a kind . . . but they remain a puzzle and a paradox.

Back at the periphery of alien contact is Erle Cox's 1925 novel, *Out of the Silence*. This, set in Australia, described the finding of a subterranean storehouse of wonders, together with a beautiful girl in suspended animation. When resuscitated she explains that she is one of two survivors of a fantastically advanced human civilization which was destroyed by an unspecified natural catastrophe millions of years before. In the subterranean chambers around her are all the science and technology of her race.

The alien in this novel is the girl — and her male companion, still in suspended animation in a similar chamber beneath the Himalayas. Although she appears fully human, her almost limitless intelligence and powers, technological and extrasensory, make her a wild factor, with tremendous potential for good or evil. She wishes to help the human race, but upbringing has given her such an alien outlook that, among other things, she wishes to exterminate all the world's non-white population. Although she is killed and her advanced technology destroyed in an over-simple ending, she has posed as much of a threat to the world as any invading extraterrestrial ever did.

Aliens do not necessarily have to be either extraterrestrial or from another time; they may be living, unsuspected, somewhere on Earth. Although some pretty strange creatures have turned up inside the Earth in various books, these are most often prehistoric animals of recognizable types, as in Jules Verne's *Journey to the Centre of the Earth*. An exception are Lord Lytton's mental and physical supermen, the Ana, in *The Coming Race*, which live just below the ground, rather than at any great depth.

Various intelligent races have been predicted to exist on the ocean floor at great depths. "In the Abyss" was H. G. Wells' 1896 story on this theme, in which a scientist descends five miles in a bathyscaphe. Down there he discovers a civilization of reptilian bipeds who are clearly intelligent. They inhabit a luminous city, to which they tow the bathyscaphe, to a temple where they worship it (or its occupant). The scientist escapes when the rope tethering his craft to the ocean bed is sawed through by rubbing against the temple's altar.

Being either extremely intrepid or else extremely foolhardy, he makes a second descent . . . from which he never returns. Obviously, communication with such a civilization would be close to impossible due to pressure differences, although Wells himself seemed to believe that the existence of creatures like that was not impossible.

A rather similar story, which must have seemed plausible at the time of its initial appearance, is Sir Arthur Conan Doyle's "The Horror of the Heights", published in *Strand Magazine* in 1913. This postulates the existence of dangerous creatures high in the air — at 40,000 feet and above.

The story is set in about 1924, when the very latest flying machines are just able to rise to that height. The creatures themselves, modelled on jellyfish and stingrays, are so fragile and tenuous in structure as to be translucent and little more than gaseous. There are several species, all larger than the aircraft which is investigating them. The jellyfish type is

> far larger . . . than the dome of St Paul's. It was of a light pink colour veined with a delicate green, but the whole fabric so tenuous that it was but a fairy outline against the dark blue sky. It pulsated with a delicate and regular rhythm. From it there depended two long, drooping tentacles, which swayed slowly backwards and forwards. This gorgeous vision passed gently with noiseless dignity over my head, as light and fragile as a soap-bubble, and drifted upon its stately way.

Others are aerial serpents, twenty or thirty feet long, but the most dangerous kind is a huge ray, fast-flying with a "curved and cruel" beak. On the first encounter the protagonist saves himself by firing a shotgun and penetrating a gas-bladder on the monster's back. He goes up again; later his headless body and scribbled journal are found on the ground.

These are aliens that never were, but exciting ones.

A similar story, from which Doyle may have taken his idea, was "The Air Serpent" by Will A. Page which appeared in *The Red Book Magazine* in 1911, although this tale was less impressively written.

The far future is rife with alien lifeforms, even if some (or most) of them are evolved forms of humanity. Perhaps the most obvious of these forms are the Eloi and Morlocks in *The Time Machine*. Mankind, by the year 802,701, has diverged into two forms, the simple, childlike Eloi, only four feet tall and with a "Dresden-china type of prettiness", and the ugly, ape-like Morlocks who live below ground. The latter are industrialists, producing clothing and other goods for the indolent Eloi. But while the Eloi live on fruit, the Morlocks prey upon the Eloi, so their relationship is a form of symbiosis. It was intended by Wells to symbolize the proof not so much of Darwinian as of Marxian theories. Still, the Time Traveller is able to communicate, if only in simple terms, with the Eloi, while the Morlocks take away his time machine and do their best to kill him. (This was yet another case of the ugly alien being untrustworthy and coming to blows with a contemporary human, while the beautiful alien becomes Man's friend: a dangerous and potentially xenophobic theory, because in reality no aliens are likely to be beautiful in our eyes.)

S. Fowler Wright's novel *The Amphibians* (1925), and its sequel *The World Below* (1929), show the world 500,000 years hence (reached by another time machine, naturally) where there are at least four intelligent nonhuman races. The Amphibians are graceful fur-covered humanoids, telepathic and almost immortal. They consider the narrator to be a barbarian for wearing clothes, but they are at least reasonably friendly towards him. There are also the Dwellers, giant humans who rule the caverns under the Earth, and the Killers, "bright worm-pink" humanoids, who rule the surface of the Earth. Yet another group are "a hairless, dead-white, ape-like, frog-mouthed form, a width of jaws in a flat skull, and small malignant eyes". They are very ugly, and the narrator, quite naturally, attacks them without stopping to think.

When considering the alienness of future man, though, the standard novel dealing with the subject is Olaf Stapledon's *Last and First Men*, which narrates a whole future history from the present to that time, two thousand million years hence, when a nearby star is about to become a supernova, destroying all men. But men have changed much over that period, evolving, remaking themselves, and changing planets twice. The "Last Men" are more alien to us than any of the extraterrestrial races which other writers have imagined. And surely this is the case: the most alien creature of all is Man.

8 THREE HUNDRED YEARS HENCE

SERIOUS PREDICTION

However much the writer of a tale of the future intends his work as satire, perhaps, or as escapist fiction, there can be few who do not hope that a few elements of their stories will, in time, come true. This does not apply only to wish-fulfilment fiction, of course; although the authors of that hope to see it come true, not many are sufficiently fanatical to believe in it, and perfect states — utopias — are the type of prediction least likely of all to come ture.

The eventual coming-true of predictions is not necessary for their inclusion here; a serious intention is enough, and this will enable some very odd and unworkable prophecies to be examined. Apart from fictional works which may include a great deal of seriously intentioned prediction (W. D. Hay's *Three Hundred Years Hence* and Hugo Gernsback's *Ralph 124C41+* are good examples) there are many nonfiction books which attempt to predict the future, or at least some narrow areas of it.

In fiction the most common area of prediction has been technological, and one of the main symbols of advanced technology has always been air travel. Most novels set some way in the future (more than five or ten years, say) extrapolate from the state of knowledge of the time and feature advanced balloons, airplanes or other flying vehicles. Novels such as *A Voyage to the Moon* by "Aratus" (1793), Mary Shelley's *The Last Man* (1826), Jane Webb's *The Mummy! A Tale of the Twenty-Second Century* (1827) and Mary Griffith's *Three Hundred Years Hence* (1836) all include advanced, although not very advanced, balloons.

One of the earliest uses of flying machines other than balloons is in Herrman Lang's *The Air Battle* (1859) where there are "aerials", which seem to be able to travel horizontally and vertically at enormous speed. Their means of propulsion is not mentioned, though they come in all sizes and some are very large indeed, containing thousands of men and having "five thousand camel-power" engines. Elsewhere a consumable power source of some kind is indicated.

The inventive W. D. Hay suggests numerous types of flying machines in *Three Hundred Years Hence* (1881). There are balloons whose canopies contain the extremely light lucegen gas; the canopy is positioned below rather than above the car. "The car was thus immersed, as it were, in a bladder covering it externally but leaving it open above; it sat in its balloon just as it might in water." Even the author concedes that such a design might tend to lead to instability and turning turtle. To prevent this he uses a powerful magnet which is attracted to the Earth's magnetic field. Thus stabilized the "Lucegenostat" is able to carry considerable weights of freight or passengers.

Yet these are superseded by even more powerful aerial machines, working on new principles. The lift is provided by "basilico-magnetism", for greater power and greater safety. The locomotive power may come from "generated heat and electricity", which causes a pair of fans modelled on birds' wings "extending along the sides of the craft from stem to stern" to flap. This type is known as the "alamotor" and is used for small utilitarian craft, for agricultural purposes and the like. The "spiralometer" is driven by one or more propellers of the "pusher" variety normally placed at the stern. "Heat and electricity give the motive power, and this form is the most generally employed on aircraft." For really heavy loads the "zodiamotor" is available, being powered by the naturally occurring "zodiacal electricity". When Hay says that "it is that which holds together the elements of air" he can be construed (just) as referring to atomic energy. At any rate, his various flying machines are able to lift any weight and to travel at a thousand miles an hour, "though seldom employing more than half that rate".

Albert Robida was less adventurous in his predictions. Looking less far ahead than Hay but from a similar starting point, he stuck with balloons of simple theory, although of various complex shapes, until well after the Wright brothers had flown. Only in his later years, after World War I, did he begin to include propeller-driven aircraft in his predictions.

Jules Verne invented a new shape of air vehicle — the air clipper, a flat-bottomed hull with thirty-seven propeller-bearing masts and another larger propeller screw at either end. This was Robur's *Albatross* in *Robur the Conqueror* — also known as *The Clipper of the Clouds* (French publication 1886, English 1887). The multimasted flying ship was borrowed by others, including George Griffith for *The Angel of the Revolution*. Similar ships, but without masts, appeared in E. Douglas Fawcett's *Hartmann the Anarchist* and Rudyard Kipling's two stories of the Aerial Board of Control. The interesting — and downright dangerous — connection between all these craft was that they had open decks where crew and passengers walked about during flight.

Not all the early fictional vehicles conformed to one of these two patterns — balloon or ship of the air. When Verne's Robur makes his reappearance as the *Master of the World* (French publication 1904, English 1914) he comes in a most curious vehicle, a combination of ship, submarine, automobile and aircraft, with a pair of swing-out wings.

Presumably this story was written before the Wright brothers' first flight in December 1903 — not that Robur's *Terror* resembles their biplane in the slightest.

Yet in the years after 1903 the familiar airplane shape, with one or more propellers at the front, became standard in fiction. In H. G. Wells' *The War in the Air* (1908) there are several types of monoplane and biplane, one with flapping wings, as well as dirigible type airships which act as aircraft-carriers. Nine years later in *The Messiah of the Cylinder* (1917) by Victor Rousseau there are ordinary airplanes which work by solar power — the story was set in 2010. R. H. Benson calls his aircraft "volors" in both *Lord of the World* (1907) and *The Dawn of All* (1911), but does not describe them with any precision; while in *The Unknown Tomorrow* (1910) William Le Queux refers to "nearly everybody possessing his own aeroplane" — "everybody" presumably meaning only the rich, because in his tale the poor are nearly starving and the UK is sliding deeper into economic depression with each passing day — a startlingly accurate prediction of today, one may feel.

The idea that small airplanes (not just helicopters) would be able to use city rooftops for take-off and landing was a popular one in fiction between the wars. For example, Robida drew pictures of it, and all the Alphas in Aldous Huxley's *Brave New World* have personal aircraft, which are kept in rooftop hangars. The serious predictors, too, seemed to favour this system. But then nearly all the aircraft prior to 1939 were fairly light in weight and did not need the heavy-duty stressed-concrete runways necessary today.

Yet there are never enough aircraft for everybody to travel by air. In Hay's *Three Hundred Years Hence* all roads and railways are ploughed up for crop-growing, but one can presume that most of the world's 130 billion people are not given the opportunity to travel around very much from city to city. Hay seems to have been the first to think of a "sub-terrane" earth-borer — which could cut holes at two to five miles per hour to any depth — but he did not extend the idea by reinforcing such holes and running trains through them.

It was left to Albert Robida to suggest the widespread use of long-distance pneumatic tubes, below and above ground and along the ocean beds; he even has a transatlantic tube. A manmade tunnel right through the centre of the Earth occurs in William Wallace Cook's *A Round Trip to the Year 2000* (1903), where at each Universal Tube Station in the USA is a notice proclaiming "Daily Drops by Comfortable Cars to China and Way Stations". Hugo Gernsback's prediction is a little more restrained in *Ralph 124C41+*: a subatlantic tube which runs in a dead straight line between New York and Brest, ignoring the Earth's curvature, and penetrating 450 miles below the surface at its midpoint. Astonishingly, at that depth, tube, train and passengers are unaffected by the extremely high temperatures in the Earth's mantle.

Moving belts for pedestrians in towns and cities have become a cliché of science fiction. Their earliest appearance seems to have been in Frank R. Stockton's 1898 novel *The Great Stone of Sardis,* where the New Jersey Bridge is, by 1947, divided into two steadily moving strips. There are some shelters at intervals on the strips, though what happens when these reach the end of the bridge is not divulged.

Presumably H. G. Wells had the same idea at the same time, for although his *When the Sleeper Wakes* was published the following year, 1899, it had been written, according to Bernard Bergonzi, during the winter of 1897-8. Here the system of moving belts is more sophisticated, obviously clearer in the author's mind. This system, in the roofed-over London of 2100, is three hundred feet across, with a stationary centre lane and gradually faster moving strips, each on a slightly higher level, to either side, with the outermost lanes "rushing along as fast as a nineteenth-century express train". There are seats and kiosks on the strips, although the problem of what happens to them at the far end is still not solved. The means of getting onto the moving strips in the first place is also somewhat obscure; presumably there is frequent access by stairs or escalators to the centre strip.

During the pulp-magazine era of the 1930s and 1940s hardly a futuristic city existed without its moving pavements, although the "father of the science-fiction pulps", Hugo Gernsback himself, in *Ralph 124C41+* solved the problem of moving large numbers of pedestrians swiftly in another and much sillier fashion. He provided each of them with electrically powered roller skates, the power being picked up from the metallic pavement surface. Mind you, the sight of New Yorkers travelling to and from work by skateboard is becoming more common.

In 1940 the moving pavements were extended to intercity travel by Robert A. Heinlein in one of his early stories, "The Roads Must Roll", which appeared in *Astounding Science Fiction* in June of that year.

Although predictions of space travel and space exploration are dealt with together in Chapter 7, this is a subject which is at the heart of much serious speculative fiction.

In fact, in this context, very few early interplanetary novels succeeded in prophesying *anything* correctly, either hardware items or planetary conditions. Few of the spaceships use rockets to provide motive power, most relying on a launching gun (Verne's *From the Earth to the Moon),* a gravity repulsion system (Griffith's *A Honeymoon in Space* and Wells' *First Men in the Moon),* some other kind of new force —magnetic in Gustavus W. Pope's *Journey to Mars* (1894), "apergy" in Percy Greg's *Across the Zodiac* (1880), and unspecified in John Munro's *A Trip to Venus* (1897) — or even atomic energy (Garrett P. Serviss' *A Columbus of Space* (1911)).

The first space station appeared as early as 1869. This was an artifical satellite designed as a navigational aid to ships at sea, which all sounds very scientific and farseeing until one learns that it was made out of bricks and launched — prematurely, with its builders still inside — by means of various mechanical devices! This was in "The Brick Moon", a story by Edward Everett Hale, serialized in *Atlantic Monthly,* and published in a collection of Hale's stories in 1872.

The Martians in Kurd Lasswitz's *Two Planets* (in German 1897) have a satellite poised above Earth's North Pole, and in the same year John Munro's *A Trip to Venus* speculated on the possibility of a space station. In fact Munro's book was among the most thoughtful of early interplanetary fiction, mentioning multistage rockets, parachutes for planetary landings, regular flights between Earth, Mars and Venus, and multigeneration starships.

In the era of the pulp science-fiction magazines space technology blossomed, with ever-faster ships travelling to ever more remote destinations — for example, *Outside the Universe,* surely the most remote journey of all, by Edmond Hamilton in *Weird Tales* (1929) — but the gain in scientific accuracy was minimal.

In those early stories all the planets and moons of the Solar System were, at one time or another, blessed with an Earth-type atmosphere, and served as the home of intelligent aliens. These inaccuracies were not necessarily the fault of the author; the foremost astronomers of the day were often enthusiastic, or at least uncertain, about the possibilities of Earth-type conditions on other worlds.

Many authors realized that the civilization of the future could not progress technologically without being in possession of a plentiful and efficient source of power. As early as 1772, Mercier says in *Memoirs of the Year 2500* that "We have formed artifical torrents and cataracts, by which is acquired a force sufficient to produce the greatest effects of motion", which suggests hydroelectric power.

Just over a century later W. D. Hay mentions various power systems in *Three Hundred Years Hence.* Geothermal heat is tapped, although it is surprising that this should be needed, for two new power sources are discovered in his version of the future. There is a mechanical friction (or clockwork-friction) machine, which makes use of the "magnetic principle" to operate as a heat-generator. "The machine occupied no great space — one or two cubic feet — required no fuel, sent a stream of heat through a stoveful of fire brick, rendering it red-hot and maintaining that temperature, could be regulated by the turn of a handle, was cheap, and only required the renewal of certain iron bars and wheels at distant intervals." But the Basilic Force is also discovered. This force seems to involve the tapping of the life force, giving Man direct organic control over all energy forms — a far-reaching advance indeed, and one which would seem to make even today's power systems redundant.

André Laurie in *The Conquest of the Moon* (first English publication 1889) gets all the power necessary to operate the electromagnets which pull the Moon down to the Earth from solar-heat condensers — large conical dishes of copper which soak up the heat of the Sun's rays.

His countryman and occasional collaborator, Jules Verne, mentioned many different systems of power in his novels. In one of his short stories, "In the 29th Century", he mentions nearly all of them: wind, water, solar and geothermal.

Slightly earlier, in 1894, John Jacob Astor mentioned all of these power sources in his *A Journey to Other Worlds*. He even has broadcast electrical power to drive air vehicles.

There is broadcast power, too, in Gernsback's *Ralph 124C41+*, although this seems to be entirely derived from solar energy — an idea remarkably similar to that behind the NASA scheme for Satellite Solar Power Stations, which are to convert solar energy into microwaves which can be beamed down to Earth, there to be in turn converted into electrical power.

H. G. Wells favours wind and water power (monopolized by the Windvane and Waterfall Trust) in *When the Sleeper Wakes* and "A Story of the Days to Come".

Later, in the 1920s, "atomic energy" became the catchphrase; it was the power system which would replace all others and bring about utopia. This is the basis for "Nedram's" *John Sagur*, where atomic power is broadcastable to any point in the world from a single source, and it turns up at the end of *Nordenholt's Million* by J. J. Connington.

In the field of communications, everything has been aimed at increasing speed, so that one does not have to hand-write messages. This has been true not only in prediction but also in the history of the past decades.

In Robida's *Le Vingtième Siècle* (1883) the telephonoscope is a kind of television-cum-picturephone, enabling one to talk to one's friends or to bring the theatre or the day's news into one's own home. There are also nonpicture telephones which provide a news service.

Bellamy, in *Equality* (1897), forecasts the death of handwriting due to "phonographs", tape-recorded messages. His future citizens also use typewriters and telephones a good deal.

William Wallace Cook in *A Round Trip to the Year 2000* suggests, perhaps not wholly seriously, that all long-distance messages will be transmitted *via* a machine which amplifies human thoughts.

In *Ralph 124C41+* Hugo Gernsback originates a couple of new communications systems — besides making use of the picturephone and television, although the latter in a peculiarly awkward manner, whereby the broadcaster can see each member of his remote audience. There is the Menograph or mind-writer — one of Ralph's many inventions — which produces a brain-wave output: "Where the wave line breaks, a new word or sentence commences." But there is also what Gernsback calls phonetic writing, which is a wavy-line voice record — unique for each individual and capable of being read almost as easily as printed words, either by people or by machines.

In Wells' "A Story of the Days to Come" there is a new phonetic alphabet in use for printed words. Hence the name "Morris" has become "Mwres" and "th" is written as "Θ". The sign "'ets r chip t'de" means "hats are cheap today". Victor Rousseau later developed this idea into a syllabic system in his novel *The Messiah of the Cylinder*.

There are countless other examples of advanced science and technology, from the enormously useful technique of weather control — illustrated by Robida and mentioned by both W. D. Hay and William Wallace Cook — to the many technological gimmicks referred to by Hugo Gernsback. Sleep learning is one of Gernsback's more interesting original ideas. This is used to greater effect in *Brave New World* by Aldous Huxley, who also refines the idea of ectogenic birth, describing in detail the task of caring for human foetuses as they come to term in their bottles. In Frank R. Stockton's *The Great Stone of Sardis* a submarine has electric gills for extracting air directly from seawater, and in a short story by the same author — "A Tale of Negative Gravity" (1884) — there is a small, portable antigravity device. Rudyard Kipling's story "As Easy as A.B.C." makes the first use of what he calls a "ground circuit", which has come to be known in modern science fiction as a tangler field — a powerful electrically derived field which restricts movement and can be used for capturing or securing criminals.

These are just a few of the many ideas expressed.

Apart from technological innovations there are considerable numbers of changes to society which are worth considering. Food, medicine, clothing and attitudes towards women are all subjects on which authors have thought to prophesy in the course of their novels.

Taking food first, there is no meat eaten by people in either Hay's *Three Hundred Years Hence* or Bellamy's *Looking Backward 2000-1887* (although Bellamy does not think to mention it until his sequel, *Equality*). Hay's reason is lack of space: arable farming is more efficient in terms of food production per acre than is the keeping of animals for their meat, and the problem of providing sufficient food for the world's vast population would be acute if large areas had to be used only for grazing or for animal feedstuffs. Bellamy's reason is one of sentiment for the poor animals. People have come "to regard the eating of their fellow animals as a revolting practice, almost akin to cannibalism".

But in neither book is the populace hard up for substitutes. Hay writes enthusiastically of all the tropical fruits and vegetables and new strains of wheat, while Bellamy's Dr Leete talks of the great number of new flavours since 1887 and says: " . . . undoubtedly the abandonment of the custom of eating animals, by which we inherited all their diseases, has had something to do with the great physical improvement of the race."

Food preparation has been centralized in Bellamy's book. Albert Robida, however, had the same idea earlier and, in *Le Vingtième Siècle*, has several pictures of foods being factory-cooked and then piped to consumers — ending, of course, with a burst pipe and what might be described as a mess of potage.

Wells, too, has automated food preparation in "A Story of the Days to Come", although he shows only the consumption end of the process. People live not in private houses but in hotel rooms, eating communally in large dining halls. The food (for breakfast) consists of "pastes and cakes of agreeable and variegated design, without any suggestion of the unfortunate animals from which their substance and juices were derived". It is served automatically from a little box at the side of each table.

Gernsback adopts similar automation, with food being delivered in liquefied form through a mouthpiece and its type — or even the addition of salt and pepper — being controlled by pushing buttons. William Wallace Cook goes one step further in *A Round Trip to the Year 2000*, where all food is inhaled as vapour rather than being placed in the mouth and chewed. And it is interesting to note that as early as 1898 Frank R. Stockton in *The Great Stone of Sardis* warned that milk and butter were injurious to health — decades before the great cholesterol debate.

In a large number of future societies great emphasis is placed on health and fitness. In W. H. Hudson's *A Crystal Age* it is a crime to be ill, for disease has been conquered and it is perfectly possible to avoid illness by taking proper care of one's body, (in any case, the inhabitants are physically superior to modern Man). Bellamy, in *Looking Backward 2000-1887*, stresses the improved health of the American nation due to improved hygiene and adequate food. All illness is attributable to mental condition, according to R. H. Benson's *The Dawn of All* (1911), and an electrical instrument has been invented (the setting is 1973) which enables one's psychical condition to be checked: "A century ago when a man was ill they began by doctoring his body. Now, when a man's ill, they begin by doctoring his mind. You see the mind is much more the man than the body is." Gernsback can be claimed to be predating modern medical trends in the revival of frozen bodies and of those whose heart has stopped. The influenza epidemic which killed so many millions of people worldwide in 1918 is predicted (although placed in 1921) by William Le Queux in *The Unknown Tomorrow* (1910).

Among the most surprising predictions on the subject of clothing is Bellamy's in *Equality,* where paper clothes are made very cheaply, worn once and then not just thrown away but *recycled!* The manufacturing techniques are advanced enough for some paper clothes to feel like silk, for others to be waterproof and for all to be as strong as ordinary cloth. Indeed, all household fabrics, including bed-linen, curtains and carpets, are made from paper. (This is in strange contrast to a passage early on in *Looking Backward 2000-1887,* where the author mentions that there has been no change in dress or furniture between 1887 and 2000.) It is mentioned also in *Equality* that women wear trousers.

The clothes of 2100 as described in Wells' "A Story of the Days to Come" are airtight, presumably made of rubber, and are designed to be partly inflated "to suggest enormous muscles". Over this goes a silk tunic and a cloak, plus a brightly coloured and inflatable hat which resembles a cock's comb. By contrast, the clothing in *When the Sleeper Wakes,* which is supposed to have the same setting, consists mainly of long robes. Perhaps the prevailing style altered rather quickly.

In R. H. Benson's *The Dawn of All* uniforms are worn by everyone to signify their occupation or profession — a frequent theme in predictive fiction. William Wallace Cook has a unisex costume worn by all in *A Round Trip to the Year 2000;* it consists of bloomers and a small hat, and it makes it very difficult to tell the sexes apart. Presumably a loose blouse is also worn.

Attitudes to women vary considerably, from their subservience to men in Mercier's *Memoirs of the Year 2500* to a matriarchy in Hudson's *A Crystal Age* and complete domination of men by women in the rôle-reversal novels of Anson, Besant and Cross. One of the earliest predictions of female emancipation comes in Mary Griffith's *Three Hundred Years Hence* (1836), where there is complete equality with men.

Obviously, the dominance of women, or even their equality with men, was not a subject which many men could bring themselves to take seriously in the 19th century. When Robida writes of and illustrates female equality — no professions are barred to women, they fight duels, they serve alongside men in the revolutionary army — his intentions are satirical.

Edward Bellamy was one of the few men of his day who honestly believed in equality. In *Looking Backward 2000-1887* women are expected to work in the industrial army, except when having children, as men are, and they receive the same annual credit allowance as men. They have been relieved of most household chores by automation and communal eating. Bellamy also includes an interesting passage on the female form in *Equality.* Julian West, the man from 1887, has accompanied his host Dr Leete to the gymnasium to watch his daughter Edith participating in various athletic events.

Then followed contests in ball-throwing and putting the shot.

"It is plain where your women get their splendid chests and shoulders," said I.

"You have noticed that, then!" exclaimed the doctor.

"I have certainly noticed," was my answer, "that your modern women seem generally to possess a vigorous development and appearance of power above the waist which were only occasionally seen in our day."

Equality of men and women is predicted in J. D. Beresford's *Goslings* (1913) but only because of the plague which has killed off almost all men and necessitated the establishment of a different society. By 1923, when Ronald Knox's *Memories of the Future* was published, it was easier to predict women's equality because the process had already begun in several walks of life. Ayn Rand's *Anthem* (1938) shows equality of all men and equality of all women; presumably there is equality between the sexes, too, but society is organized so that men and women live in separate communities, never meeting except at appointed mating times. John Kendall's communistic state in *Unborn Tomorrow* (1933) has a shortage of women; consequently there is a falling birth rate and most men have to remain unmarried — the phenomenon is not accounted for, and neither is a solution found.

There are many other aspects of society which particular authors have commented on or extrapolated into the future. It is surprising that W. D. Hay is almost alone among pre-1945 writers of fiction to envisage a truly enormous world population within a couple of hundred years or so and to take steps to accommodate and feed everybody.

Beside this, the more limited predictions of other authors seem unimpressive. Nevertheless, Bellamy's idea of a credit system and credit cards, with no money exchanging hands or even existing, is an interesting prophecy even though our own credit system is differently based. R. H. Benson's suggestion in *Lord of the World* that Esperanto would catch on and might become the official language in the UK has proved unfounded, but history might have been different. The total roofing-over of London, as predicted by Wells in *When the Sleeper Wakes*, may still occur; after all we are a long way from the year 2100 yet, and a lot of radical changes are bound to happen before then. The total automation forecast by E. M. Forster in "The Machine Stops" is well on its way to coming true; already we possess the technical capacity to achieve it, although not for the whole world population, and some partly disabled people and invalids benefit from as wide a range of automatic devices as Forster mentions. There is as yet no widespread use of humanoid robots or androids such as those described by Cook and Čapek, but control devices at least as "clever" are already being used in factories and offices. While the temporary marriages — "companionate marriages"

— mentioned by John Gloag in *Tomorrow's Yesterday* (1932) are not officially sanctioned, they are certainly present in spirit. And let us hope that the almost total lack of privacy which characterizes society in Zamyatin's *We* will not become fact.

The natural world, too, is the subject of prediction in tales of the future. Leaving aside the wilder and more disastrous prophecies, some remain which should give us cause for thought.

Frank R. Stockton's reference in *The Great Stone of Sardis* to the whale being almost extinct — hunted out of existence — by 1947 is a few decades premature but seems well on the way to being fulfilled.

W. D. Hay describes the slaughter of all animal species — wild and domestic — until "only a few specimens of them remain for curiosities", and this is something which mankind would have to consider if the world population ever rose as high as, say, thirty billion, let alone the 130 billion which Hay anticipated.

A new glaciation will almost certainly affect the Earth within a few thousand years unless by that time Man possesses the technology to prevent it. In de Tarde's *Underground Man* this forces us to retreat into the Earth's interior, where we eventually die out. In Llewellyn's *The Strange Invaders* the conditions are less severe and the ice age makes relatively little difference to mankind, which has in any case regressed due to war.

Serious "nonfiction" prediction by scientists and others with specialist knowledge has a long history.

Although some Greek and Roman historians speculated on the outcome of future battles or campaigns, the earliest notable scientific predictor was Leonardo da Vinci (1452-1519). During the last two decades of the 15th century he produced many detailed drawings, accompanied always by explanations and building instructions in mirror writing, of an enormous number of machines and technical features, some of which could or would not be built for centuries. Many of these were weapons of attack or defence — for he lived in a violent age — including improvements to hafted weapons, mechanical siege engines, chariots armed with moving scythes or flails, methods of resisting besieging forces, new types of shields for various types of soldier, designs for cannon and mortars, a primitive armoured car or tank, and manpowered flying machines. Among his nonmilitary drawings were architectural designs, new clock escapements, machine tools, lock and weir arrangements for canals, and many original gadgets. Some were refinements of existing items, others were completely new. Some were quickly put into practice while others — in particular the flying machine — were seen by Leonardo himself to be unworkable.

Another notable scientific prophet was the 17th-century Marquis of Worcester. Number 100 in his *Century of Inventions* (1663) describes a steam engine which he suggests can be used to raise water. The details are unclear, but this is generally considered to have been the first description of a steam engine. (Other contenders for this honour are Hero of Alexandria, who wrote about a very primitive steam turbine in his *Pneumatica,* in the 1st century AD, and Giovanni Battista della Porte, who went part of the way to describing a working steam engine in 1601.) The fact that the first successful steam engine was not built until 1698, by Thomas Savery, means that these earlier descriptions are all predictive. (The popular supposition that Watt invented the steam engine is false.)

Among other seriously intended predictions in Worcester's *Century of Inventions* are a perpetual-motion machine and instructions for making a man able to fly. Many other ideas — some possible, some which we see now to be totally ridiculous — were discussed and written about by scientists and men of learning over the centuries.

There were even a few social predictions, such as those by Gregory King in *Observations on the State of England* (1696). He says:

In all probability the next doubling of the people of England will be in about six hundred years to come, or by the year of our Lord 2300, at which time it will have eleven millions of people. The next doubling after that will be, in all probability, in less than twelve or thirteen hundred years, or by the year of our Lord 3500 or 3600. At which time the Kingdom will have 22 millions of souls . . . in case the world should last so long.

Yet it was not until the 19th century that books containing scientific or social appraisals of the future became common. Early in the century there were published many designs for navigable balloons or ideas for the use of balloons in warfare — these had begun to appear even before the Montgolfiers' first successful ascent in 1783. Later the speculation concentrated more on heavier-than-air machines, such as Stringfellow & Henson's Aerial Steam Carriage of 1843 (illustrations of it in flight over Britain, over the pyramids of Egypt, etc., were published widely, although only a scale model actually made it off the ground) and Langley's petrol-engined, catapult-launched "aerodrome" which could, with more luck, have flown late in 1903, beating the Wright brothers by a few days.

There was similar speculation over horseless carriages. From the 1820s a successful steam-powered car was widely anticipated. At the same time the Bristol (UK) inventor George Pocock was trying to use kites to draw carriages. In his slim but beautifully illustrated book *Navigation in the Air* (1827) he shows carriages being towed along by pairs of fairly small kites.

During the last few decades of the 19th century there was a flurry of books, pamphlets and articles published about the future. In fact, to say "the future" gives a false impression, for none considered the future as a whole — at least, not in any detail. Instead, they were specialized speculations written largely by experts who were willing to stick their necks out and predict the future of their own profession over the next ten, twenty-five or fifty years, usually saying how much of an improvement there would be if their own ideas were to be followed through.

Two of the most important of these works are *Hygeia; or, A City of Health* (1876) by Dr B. W. Richardson and *Garden Cities of Tomorrow* (1898) by Ebenezer Howard.

Richardson's *Hygeia* was just a pamphlet, originally delivered as a lecture to the Social Science Association, but it was the first publication on the subject of public hygiene to be widely read. The leading British expert on the subject, Richardson advocated public water and sewerage schemes and less crowded living conditions in cities, with wider streets and frequent open spaces and parks. He says:

> It is my object to put forward a theoretical outline of a community so circumstanced and so maintained by the exercise of its own free will, guided by scientific knowledge, that the perfection of sanitary results will be approached, if not actually realised, in the co-existence of the lowest possible general mortality with the highest possible individual longevity.

His forecast of the increased well-being which would inevitably follow such reforms was almost as embracing as that in Edward Bellamy's books and even more believable. Indeed, writers such as Bellamy were directly influenced by *Hygeia*. The spacious Boston of 2000 is based on Richardson's prescriptions, and in *Equality* Dr Leete tells Julian West: "I know that Boston Harbour water was far from being clean enough for bathing in your day, but all that is changed. Your sewage systems, remember, are forgotten abominations, and nothing that can defile is allowed to reach sea or river nowadays."

Ebenezer Howard's *Garden Cities of Tomorrow* was a seminal work in the field of town planning. First published as *Tomorrow: a Peaceful Path to Real Reform* in 1898, it was reissued in a revised form under its better known title in 1902. It has been reprinted frequently since then and is still available — an astonishing feat of stamina for any textbook.

The term "garden city" was Howard's own. The central theme of his theories is that instead of permitting large urban centres such as London to encroach into surrounding farmlands in a never-ending suburban sprawl, with few amenities and an ever-lengthening commuter trek to the central industrial and commercial areas, small satellite towns should be established. Howard's idea was that a green belt should always be maintained between the large urban centre and the garden city. Also, the latter should have its own factories and offices, providing on-the-spot employment, and its overall size should be limited — to 32,000 people. All this would, of course, require detailed planning and control at national and regional levels. The garden city would not be allowed to sprawl, but the land would be laid out in advance for house-plots, public buildings, factories, wide roads and, above all, parks and open spaces. "Town and country must be married, and out of this joyous union will spring a new hope, a new life, a new civilization."

Certainly Howard had read Richardson's pamphlet and adopted his ideas. It is very probable that in addition he had read Bellamy's *Looking Backward 2000-1887* and perhaps Hertzka's *Freeland,* deciding that utopia need not be built on the site of an old city or in the unknown hinterland of another continent, but on green field sites fifteen or twenty miles from the centre of London.

Perhaps surprisingly — for one never expects good ideas to bear fruit quickly, if at all — garden cities were established in Hertfordshire, just north of London, at Letchworth in 1903 and Welwyn in 1919. These did not conform to the circular layout or have a central park area, as Howard had suggested, but in most other respects they accorded with his plans.

A perennial speculation, which was first contemplated at least as early as 1802, reached its height of public interest in the last quarter of the 19th century, has received attention at intervals during the 20th century, and is by no means dead yet, is the construction of a tunnel or bridge across the English Channel between the UK and France. The minimum sea distance is about twenty-two miles, although the total length of any bridge or tunnel would need to be close to thirty miles.

A French engineer, M. Albert Mathieu, suggested a tunnel connection in 1802. This was before the widespread building of railways, and the tunnel was intended to be a roadway only, lit by oil lamps (neither gas nor electricity was available) and having a number of ventilation chimneys projecting above the surface of the water. Anglo-French hostilities halted that particular scheme, although others were put forward for discussion when peace returned.

At length, in the 1870s, a plan which originated with M. Thome de Gamond, a French government engineer, was agreed on by the UK and French authorities. This was to be a railway tunnel, ventilated by thirteen artificial islets, of which the central one would be fairly large with railway interchange facilities. A Channel Tunnel Company was formed, preliminary borings were made, and in 1880-82 a mile of tunnel was dug from the English side. At this stage there emerged military opposition on grounds of national security, and the UK government stopped the work.

Even the strongest commercial arguments and the introduction of several private members' bills in the UK Parliament failed to reverse this decision. Yet, thoughout the 1890s and into the next decade, the channel tunnel was a live issue. Several channel-tunnel invasion novels and stories appeared at about this time, most notably Max Pemberton's *Pro Patria* (1901), which is described fully in Chapter 2.

During the 20th century several new feasibility studies have been undertaken. In 1964 a rail tunnel was agreed in principle. Once again test borings were made; in 1975 the idea was dropped; in 1980 it was revived.

A channel bridge was first mooted in 1849. In 1870 such a project was accepted as feasible, and final plans and models were on show at the Paris Exhibition of 1889. Even the cost of £35 million (at 1889 values) was accepted. But the naval authorities vetoed the idea because of the hazards presented by the 120 supporting pillars.

Even so, H. G. Wells predicted a channel bridge in *The War in the Air*, which was published in 1908 and set only about nine years in the future: "Presently the English Channel was bridged — a series of great iron Eiffel Tower pillars carrying mono-rail cables at a height of a hundred and fifty feet above the water, except near the middle, where they rose higher to allow the passage of the London and Antwerp shipping and the Hamburg-American liners." Other schemes, such as a tube lying on the seabed or a submerged railway — a sort of wheeled submarine running on tracks and powered by electricity — have come to nothing.

It must not be forgotten that most of the subjects which occupied the writers of tales of the future were aired also in nonfiction settings in books and magazines. The magazines of the 1890s and 1900s — this was the heyday of the glossy, general interest, monthly magazine — were full of articles entitled "The Future of . . .". Without a doubt the most popular topic was warfare, either the weapons and tactics which would be employed in the next major war — *all* the pundits were wrong — or else the probable nationalities of the combatants.

Other recurring topics are transport, science, houses and women. By and large no seriously expressed opinions on the future of any of these subjects were as imaginative or even as accurate as those found in tales of the future.

Opinions on the future of women, for example, were generally that their position would remain unchanged, because most women were bound to the home by children and in any case were unfit to compete against men in the world of industry and commerce — it was a popular belief in the 19th century that women were an inferior race to men. The few women who did achieve success in the man's world were looked upon as peculiar and unfeminine, and were not expected to find the time to marry and raise daughters who would follow in their footsteps. Except in a very few cases any prophecies that women would achieve equality with men or would eventually become the dominant sex were intended satirically and accepted in the same spirit.

In 1901 was published, for the first time, a nonfiction view of the future which was universal in scope. This was *Anticipations of the Reaction of Mechanical and Scientific Progress Upon Human Life and Thought* by H. G. Wells. It has been responsible, more than any other book, for the rise of the science of futurism, which was a school of art at the time *Anticipations* was published but, since 1945, has come to mean the study of the future. *Anticipations* can be seen as a watered-down version of *When the Sleeper Wakes,* which had been published two years earlier, less politically intentioned, less frenzied, set less far in the future, yet wider in scope and much more concerned with building up a credible picture of tomorrow. Wells was looking a century ahead to the year 2000.

As he suggests in his title, Wells is concerned not only with the progress of technology but with its effects upon the whole of human society. His predictions are more restrained than in his fiction — indeed, so restrained at times as to be amusing — but this was only to be expected in a serious work, and was to set the pattern for other general nonfiction prophecies right up to the present day.

Wells predicts the development of motor vehicles — automobiles for pleasure, lorries for deliveries and 'buses for public transport — and he also highlights the necessity of isolating these faster-moving vehicles from pedestrians and horse-drawn traffic. This, he suggests, could be done by the building of special long-distance roads expressly designed — by virtue of their greater width, straightness and better surfacing — for high-speed travel on rubber tyres; he even mentions a dual-carriageway system. These roads are now with us, of course, in the shape of motorways and freeways. For the mass transport of pedestrians in cities Wells draws on *When the Sleeper Wakes* and suggests moving pavements, saying that part of London's tube system could be converted to this.

The social side of faster and better transport is something else which he accurately predicts: the stretching of commuting distances.

Indeed, it is not too much to say that the London citizen of the year 2000 A. D. may have a choice of nearly all England and Wales south of Nottingham and east of Exeter as his suburb, and that the vast stretch of country from Washington to Albany will be all of it 'available' to the active citizen of New York and Philadelphia before that date.

Obviously Wells had not read Ebenezer Howard's book on garden cities, published three years before *Anticipations.* He predicts also the steady growth of cities, of London to twenty millions and New York to forty, and foresees most of the UK as an urban region by the year 2000.

Society itself he sees as losing its former class structure based on birth and income, this to be replaced by a four-part division. The categories are: the irresponsible property owners; the non-technical manual workers, now unemployable, whom he calls "the contingents of the Abyss"; the Efficients, who are a heterogeneous group "applying the growing body of scientific knowledge to the general needs"; and a large number of nonproductive people "living in and by the social confusion". There will be no personal servant class, because automation and better design will have done away with the need. A minor domestic feature that Wells predicts with accuracy (and suitable derision) is, among a mass of imitations, an imitation fire of glowing logs in an electrically heated house.

On the subject of warfare, Wells is most restrained. He refers to trench warfare but dismisses the usefulness of submarines and tanks — this was two years before the first appearance of his story "The Land Ironclads". On aircraft he says that he is "inclined to believe that long before the year A.D.2000, and very probably before 1950, a successful aeroplane will have soared and come home safe and sound", to which he adds in an Introduction to the 1914 edition: ". . . the boldness of it!"

He forecasts the expansion of the English language to the extent that it will be understood by "the whole functional body of human society" by 2000. He looks forward to greater unity between nations and to the gradual development of a "New Republic" — a peaceful and mature world state formed by the Efficients.

Although other specialized works of nonfiction prediction continued to be published, the next significant event in this field did not come until after World War I. In 1923 a small booklet was published, *Daedalus or Science and the Future* by J. B. S. Haldane, the slightly enlarged text of a lecture he had given on the power of science to solve Man's problems and create a better future. Among Dr Haldane's predictions of the triumphs of science are greatly increased crop yields, much greater industrial efficiency, human eugenics and ectogenetic foetal development. This (the last item in particular) was controversial stuff, published nine years before Huxley's *Brave New World*, which it undoubtedly influenced.

The book led to the publishers (Kegan Paul, Trench, Trubner & Co) issuing just over a hundred other titles during the next eight years in the same binding and the same miniature format — the "Today and Tomorrow" series. These were all essays on the future of some aspect of society, although quite often two books presenting conflicting views appeared on the same subject. In fact, the second title was *Icarus or the Future of Science* (1925) by Bertrand Russell, intended as a rebuttal of

Daedalus, a much more gloomy view of the influence of science upon future man, symbolized not by Daedalus, who learnt to fly by watching the birds and building his own wings (a triumph of science, if only mythological), but by Icarus, his son, who flew too close to the Sun and was killed when the wax in his wings melted — the downfall of Man through expecting too much of science.

Later volumes, almost all with suitably symbolic mythological titles, included speculations on women, war, transport, architecture, socialism, wine, nonsense and the British Empire. Robert Graves contributed two volumes, *Lars Porsena, or the Future of Swearing* and *Mrs Fisher, or the Future of Humour.* One title, *The Next Chapter: the War Against the Moon* by André Maurois, was fiction and we have met it elsewhere several times in this book.

Unfortunately, many of the later booklets were mundane in their predictions — sometimes right, sometimes wrong, but usually unimaginative.

The most important title, and one which is still in print, is *The World, the Flesh and the Devil* (1929) by J. D. Bernal. This makes a number of astonishing scientific predictions and discusses their possible effect upon Man's future. Dr Bernal suggests that it may soon be possible to make new materials which are not just the natural materials (stone, metal, wood, plant and animal fibres) in a refined form but which are built up to our own specifications from the basic molecules of matter, tailormade to fulfil a certain rôle. This is already being done to a certain extent, but it could be more widespread and much cheaper, the object being to prepare for life on a much more crowded Earth, where all materials — especially foodstuffs — will need to be produced more efficiently from fewer resources.

The suggestion is made that Man should travel into space using rockets for the initial thrust (unless the radio-transmission of energy becomes possible), then relying on solar energy, or perhaps on the solar wind, which will be caught by the space vehicle's immense metallic sails. If Man can learn to live off solar energy and can manufacture his food from any material he can be free of the Earth. He can live in space, possibly in a sphere "ten miles or so in diameter", which would be gravitationless and could house perhaps 20,000 to 30,000 people. This idea for a space colony — in what is now known as a "Bernal sphere" — was a staggering one for 1929, and it is currently regarded, in an only slightly modified form, as a strong possibility within a few decades.

Another area of prophecy in this book covers the changes which Man makes to himself. The addition of nonorganic spare parts inside the body is mentioned, although this had scarcely begun in 1929. More importantly, Dr Bernal refers to the deliberate altering of Man's shape by surgical manipulation of the "germ plasm" — in other words, genetic engineering. He speculates on the possibility of keeping the brain alive after the body has grown too old or has been injured beyond repair. The disembodied brain could be housed in, or connected to, an artificial body of almost any shape, so long as a fresh blood supply was assured. The sensory areas of the brain could be connected up to artificial sensory organs and limbs, though these could be fairly easily replaced for different jobs or changed conditions. (The disembodied brain was swiftly taken up as a plot element by the science-fiction writers of the time and became a cliché in the pulp magazines of the 1920s and 1930s.)

The disembodied brain would conceivably be better off than the normal man in a human body because it would be more adaptable and possibly would be able to achieve direct electrical communication with other disembodied brains. Perhaps compound or complex minds could be formed. These could "extend their perceptions and understandings and their actions far beyond those of the individual". It is clear that some of these ideas and the spiritual changes they would lead to in mankind were influential upon Olaf Stapledon and are reflected in his novel *Last and First Men* (1930).

During the 1920s and 1930s several general books about the future were published, following the pattern established in Wells' *Anticipations* but tending to concentrate a little more on the nuts-and-bolts side of technology and a little less on social changes.

One such was A. M. Low's *The Future* (1925). Although this is generally enthusiastic about technology's ability to provide everything which Man could possibly desire, there is a warning about the potential for evil as well as good: "Unless the advance of science is closely accompanied by an equivalent progress of moral and critical ideas, scientific discovery may unleash powers that could ultimately destroy civilization."

Also, this is one of the earliest nonfiction books to warn that the future would almost certainly seem strange and unattractive to us if we could see it, because it would be aimed at pleasing our descendants rather than ourselves, and they would have different criteria for happiness and desirability. For example, Low predicts that by about AD3000 there will be universal baldness of both men and women as well as some slight atrophying of legs due to underuse. In fact, everybody will have a poorer physique and less acute senses. Food will have become much less important and will be reduced to a single, probably concentrated, meal per day. There will be much greater governmental control over life and liberty, and clothes will be simple one-piece garments wearable by people of either sex.

None of that sounds much fun, but on the other hand there will be many technological marvels, including broadcast power, roofed-over cities (with aircraft landing on the roofs), matter transmission and eventually, perhaps, telepathy. Illness will be prevented by psychological techniques, and organ transplants and rejuvenation will increase the human lifespan.

In a second assault on the future in the enlarged and rather more thoughtful *Our Wonderful World of Tomorrow* (1934) Low adds a few topics. One particularly good idea is his suggestion that there should be a Ministry of the Future. Although its functions are more in the field of technological and resource planning and information than the relief of stress, this still comes across as a forerunner of Alvin Toffler's approach in *Future Shock* (1970).

The values of efficient weather forecasting and weather control are stressed. There are detailed descriptions of the ways in which the men of the future will pamper themselves in oval rooms kept at exactly the right temperature and humidity, with instantly adjustable wall coloration and armchair controls for food, drink, entertainment, the admission of visitors and even for page-turning! Everything that can get dirty — such as clothes, crockery, cutlery, bedclothes, etc. — will be disposable. Human beings will become immersed in all this armchair luxury and will begin to live alone.

The Earl of Birkenhead produced a careful and restrained summing-up of contemporary thoughts on the future in *The World in 2030* (1930). It is a mainly optimistic work which adds nothing new but relies on science to create a bright future *via* eugenics and atomic energy.

Much more forthright and dogmatic is *A Short History of the Future* (1936) by John Langdon-Davies. Its definiteness, naturally, leads to a number of seriously wrong predictions but makes the book more enjoyable to read. His most perceptive statement is this: "We would prefer to be living in the past, and since the present is not the past, we hope that the future may be." This is very true, and accounts not only for the pastoralism displayed in books like Morris' *News From Nowhere* and Hudson's *A Crystal Age* but also for many of the wish-fulfilment novels which have been written about technological utopias; these are too often improved versions of the past and present rather than genuine prophecies of the future.

A Short History of the Future makes twenty-four categorical prophecies, of which only about half a dozen have come true or stand any chance of doing so. Although the author says that his ideas are not wish-fulfilment dreams but will inevitably come to pass, this seems to apply only to the short-range prophecies. A couple of examples of these are: "There will be no war in Western Europe for the next five years [from 1935]" and "Democracy will be dead by 1950". A couple of wish-fulfilment prophecies which have not come true are "By 1960 work will be limited to three hours a day" and "Abundant new raw materials will make food, clothing and other necessities universally obtainable" (again referring to 1960). It is suggested that birth control will be so widely adopted and international control of population so complete that eventually — no timescale is given — "England will have a population one tenth of its present size" and "Large tracts of America will go back to the primeval wilderness". The author also subscribes to the melting-pot theory of genetics, pronouncing: "By A.D.4000 the race problems will all be solved. There will be one race in the world, with a pale coffee-coloured skin, mongoloid eyes, rather shorter than the average Englishman of today."

In the same year (1936) appeared *After Us or The World as it Might Be* by J. P. Lockhart-Mummery. This is a prescriptive work, good on the biological sciences — the author was a surgeon — but unsure in other areas. Most interesting are the chapters on the controlled breeding of animals and humans. "There are hardly any limits to the possibilities of what can be achieved by artificial breeding of living forms." To illustrate this he proposes the use of mutated tigers as guard-dogs or for track-racing, and the use of moles and guinea pigs for digging gardens and trimming lawns!

As regards humans, he is a strong proponent of governmental eugenics schemes in order to control population levels while improving the quality of mankind. "Were the birthrate to continue increasing at the rate it has done during the last sixty years it would take only another two hundred years before there would be neither food nor standing room for man upon the earth." He recommends the sterilization of almost all male children, with only a few, embodying "selected strains", being allowed to remain fertile. Women would be allowed to have children only by permit, and the conception generally would be by means of artificial insemination.

There is an early reference to the growing of meat for food in laboratory tissue cultures, so removing the need for much farm livestock, while other foods (presumably dairy products) will be laboratory produced directly from cellulose. However, the author derides the common fallacy of food in tablet form. Although future food will be artificial it will resemble current food except for being more wholesome, nutritious and full of flavour.

J. P. Lockhart-Mummery's ideas on future technology are less well considered. His future London is spacious but a bland copy of earlier predictions. He dismisses atomic energy, warns against the possibility of drawing the Moon too close to the Earth if tide-power is "exploited over a long period of time", and makes some silly predictions about rocket propulsion.

During World War II, as during World War I, quite a number of books were written predicting the immediate future — the possible outcome of hostilities, the means by which the war might be paid for, the reconstruction, and suggestions for ensuring world peace. An example is Douglas Reed's *All Our Tomorrows* (1942), which we know already, of which only the last third is predictive.

Since World War II there has been an explosive increase in the numbers of books of serious futuristic speculation published. We will look at some of these in the last chapter, but here we can note that, with comparatively few exceptions, nonfiction has taken over from fiction as the medium for the seriously predictive speculator.

9 LAST AND FIRST MEN
PHILOSOPHICAL INTENTIONS

The authors' reason for writing some tales of the future is to put across a philosophical message. This is not just a simple dire warning or promise of utopia — at least, not normally — but rather an attempt to impress upon the reader a way of life to be followed, a way of life to be avoided, or a new way of looking at the world.

There are all manner of different approaches and different philosophies here. The idea being put across may be as restricted as a single scientific theory — such as Lamarckism, upon which George Bernard Shaw based his play *Back to Methuselah* (1921) — or it may be an all-embracing philosophy of life and outlook — such as the free moral will of Kantism, which Kurd Lasswitz not only followed himself but had all his characters, human and Martian, adhere to in *Auf Zwei Planeten* (1897).

Sometimes the philosophy is presented in the form of a utopian society which has risen above the evils of the past because mankind suddenly saw the light and began to embrace, for example, utopian socialism, as in Edward Bellamy's *Looking Backward 2000-1887* (1888). At other times the philosophy is implicit in a dire warning as an individual realizes that the society in which he lives is totally mistaken in its beliefs and organizational style, as in *Anthem* by Ayn Rand, first published in 1938. Or it might take a world war and the death of virtually everybody in the world before the philosophy can be developed and understood, as is the case with Alfred Noyes' novel *The Last Man* (1940).

The philosophical ideas themselves are a mixture of political, religious, economic and scientific beliefs, although it is misleading and unfair to assign such labels. Indeed, most predictive novels have some philosophical content, generally political; and it is to political philosophy that we will devote most of our attentions in this chapter.

The two most important novels in this philosophical category in terms of effect — because they were both very influential, selling large numbers of copies in many countries and leading to the foundation of societies which tried to put their respective philosophies into practice — were Bellamy's *Looking Backward 2000-1887* and Theodor Hertzka's *Freeland* (1891).

Looking Backward 2000-1887 is a detailed description of an ideal state which exists in the USA and most of the rest of the world in the year 2000, as contrasted with the conditions (particularly in Boston, Mass.) in 1887, the year of writing.

For most of the 20th century the USA has been a communist state, with all work, production and enterprise being centrally controlled and all workers — of whatever trade, grade or age — receiving the same wage, paid as credit. This credit allowance is generous but is exchangeable only at a public store. There is no private manufacturing of any sort, so no competition or advertising exists. Nor is there very much freedom, because the nation is the sole employer and sole provider of all goods and services.

It is rather surprising not only that such an anti-capitalist scheme should have been put forward as an ideal by a 19th-century American but that it should have been so widely accepted by other Americans. The book went into many editions very quickly, selling well in excess of a quarter of a million copies in the USA alone. (Before me as I write I have a copy of the 22nd UK edition, which is dated October 1891 — only two years after the book first appeared in the UK.) It was translated into many European languages and led to the publication of a good number of sequels — only one of which, *Equality* (1897), was by Bellamy himself — and associated utopian socialist tracts, and, naturally, to some rebuttals, the most notable being William Morris' *News From Nowhere* (1891). Societies were formed, particularly in the USA, to discuss and promulgate Bellamy's ideas.

The main reason for this unquestioning acceptance of communism by the greatest supporters of capitalism was that Bellamy had cunningly provided a sugar-coating for his message. Although very early in the book 19th-century society is compared to a coach, drawn by the downtrodden masses and bearing the idle rich, most of the book's pages are devoted to showing the awakened sleeper of 1887, Julian West, how wonderful life is in the year 2000.

There is a universally high standard of living, with full employment, good working conditions, retirement on the same high income at the age of forty-five, magnificent housing, free medical treatment, and a host of other improvements over the society of 1887. In fact the people of 2000 all seem to live as well as — or better than — the idle rich of 1887, such as Julian West, except that there are no personal servants; these have been replaced by machines for house cleaning, etc., and area restaurants for family eating.

The rise in the standard of living is claimed by the author to stem from greater efficiency of production (because there is no competition), lack of waste (because all men are working for the common good and because all demand for goods is accurately known), no monetary system to complicate matters, and no government administration to consume a tithe of all production — technological innovation is *not* cited as a reason. But Bellamy's flow of argument is so convincing, so reasonable, that if one does not stop to think one is totally won over to the system without ever realizing what it represents. Bellamy is very clever, "solving" all the problems of his age and offering something to almost everyone: food for the poor, jobs for the unemployed, better conditions than they could ever have imagined for the militant unionists, education for the young, security for the old and equality for women. People of ambition may still achieve great power, although they need to work their way up by proven merit and cannot buy their way to the top through inheritance, family connections or bribery. Even the rich capitalists like Julian West are supposed to have realized, in a flash of insight, that they have always been useless, leeches on society, and to have made amends by rushing out joyously to get an honest job. The only groups to whom Bellamy does not offer a carrot of some kind are lawyers (the profession is abolished, with only lay judges remaining), bankers (made obsolete by the substitution of credit for money because, of course, one does not need bankers to operate a credit system; this is a dreadful mistake which Bellamy tries to cover up in *Equality*), bureaucrats (there are none) and negroes (who are not mentioned — perhaps because he did not wish to antagonize his readers too much).

The central feature of Bellamy's utopia is the army of industry, comprising all able-bodied citizens, male and female, between the ages of twenty-one and forty-five, who choose their occupations according to natural ability and personal preference — conditions of work are varied to make the supply of labour in each trade fit the demand. This is organized on military lines (the armed services, incidentally, have been abolished). The professionals and intellectuals are organized in associated corps, as are those who are not able-bodied. There is a hierarchy of command, the most efficient men being promoted, but the author seems to think that an entire nation can be run smoothly and efficiently by a relative handful of supervisors, who are not specialist administrators, without the help of a bureaucracy. Obviously Edward Bellamy's fictional 20th century did not produce either Parkinson's Law or the Peter Principle.

Dr Theodor Hertzka was a well known Viennese economist. His book *Freiland: ein sociales Zukunftsbild* was published early in 1890, and an English translation, *Freeland: A Social Anticipation,* appeared in June 1891.

The nub of his philosophy was that the most efficient and most desirable system for industrial production was the workers' cooperative. He is not recommending communism — although he did believe that the means of production, including land, should be jointly owned by all — but a very direct and participative form of capitalism. As he says in his preface to the book: ". . . if interest can be dispensed with without introducing communistic control in its stead, then there no longer stands any positive obstacle in the way of the establishment of the free social order."

In order to demonstrate the enormous benefits of such a system he wrote *Freeland,* which is a lengthy and detailed description of its practical application through the establishment of a new community in the high plateau region of East Africa, near Mount Kenya. (This was largely unknown territory in 1890, having been visited by just a handful of European explorers — including Stanley.) The International Free Society is founded for this purpose, and it sends out an advance party of two hundred men to find suitable sites and begin clearing the land and laying out streets and buildings.

The trek inland from Mombasa takes thirty-eight days, and although it is hard work it is accomplished without setbacks. Peaceful relations are established with native tribes including the Masai and Kikuyu. The initial settlement in an attractive valley is christened Eden Vale.

Membership of the society grows exponentially and new settlers flock to join them. A regular route from the coast is established, with waggons using it every day to bring in new settlers and take out the colony's excess products, initially grain. Groups of men of each trade get together to form cooperatives, always acting in perfect harmony. All are joint entrepreneurs; none are employees. They bring their wives and children with them, of course and, in the hope of providing wives for the single men, many women teachers are engaged at attractive salaries.

The laws of Freeland are as follows:

1. Every inhabitant has an equal and inalienable claim upon the whole of the land, and upon the means of production accumulated by the community.

2. Women, children, old men, and men incapable of work, have a right to a competent maintenance, fairly proportionate to the level of the average wealth of the community.

3. No one can be hindered from the active exercise of his own free individual will, so long as he does not infringe upon the rights of others.

4. Public affairs are to be administered as shall be determined by all the adult [above twenty years of age] inhabitants of Freeland, without distinction of sex, who shall all possess an equal active and passive right of vote and of election in all matters that affect the commonwealth.

5. Both the legislative and executive authority shall be divided into departments, and in such a manner that the whole of the electors shall choose special representatives for the principal public ,departments, who shall give their decisions apart and watch over

the action of the administrative boards of the respective departments.

Within a year the colony of Freeland has 95,000 inhabitants. New townships have been founded over quite a wide area. A railway line is soon to be built to Mombasa. The workers find that they are able to achieve a higher standard of living by cutting out the idle land-owning, interest-earning class. Prices are lower and wages higher than in Europe or the USA. The Freelanders are able to export large quantities of foodstuffs and, eventually, manufactured goods. "At the close of the fourth year the population of Freeland had risen to 780,000 souls. A great part of Eden Vale had become a city of villas, which covered forty square miles and contained 58,000 dwelling-houses, whose 270,000 occupants devoted themselves to gardening, industrial or intellectual pursuits."

The natives of the area are treated very well. Far from being used as cheap or slave labour they are educated and encouraged to achieve prosperity through efficient agriculture.

Twenty-five years after its foundation — that is, about the year 1918 or 1920, although Dr Hertzka never mentions specific years — Freeland has a population of 42 million, of which 26 million are white settlers, with more than another million arriving each year. Some 22 million acres of land are being farmed, with two harvests a year, and, unsurprisingly, Freeland has become the most prosperous nation in the world.

This is, of course, an unashamed wish-fulfilment fantasy. Dr Hertzka was so overwhelmed by the vision of workers' cooperatives that he considered them a panacea for "protective duties, cartels and trusts, guild agitation, strikes" and all similar industrial ills.

The author's enthusiasm was initially infectious; an International Freeland Society was formed and "a suitable tract of land in British East Africa, between Mount Kenya and the coast" was placed at its disposal. Local Freeland societies were founded in many cities and towns of Europe, the UK and the USA, although particularly in Austria and Germany. But the dream of utopia was never fulfilled. A small group of just sixteen colonists set out to found their Freeland, but the practical difficulties proved more acute in reality than on paper.

Quite a number of other authors have put forward a proposed system of political and economic organization through the medium of a tale of the future.

News From Nowhere (1891) by William Morris was written partly as a satire on Bellamy's *Looking Backward 2000-1887,* presenting an off-beat picture of England in about 2100 as a socialist state. Yet this is not Bellamy's highly organized socialism; instead it is a largely informal system by which people work because they want to at whatever job takes their fancy, and consume whatever they need. There is no national government and no organized industrial production. Everything is small-scale, local and antitechnological, whether it is a project, like house- or bridge-building, or a trade like weaving or cobbling. As in *Looking Backward 2000-1887*, there is no money used, but there is no credit or value system, either.

Perhaps Morris' system could be described as true communism; it is patently unworkable for any community larger than a village, and even then would result in technological regression, but this was just the sort of society which Morris was idealizing, in contrast to Bellamy's soulless and hive-like recommendation.

An interesting comparison with both *Freeland* and *Looking Backward 2000-1887* can be found in *Caesar's Column* (1890), by Ignatius Donnelly, another book which we have met before. After the destruction of the capitalist oligarchy which has ruled the USA, the socialist narrator and his friends escape by airship to Uganda, where they found a utopian society. The details of this are sketchy, but it seems to be a kind of limited capitalism, subject to strict governmental control by the elected parliament of the citizens. Interest on money is forbidden, although the accumulation of wealth is allowed, up to a certain maximum. Certainly there are employers and landowners, and money is retained, although the use of gold as its basis is discontinued. This was written after the publication of *Looking Backward 2000-1887*, although it seems to owe little to Bellamy's book, and was being produced at the same time as *Freeland*, so that the East African location and limited capitalist system are coincidences.

The socialist message is put across strongly by Jack London in *The Iron Heel* (1907), although only by counter-example, since the setting is the USA under a brutal capitalist oligarchy. Ayn Rand uses a similar approach with the opposite intention in *Anthem* (1938), detailing a totally repressive far-future communist state in order to show by contrast how free and individualistic one is allowed to be under non-collectivist régimes.

A more ambivalent stance is adopted by J. D. Beresford in his novel *Revolution* (1921). He shows a workers' revolution in the UK during the early 1920s and the formation of local cooperative committees, as in Russia. Although there is a right-wing counter-revolution in little more than a year, one feels this ending was put in because it was more acceptable to the (essentially conservative) reading public. Yet the novel shows communism in the UK working in the short term, and the author suggests his own sympathy with it.

Several authors have written novels aimed at opposing the existence of totalitarian government, whatever its form, without particularly upholding or condemning either communism or capitalism. These are dire warnings, dystopias, of course, but more than that they are arguments for the liberty of the individual. In H. G. Wells' *When the Sleeper Wakes* (1899) it is the Council of Trustees, controlling the labour Companies which employ half the world's population, who are the culprits. In *The Messiah of the Cylinder*, Victor Rousseau's 1917 novel, it is an atheistic totalitariansim, developed from Marxism but reinforced by an insane eugenic idealism. And in Sinclair Lewis' *It Can't Happen Here* (1935) it is fascism controlling the USA in imitation of the situations prevailing in Germany and Italy, but including some accurate anticipation of concentration camps and widespread executions without trial. In addition to appealing for individual freedom, the Lewis novel also makes the point that it is up to the individual to claim and maintain his rights by speaking out; too many totalitarian régimes have come into existence because the silent majority remained silent while their rights were stripped away.

A final philosophical observation on the struggle between right and left, between capitalism and communism, comes from Leslie Beresford, writing as "Pan", in *The Great Image* (1921). Against the bloodletting of an unsuccessful workers' revolution, set in the UK about a hundred years ahead, he suggests that the world is divided into Jacobs, who always succeed, gaining rank, power and money, and Esaus, who always occupy the lower rungs. The author intends this as an argument against communism, but it can equally well be interpreted as an argument for or an acceptance of a meritocracy.

An important category of philosophically motivated novels is that of the antiwar books which were particularly prevalent during the 1930s.

Sometimes war is prevented, or peace imposed upon warring nations, by means of a new invention. In *Armoured Doves* (1931) by Bernard Newman it is a League of Scientists, formed specifically to oppose war, which stops a Turko-Italian war in 1954 by means of a "Peace Ray" which disintegrates all copper and puts naval vessels out of commission, and later, in 1961, develops a "Magnetising Ray" to prevent a Franco-German war. (The first of these two ideas seems to have been adapted from C. J. Cutcliffe Hyne's *Emperor of the World* (1910), where a "New Force" which can reduce iron to a yellow sludge is used to prevent an Anglo-German war, though Hyne's intention was to create an escapist farce, not to promote pacifism as a philosophy.)

The Man Who Could Stop War (1929) by William Penmare (a pseudonym for Mavis Elizabeth Nisot) concerns a young inventor who is not particularly antiwar until the secret of his new explosive is obtained from him by threats and is about to be used by the Russians as a preliminary to European invasion.

A rather different antiwar tactic is adopted in Eric Linklater's *The Impregnable Women* (1938), a version of the Lysistrata story, with women in the UK and other countries organizing love-strikes and take-overs of strategic buildings in an attempt to end a mid-'forties European war.

A much more thoughtful and serious treatment of the antiwar message appeared in 1940: *The Last Man* by Alfred Noyes. Set in the early 21st century, it opens with the death of almost everyone in the world through the agency of a weapon of last resort — an "all-pervasive etherial wave" which stops the human heart. The only survivors appear to be those who were deep underwater when the weapon was unleashed.

At first the protagonist, Mark Adams, believes himself to be the sole survivor. He wanders the deserted streets of towns in England, France and Italy — reminiscent of Lionel Verney in Mary Shelley's *The Last Man* — scarcely able to comprehend so many dead bodies.

> And how are we to mourn for the universe? Let the angels of God
> do that. I could weep for one or two, or a hundred, or a thousand;
> but how is it possible to weep for mankind?

In fact the corpses become chalky after a day or two and after a couple of weeks begin to disintegrate and flake away, which solves the problem of disposal.

Mark finds evidence of another survivor — a woman — but he has an agonizing task tracing her in the depopulated wilderness of Europe. At last he makes contact with her, a young woman named Evelyn Hamilton — the symbolism of the names should strike you at once! A mad scientist has also survived — a necessary plot element, perhaps, but not a particularly credible one — and a large group of monks and villagers at the village of Assisi.

The message here is that Man's own iniquities will destroy him unless he learns to live in peace with God. The people of Assisi had faith and were spared, while Mark and Evelyn have been steered towards Assisi to join them.

The theological philosopher C. S. Lewis wrote three novels which explored the nature of Man, his failings and his virtues. Of these three — *Out of the Silent Planet* (1938), *Perelandra* (also known as *Voyage to Venus;* 1943) and *That Hideous Strength* (1945) — only the last is predictive, having a near-future setting.

The belief that Man is capable of being made into a better person by some external force (which may be interpreted as God) and will for this reason give up war turns up in H. G. Wells' *In the Days of the Comet* (1906). The external force manifests itself as the green vapours, affecting all of mankind, from a comet which comes close to the Earth.

In fact this was intended not as a religious novel but as an early attempt by Wells to create a socialist utopia; it was certainly less deep and more speculative than his *A Modern Utopia* (1905).

His *The World Set Free* (1914), was an irritating and largely unsuccessful attempt to lay out a future history culminating in a utopian world state.

But his most dramatic and enjoyable assault on the theme of a utopian state came in 1923, with the publication of *Men Like Gods,* where a handful of English people from the early 1920s are shunted into a parallel universe — the same one as that lived in by the narrator of *A Modern Utopia,* but a thousand years more advanced — where a remarkably utopian society exists. The reactions and lack of flexibility of normal English people can be observed — and enjoyed.

The culmination of his ideas on achievable utopias is to be found in *The Shape of Things to Come* (1933), where an evolved world state is described in detail. The world state in his later novel, *The Holy Terror* (1936), is very much a dystopia.

Olaf Stapledon in *Last and First Men* (1930) shows many successive world states, some of them describable as utopian, in the longest and most ambitious future history of all, yet his intention was not to make points about the achievement of utopia but to discuss the changing (and developing) spritiual qualities of mankind through many different incarnations. At first it is Man's inherent personality faults which bring disaster. When a more mature stage of development has been reached, with greater harmony between Man and his environment and between man and man, the spiritual peace is upset by external forces which drag down the later races of Man time and time again. For millions of years Man is tortured by guilt over his destruction of an intelligent species on the planet Venus, for example.

He arises each time greater than before, but having at last achieved a physical and mental balance which provides perfect spiritual tranquillity he finds that his extinction by a cosmic disaster is unavoidable. Perhaps this spiritual tranquillity was the purpose of Man's existence and, having achieved it, his existence was deliberately ended by a greater power.

Last and First Men is probably the single most important predictive novel whose intentions are philosophical — indeed, it ranks highly among philosophical fictions of any kind; in this context, it is interesting to note that it is the only novel ever to have been published under the otherwise exclusively nonfiction "Pelican" paperback imprint. Stapledon's imaginative visions of the future forms of Man are entrancing and often very beautiful; the impartiality of his narration (in theory by a member of the Last Men) not only conveys a certain sense of historical realism but also puts across just as effectively as the enormous scope of the book the relative unimportance, on the cosmic scale, of generations of mankind; and the sober beauty of much of his writing provides a perfect setting for his profound ideas.

Stapledon did, of course, write several other philosophical novels. In *Odd John* (1935) he describes the emergence of a superman. This is no altruistic superhero figure but a creature who, although born of man and woman, operates on a remote and quite different intellectual plane from the rest of us. Stapledon uses the novel as a vehicle to question all of our fundamental beliefs — not necessarily to oppose them, just to show that a being mentally far in advance of ourselves may have totally different ethics. The results can be frightening — especially when Odd John questions the wrongness of murder, for example, at which he has tried his hand.

Star Maker (1937), while not truly predictive, is also of interest to us as a philosophical work — and, in a way, it is the alien-contact novel to end all alien-contact novels. The narrator, while staring at the stars one night, feels his mind drawn off into the cosmos for an unspecified reason (a clumsy device, perhaps, but the clumsiness is irrelevant). Floating freely and at infinite speed his mind explores other worlds peopled by bizarre but well realized alien societies. It then makes contact with a number of alien dissociated minds which are exploring the Universe much as his is, and they resolve to search for the answer to the fundamental question of the cosmos, to seek the Star Maker himself.

Among other works, Stapledon wrote also a charming science-fiction novel, *Sirius* (1944). Sirius is a dog whose intelligence has been artificially raised to the level of a man's, or even beyond. His "creator" dies, but a deep bond of love exists between the dog and his "creator's" daughter — a bond so deep that other people, unhappy anyway with the idea of a superintelligent dog, or even any creature more intelligent than themselves, become incensed. Sirius is hunted down and killed: he pays the price for being different, for being intelligent.

In all of these books it may seem that Stapledon is stressing the insignificance of mankind. That this is not true is perhaps best exemplified by a few words he puts on the lips of the member of the Last Men who narrates *Last and First Men*. After describing all the forms, triumphs and tribulations of mankind over a vast period, and stating that the Last Men are now awaiting, in dignity, unavoidable doom, the narrator makes a very simple statement: "It is good to have been Man."

Despite it all, it is good to have been Man. This is a philosophy which concerns itself not merely with political utopias or individual aspirations but with the entire lifespan of an intelligent species.

10 THE SHAPE OF THINGS TO COME

THE FUTURE SINCE 1945

Since 1945 predicting the future has been a growth industry. Science fiction — of which tales of the future comprise the major part — has tended to sell more copies of more titles in almost every successive year. Futurism, or futurology, has become institutionalized — a suitable subject for academic study — resulting in a considerable output of books and articles. In fact, hundreds of books have been published since 1945 in each one of my chapter- categories. To do justice to these — or even to analyze them in the same way as I have treated the works dating from 1800 to 1945 — would require far more space than is available here.

What I hope to achieve in this final chapter is to show how some of the trends of the last eight chapters have been maintained while others have changed direction or even disappeared. At the risk of seeming trite, I must mention that the shape of prediction is bound to change with time, if only because all prediction is a reflection of, or an extrapolation from, a moving baseline — the time of writing. Additionally there are fashions in prediction, in terms of content, intention and style, perhaps to a greater extent than in other areas of fiction or nonfiction.

Dire warnings are still very much in evidence, still anxious over the same ugly threats to human existence, although a couple of new ones have been added. The tenor of most such novels has been pessimistic, showing a devastated Earth without much hope for the survival of mankind.

Warnings of war and alien invasion in particular follow this pattern. War means nuclear war — a total war from which there can emerge no winners. Some authors have found it necessary to exaggerate the power of nuclear devices, showing the Earth reacting in a spectacular manner with worldwide volcanic eruptions, or being pushed out of its orbit or blown apart to form a new asteroid belt. Much more chilling, though, is the slow spread of radiation as portrayed in Nevil Shute's *On the Beach* (1957). Even those people deep underground in shelters will not necessarily survive, as Mordecai Roshwald shows in *Level 7* (1959). The grimmest of alien invasion stories is *The Genocides* (1965) by Thomas M. Disch, which shows the Earth being used as a crop-growing planet by unseen aliens, whose plants grow too swiftly to be coped with.

Humanity is fairly quickly and easily obliterated by these superior invaders — just as we would eliminate a garden pest.

Of all political warnings the most vivid is the horrifying totalitarianism of George Orwell's *Nineteen Eighty-four* (1949), where Big Brother watches you through every TV screen, where dissenters are tortured psychologically using their own worst fears. The state demands absolute, unquestioning obedience from its subjects. As the interrogator, O'Brien, says to Winston Smith, the protagonist, "If you want a picture of the future, imagine a boot stamping on a human face — for ever."

The target for political dystopias since 1945 has been dictatorial government much more than either political extremes as such. The rallying call has been "Freedom for the individual", whether the dictatorship has been of communist Russia over the UK, as in Constantine Fitzgibbon's 1960 novel *When the Kissing Had to Stop*, of Japan over the USA, in *The Man in the High Castle* (1962) by Philip K. Dick, or manifested as the suppression of information by the burning of all books, as in Ray Bradbury's *Fahrenheit 451* (1953).

As technology has developed and spread to affect every part of the world and every facet of our lives, so the opportunities for its misuse have been magnified at least proportionately. Since 1945 it has become fashionable and then hackneyed to show how the many tentacles of technology are oppressing Mankind. The nuclear warning is repeated here, in novels like Poul Anderson's *Twilight World* (1961) where high levels of radiation cause sterility and hideous mutations for generations.

The more immediate problem of manmade ecological disaster has been most convincingly put over in the unrelieved grimness of John Brunner's *The Sheep Look Up* (1972), which shows how the many and various forms of land, sea and air pollution, each merely annoying on its own, can combine to make life on Earth impossible. Although manmade air and water pollution were mentioned in earlier prediction, this is essentially a new subcategory. Among the other areas of technology warned against is the computer, in another Brunner novel, *The Shockwave Rider* (1975).

Although multitudes of natural disasters have been described in detail it is noticeable that the warning given has not really been of a virus which kills all grasses — *The Death of Grass* (1956) by John Christopher — or of a mutated mobile plant — *The Day of the Triffids* by John Wyndham, from 1951 — or of Earth's collision with a comet — *Lucifer's Hammer* (1977) by Larry Niven and Jerry Pournelle — but of the fragility of our civilization and the ease with which it can be upset so as to bring about a temporary or permanent return to the law of the jungle.

The possible misuse of power was not identified as a separate category in Chapter 2, despite novels like S. Fowler Wright's *Power*. Now, when so much more power is available, when so many people have access to nuclear triggers, there is the ever-increasing possibility of the world being held to ransom not by a particular nation (which has everything to lose) but by, for example, the crew of a nuclear submarine, as in *A Small Armageddon* (1962) by Mordecai Roshwald. Apart from technological power there is physical power — the misuse of a natural extrasensory talent. This is the situation in Ursula Le Guin's *The Lathe of Heaven* (1971), where a man is endowed with the power to change the world through his dreams.

A completely new category of warning has sprung up around overpopulation. While W. D. Hay's *Three Hundred Years Hence* accepted overpopulation and coped with it — and while very few other pre-1945 authors bothered to mention it — overpopulation has become a leading agent of future disaster in recent years. One of the best known of these novels is Harry Harrison's *Make Room! Make Room!* (1966), which was filmed as *Soylent Green* (1973). A noted satire on the theme is *The World Inside* (1971) by Robert Silverberg.

War is an area of prophecy which has changed out of all recognition over the last sixty-five years, one which has become more important but less featured since 1945. The 19th-century glorification of war has barely surfaced since 1914 except in some juvenile novels. Widespread pacifism has meant that future wars have become a less important category, with the threat of war and its aftermath being used as backgrounds but war itself rarely being the main subject (at least, on Earth) except satirically, an example being *The Iron Dream* (1972) by Norman Spinrad, a spoof wish-fulfilment novel by "Adolf Hitler" in which the genetically impure are slaughtered in an orgy of violence.

Now future European wars and their consequent invasions of the UK, once so popular, have become almost extinct, although one must not overlook the bombing of London in *The Old Men at the Zoo* (1961) by Angus Wilson, nor the impeccably researched "future history" *The Third World War* (1979) by General Sir John Hackett and others.

Both enemies and weapons have changed. All post-1945 predictions bear in mind the fact that power blocs exist which would tend to make any two-nation war into a world war, with the USA and Europe on one side and the USSR and/or China on the other. Alternatively, there are wars between Earth and alien races — a more popular theme which has managed to sidestep pacifist feelings by explaining that "they started it", or "they're not really intelligent — just blobs". Robert Heinlein has been accused of glorifying war in *Starship Troopers* (1959), where the technologically aided soldiers of Earth kill large numbers of aliens — although other commentators have defended the novel as being either for children or a satire. A more obvious satire on war with aliens is *Bill, the Galactic Hero* (1965) by Harry Harrison; although the ridiculous nature of trying to pursue war against alien creatures, often for mistaken reasons, over distances of many light years is shown up best by Joe Haldeman in *The Forever War* (1974). A recent nonfiction excursion into all aspects of war, from the near to the extremely remote future, is to be found in *War in 2080: The Future of Military Technology* (1979), by David Langford.

As for weapons, the increasing power of the "absolute deterrent" means that there is an ever-present threat of most of the world being instantly devastated with no more than five or ten minutes' warning. No all-out war on Earth can last very long in the future unless, as Philip K. Dick (among others) has predicted, all the fighting is done by robots which will automatically replace themselves, never knowing or caring that their original human designers are all dead.

Satire has come to be spread more thinly during the last thirty or forty years; while very few tales of the future have been wholly satirical, there have been strong elements of satire in a greater proportion of them than previously. Also, futuristic satire has been more commonly provided by authors who do not normally write science fiction, such as John Bowen in *After the Rain* (1958), Brigid Brophy in *Hackenfeller's Ape* (1953) and Michael Young in *The Rise of the Meritocracy* (1958), or by authors who claim never to write science fiction, such as Kurt Vonnegut Jr. (whose work all tends to be satirical).

One of the most consistently humorous of satirists is Ron Goulart, whose brief, zany novels written in a very spare, almost skeletal, style are all satires of life in contemporary California, even when set in the far future on alien planets. Most of Robert Sheckley's work is strong on light-hearted satire, particularly where he features the reversal of contemporary mores. One of R. A. Lafferty's earliest novels, *Space Chantey* (1968), is a hilarious outer-space parody of Homer's *Odyssey,* while John T. Sladek has produced some renowned parodies of other science-fiction writers besides contributing two novels which include satirical elements.

Among sharper satires is Robert Silverberg's *The World Inside,* on population control. He postulates a future in which the people of Earth are encouraged to breed as quickly as possible. All seventy billion live in immense self-contained cities a thousand stories high, with most of the land being devoted to food production. They are all happy and healthy, but their civilization is racing madly towards the point where Earth's resources will not be able to stand it.

William Kotzwinkle's *Doctor Rat* (1976), narrated by a laboratory rat, is an outrageous black comedy.

Frederik Pohl has written a number of more-or-less bitingly satirical stories and novels, including *The Space Merchants* (1953) — about a future in which the world is run by advertising agencies — in collaboration with C. M. Kornbluth.

The weird political situations so carefully detailed in some of Jack Vance's novels are satires of contemporary situations, with the planet Koryphon in *The Gray Prince* (1974) being South Africa and the eponymous planet Wyst: Alastor 1716 (from the 1978 novel) representing the UK.

Some of the leading satirical writers in the science-fiction field at the moment are eastern Europeans, most notably the Pole Stanislaw Lem and the Czech Josef Nesvadba.

Escapism has been a well populated category since 1945. Although it contains some well written and extremely entertaining books which just happen not to possess any kind of message, it is also a convenient repository-classification for a great deal of rubbish. It is inevitable that a great many tales of the future should be substandard, partly because there is a low-quality end to every genre of fiction and particularly because science fiction has been a rapidly expanding market area with a largely undiscriminating readership.

Recent escapist novels may still be divided into tales of disaster, voyages (which must include quests of various kinds, such as the growing subgenre of futuristic detective stories) and a miscellany of others.

The disasters come in a multitude of forms: too much heat, too little heat, too much water, too little water, plague, war, infertility, cosmic disaster and many more. Normally the aftermath is shown, too, and just as often it is *only* the aftermath which is shown, the story being set some decades or centuries after the breakdown of civilization.

Both the disaster — a new disease — and the aftermath are given in the well known *Earth Abides* (1949) by George R. Stewart, although most of this fine novel is devoted to the founding of a new pastoral society in the USA by the few survivors. Although Stewart is an American, the disaster story has been a particularly UK fashion since 1945, with important contributions from John Wyndham, F. G. Rayer, Richard Cowper and Christopher Priest.

In Isaac Asimov's *Foundation* trilogy (1951-3) the disaster is the break-up of a galactic empire. A fine post-nuclear-disaster novel is *Dr Bloodmoney* (1965) by Philip K. Dick.

Two post-disaster stories which also happen to be journeys are Piers Anthony's *Sos the Rope* (1968), which is the story of a strange future where advanced technology still exists but most of the population are barbarians in a culture where martial arts have been institutionalized, and *Hiero's Journey* (1975) by Sterling E. Lanier, an adventure story involving many kinds of mutated — which in this instance inevitably means "giant" — animal life.

Other journeys include multigeneration starship voyages, especially where the descendants of the original crew have regressed and the mission has been forgotten, as in *Non-Stop* (1958) by Brian W. Aldiss. Very nearly all space adventures fall into this category, although alien contact stories will be mentioned below. (One of the major areas in which post-1945 predictions have been made redundant by events is in the field of space travel. There are many examples from the 1950s which show the first rocket to the Moon as a backyard venture, or at least the result of research by a private corporation.) The level of technological accuracy varies from being highly sophisticated and hence thoroughly credible, as in the case of works by Arthur C. Clarke, Hal Clement and Larry Niven, to the scientifically illiterate contributions by far too many minor writers.

Journeys may be through time, like Robert Silverberg's highly amusing time-paradox novel, *Up the Line* (1969), or they may be quests for knowledge, including futuristic detective/thriller stories such as *The Stainless Steel Rat* (1961) and its sequels, by Harry Harrison, and Jack Vance's "Demon Princes" books, beginning with *Star King* (1964).

Wish fulfilment has been forced to change its spots, because few people believe that the future will bring about utopia. The ideal states which have appeared since 1945 have been strange ones, while nearly all wish fulfilment has been manifested as personal power.

The problems of post-1945 industrialization and population growth have led to a disillusionment with the future. Perhaps the only writer to attempt to create a socioeconomic utopia has been Mack Reynolds. Drawing heavily upon Bellamy's *Looking Backward 2000-1887* he has produced two novels, *Looking Backward from the Year 2000* (1973) and *Equality in the Year 2000* (1977), which bring Bellamy's vision up to date by adding technology. But the Marxist-based equality of income is retained, even though a very high level of technological unemployment exists.

Almost all other predictions have been dystopian, except for a continual current of technological optimism from such writers as Arthur C. Clarke, who has always predicted that science would bring about a much better world, given time. Most of his novels demonstrate this, particularly *The City and the Stars* (1956), although elsewhere he suggests that the high-technology utopia can be established only on Mars or the Moon.

Occasionally there are still fairy-tale predictions of a new principle being discovered and applied overnight — of the unlimited-power-without-fuel variety — as in Robert A. Heinlein's *Sixth Column* (1949; also published as *The Day After Tomorrow*), where half a dozen men in the invaded USA succeed in driving out the PanAsians and turning defeat into victory. A smaller-scale version of this is the boy who defies the authorities in an antiscience future to reinvent the hot-air balloon, in *The Cloud Walker* (1973) by Edmund Cooper.

A different approach was adopted in Christopher Priest's novel *A Dream of Wessex* (1977), where a government project is set up to speculate on the creation of a better world of the future through the programmed joint dreams of its members. Samuel R. Delany's massive and complex novel *Dhalgren* (1975) is set against the background of a strange, isolated and half-deserted American city which has become a kind of "hippie heaven".

Small utopian communities, usually following the pastoral tradition of W. H. Hudson's *A Crystal Age* in banning or strictly controlling all technology, have occurred in recent tales of the future, despite the fact that it would be impossible to apply such an idea to any significant portion of the world.

In the far future it is possible to postulate a smaller Earth population or a wide-flung commonwealth of sparsely settled planets. Against such backgrounds there can be utopian societies and many wonderful scientific discoveries. Even immortality, that centuries-old dream, would be credible in those circumstances. As it is, immortality has generally needed to be restricted in some way to avoid the creation of an impossibly large population. Typical books are James Gunn's *The Immortals* (1962) and Jack Vance's *To Live Forever* (1956).

The most important and most common area of wish fulfilment over the last thirty years has been the "superman" theme, usually seen as arising from the possession of one or more extrasensory talents rather than sheer physical strength. The earliest stories on the theme, such as J. D. Beresford's *The Hampdenshire Wonder* (1911) and Olaf Stapledon's *Odd John* (1935) were not set in the future, although they established the commonest fate of the talented person — to be an outcast, an oddity. Sometimes the development of these powers is due to excessive radiation — in *The Chrysalids* (1955) by John Wyndham, for example — and a number of mutants band together for protection. More often the protagonist believes himself to be unique, only meeting up with a similarly talented female in the last few pages, as in Eric Frank Russell's *Three to Conquer* (1956) and Wilson Tucker's *Wild Talent* (1954). Although telepathy is the commonest talent, many others have occurred, including knowledge of the future, shape-changing and fire-raising.

Alien contact is a theme which has continued to develop over the last century or so. Instead of the humanoid aliens which seemed to exist on every planet of our Solar System, Man has had to travel much further and the aliens encountered have been much more strange in appearance and behaviour.

A large proportion of post-1945 tales of the future have featured alien contact. There is a quality spectrum from outstanding to abysmal, but at the upper end authors have achieved great subtlety in their descriptions of aliens and human-alien relationships. No longer need human and alien fight at first sight, however distasteful they find each other's personal appearance; complexity has sprung from a realization that human and alien need have absolutely nothing in common, either physically or mentally. This means that alien races are not more or less intelligent, or more or less advanced, than us; they are just different.

During the 1970s it seems to have been the fashion for the better authors to have made their aliens either as enigmatic as possible or else better "people" than we are. Frederik Pohl has best captured this enigmatic flavour in *Gateway* (1977) by showing us his aliens only through their artifacts. In particular, these are working spaceships — a space-station full of them — with obscure controls whose operation can be discovered by trial and error. Both the inherent betterness and the obscurity of aliens are demonstrated by Robert Silverberg in such novels as *Downward to the Earth* (1971) and *The Man in the Maze* (1969). Perhaps the most imaginative creator of alien lifeforms over the last fifteen years has been Larry Niven, in such books as his collection *Neutron Star* (1968) and, with Jerry Pournelle, the novel *The Mote in God's Eye* (1974).

Before it was possible for books like those to be written or appreciated, the groundwork had to be done by other writers in the 1950s and early 1960s. In 1961 Philip José Farmer's *The Lovers* had appeared, about an illicit sexual relationship between a human and an alien who was outwardly human but actually insectoid. In 1957 there was *The Black Cloud* by Fred Hoyle, about a vast gaseous cloud which proves to be an intelligent being entering the Solar System. Hal Clement contributed several excellent novels on peculiar aliens and their planets, particularly *Mission of Gravity* (1954) and *Cycle of Fire* (1957).

Alien invasions of Earth were fashionable during the 1950s, with a number of unconvincing films being released and quite a lot of books appearing; it is a theme which still receives some attention, and a couple of examples are the urbane and witty *The Interpreter* (1960) by Brian W. Aldiss and the marvellously alien *Lords of the Psychon* (1963) by Daniel F. Galouye.

The serious predictions in post-1945 tales of the future have varied from the highly perceptive to the inexcusably idiotic. Of course, this is a dangerous thing to say because, to quote Arthur C. Clarke's Third Law: "Any sufficiently advanced technology is indistinguishable from magic." But there is a great difference between extrapolating from up-to-the-minute science and guessing wildly without any knowledge of the current state of science — or, occasionally, without even much knowledge of basic science.

In the 19th century scientific knowledge was not only much less advanced — many of the things we take for granted today, such as computers, heart-transplants, Inter-Continental Ballistic Missiles and ball-point pens, were not predictable even by means of the most fanciful extrapolation — but it was concentrated in a very much smaller proportion of the population and information was not easily accessible to others. This meant that fictional predictions which contradicted known facts, scientific laws or widely respected theories were still acceptable among readers of novels.

The situation is very different today, when the most recent findings in any field of science are with few exceptions freely available (although perhaps not comprehensible) and a much larger proportion of the readership is scientifically trained.

There is room for only a few examples of interesting predictions in fiction. Human cloning is a theme which has gradually received more attention from writers of fiction as scientific research into DNA and animal cloning has progressed. Some novels have shown human cloning being achieved for the first time — such as Kate Wilhelm's *Where Late the Sweet Birds Sang* (1976) — while others have assumed it as a common technique for body duplication; for example, *The Ophiuchi Hotline* (1977) by John Varley. Public interest in the subject was increased dramatically with the 1978 publication of *In His Image: the Cloning of a Man* by David Rorvik, which claimed that a human clone had been successfully produced, although this claim has been totally discredited.

The recording of the whole contents of a person's mind — memory and personality — has been assumed in several novels, perhaps most convincingly in Robert Silverberg's *To Live Again* (1969). Preparing a man for survival on Mars was the theme of *Man Plus* (1976) by Frederik Pohl, in which there was only a small degree of extrapolation of present-day surgical and prosthetic techniques.

On the hardware side of science, Larry Niven has produced an eminently believable description of a worldwide matter-transmission system for personal and freight transportation and an analysis of its effects upon human society in the story "Flash Crowd" (1973).

Arthur C. Clarke has predicted many advances in his novels and stories. In his latest novel *The Fountains of Paradise* (1979) is a space elevator — a very long bridge between Earth and a satellite in geostationary orbit; the idea is feasible but the materials for its construction do not yet exist. Some of Clarke's earlier novels show expeditions to the Moon and Mars; his predictions here have been superseded by events and by increased knowledge of those worlds.

Perhaps the greatest conceivable engineering feat would be the construction of a Dyson sphere — a thin shell of matter at Earth-orbit distance which would totally enclose the Sun, giving a living space equivalent to hundreds of millions of Earths. The idea came from a renowned physicist (Dr Freeman Dyson), and Bob Shaw has based a novel on it: *Orbitsville* (1975).

There was a recent fashion for predictive stories about black holes, after they had received official sanction from leading astrophysicists in the early 1970s. Larry Niven, in particular, has written several stories involving black holes.

Nonfiction predictions have boomed since 1945 in an even bigger way than have predictive tales. Very detailed pictures of the future, in terms of population, energy, standard of living, food supplies and natural resources have been prepared by a number of organizations, working from the latest available statistics and making various assumptions about trends. As one might expect, not just one picture of the future has been derived from this, but a spectrum of possibilities varying from utopia to disaster. The two major views are known as Technological-Optimism and Neo-Malthusianism.

The technological optimists, chief spokesman Herman Kahn, believe in the power of new technology to provide (or enable the tapping of) new sources of energy, to give us access to new stocks of raw materials and to raise the standard of living continuously. They favour more education, more capital expenditure and more development of technology, giving a high rate of economic growth. They see no problems which are not soluble by means of technology. This view is presented best in various books written by Herman Kahn, such as *The Year 2000* (1967) in collaboration with Anthony J. Wiener and *The Next 200 Years* (1977) in collaboration with William Brown and Leon Martell.

The Neo-Malthusians have a pessimistic view of the future. They believe that world resources are running out, that world population is already too large to cope with, that technology creates more problems than it solves, and that any further economic growth will make the situation even worse. They favour the conservation of resources and the use of nonexhaustible power sources — wind, water and solar. Yet, even given halts in industrialization, population growth and use of scarce resources, the Neo-Malthusians are pessimistic and foresee economic disaster with widespread pollution and starvation within forty years. This position and the computer models which back it up are set out in *The Limits to Growth* (1972) by Donella H. Meadows *et al.*

Many other books have appeared over the last thirty years dealing with specific elements of the future. A. M. Low produced more mainly technological predictions in *It's Bound to Happen* (1950). Several books appeared during the 1950s describing the future of the US space program, with designs and approaches which are now obsolete, including *The Conquest of Space* (1950) by Willy Ley and *The Exploration of Mars* (1956) by Willy Ley and Werner von Braun, both with illustrations by Chesley Bonestell.

During the 1970s space-travel speculators have concentrated more on interstellar exploration, perhaps by the projected Daedalus starship, and on working out the best designs for orbiting space colonies — on which subject see *The High Frontier* (1977) by Gerard O'Neill and *Colonies in Space* (1977) by T. A. Heppenheimer. Looking much further ahead, to mankind's long-term future, Adrian Berry has written *The Next Ten Thousand Years* (1974).

However, as Alvin Toffler has warned in *Future Shock* (1970), if mankind does not find ways of reducing, avoiding or otherwise coping with the increasing stress that the future is bringing, civilization will not be able to continue.

Among other topics covered in specialist books are the futures of war, architecture, London and the evolution of Man. There is even R. C. Churchill's *A Short History of the Future* (1955) which attempts to construct a world history of the next few thousand years based on various predictive novels of the 1940s and early 1950s.

Philosophical intentions contained in tales of the future since 1945 have been at least as diverse as those prior to 1945. The political and religious questions remain but, as the genre has attracted more adventurous and deeper-thinking writers over the last couple of decades, other philosophical or metaphysical subjects have been approached, including the subjectivity of perception, the reach of the mind and various problems of sex and identity.

Amongst others, George Orwell in *Nineteen Eighty-four* (1949) and David Karp in *One* (1953) attack totalitarianism — they seem to be putting forward alternatives of freedom and democracy without being specific as to details; many of the far futures of Isaac Asimov, Jack Vance and others have returned to the feudal system; Ursula Le Guin seems to be recommending a pacific form of anarchy in *The Dispossessed* (1974); and Mack Reynolds suggests Marxism in *Looking Backward from the Year 2000* and its sequel.

While Walter M. Miller examines the problems of Christianity, especially insofar as the Church acts as the custodian of knowledge, in a post-atomic war future in *A Canticle for Leibowitz* (1958) and Robert Silverberg searches for a scientifically based religion fit for the future in *To Open the Sky* (1967), James Blish tackles the more basic problem of original sin — or rather the lack of it — in *A Case of Conscience* (1958). A race of intelligent aliens appears to be existing in a Garden-of-Eden state, ignorant of sin but ignorant of God, too. They are Christians in all but name, yet because they do not believe in God they must be the creations of Satan.

The difficulties associated with perception — with subjectivity and objectivity and various states of reality — are analyzed (subjectively, at least) in Samuel R. Delany's *Dhalgren*, which examines also problems of identity, creativity and commune living, among other things, and more rigorously in some of Ian Watson's novels, particularly *Miracle Visitors* (1978) and *God's World* (1979). Sexual equality and gender rôles have been dealt with in such works as Theodore Sturgeon's *Venus Plus X* (1960) and Ursula Le Guin's *The Left Hand of Darkness* (1969), in both of which a single bisexual gender is postulated, and in Joanna Russ's rampantly feminist *The Female Man* (1975).

To predict the future of tales of the future is to risk self-parody. Due to the lag between writing and publishing, all existing tales of the future are rooted in the past — to the environment in which they were created. To that extent they are all obsolete, describing the shapes of futures past, although some of their predictions may still come about.

Yet I would not call them
Voices of warning, that announce to us
Only the inevitable. As the sun,
Ere it is risen, sometimes points its image
In the atmosphere — so often do the spirits
Of great events stride on before the events,
And in today already walks tomorrow.

(Coleridge's translation of Schiller's *Wallenstein*)

BIBLIOGRAPHY

Aldiss, Brian W.: *Billion Year Spree: The History of Science Fiction*, Weidenfeld & Nicolson (London), 1973

Amis, Kingsley: *New Maps of Hell*, Harcourt, Brace (New York), 1960

Armytage, W.H.G.: *Yesterday's Tomorrows*, Routledge & Kegan Paul (London), 1968

Bailey, J.O.: *Pilgrims Through Space and Time*, Argus (New York), 1947

Bergonzi, Bernard: *The Early H.G. Wells*, Manchester University Press (Manchester), 1961

Bernal, J.D.: *The World, the Flesh and the Devil*, Kegan Paul, Trench & Trubner (London), 1929

Birkenhead, Earl of: *The World in 2030*, Hodder & Stoughton (London), 1930

Bleiler, Everett F.: *The Checklist of Fantastic Literature*, Shasta (Chicago), 1948

Churchill, R.C.: *A Short History of the Future*, Werner Laurie (London), 1955

Clareson, Thomas D. (ed.): *S.F.: The Other Side of Realism*, Popular Press (Bowling Green, Ohio), 1971

Clarke, I.F.: *Tale of the Future*, Library Association (London), 1978

Clarke, I.F.: *Voices Prophesying War 1763-1984*, Oxford University Press (Oxford), 1966

Clarke, I.F.: *The Pattern of Expectation*, Jonathan Cape (London), 1979

Dunne, J.W.: *An Experiment with Time*, Faber (London), 1927

Geoffrey of Monmouth: *The History of the Kings of Britain*, Penguin (London), 1966

Glass, Justine: *They Foresaw the Future*, G. P. Putnam's Sons (New York), 1969

Haldane, J.B.S.: *Daedalus, or Science and the Future*, Kegan Paul, Trench & Trubner (London), 1923

Hillegas, Mark R.: *The Future as Nightmare*, Oxford University Press (New York), 1967

Howard, Ebenezer: *Garden Cities of Tomorrow*, Faber (London), 1965

Kahn, Herman (with William Brown and Leon Martell): *The Next 200 Years*, Associated Business Programmes (London), 1977

Langdon-Davies, John: *A Short History of the Future,* Routledge (London), 1936

Ley, Willy: *The Conquest of Space,* Sidgwick & Jackson (London), 1950

Locke, George: *Voyages in Space,* Ferret Fantasy (London), 1975

Lockhart-Mummery, J.P.: *After Us,* Stanley Paul (London), 1936

Low, A.M.: *The Future,* Routledge (London), 1925

Low, A.M.: *Our Wonderful World of Tomorrow,* Ward Lock (London), 1934

Low, A.M.: *It's Bound to Happen,* Burke (London), 1950

Nicholls, Peter (ed.): *The Encyclopaedia of Science Fiction,* Granada (London and St Albans), 1979

Nicolson, Marjorie Hope: *Voyages to the Moon,* Macmillan (New York), 1948

Papp, Desiderius: *Creation's Doom,* Jarrolds (London), 1934

Pizor, Faith K., and Comp, T. Allan: *The Man in the Moone,* Praeger (New York), 1971

Reed, Douglas: *All Our Tomorrows,* Jonathan Cape (London), 1942

Russell, Bertrand: *Icarus, or the Future of Science,* Kegan Paul, Trench & Trubner (London), 1925

Richardson, Dr B. W. : *Hygeia; or, a City of Health,* pamphlets, 1876

Stableford, Brian M.: "The Utopian Dream Revisited: Socioeconomic Speculation in the SF of Mack Reynolds", in *Foundation 16* (London), 1979

Stearn, Jess: *The Door to the Future,* Muller (London), 1964

Tuck, Donald H.: *The Encyclopaedia of Science Fiction and Fantasy* (2 volumes to date), Advent (Chicago), 1974, 1978

Wells, H.G.: *Anticipations,* Chapman & Hall (London), 1901

ACKNOWLEDGEMENTS

In particular I should like to thank Brian Stableford for his many helpful suggestions and for the loan of written and illustrated material including illustrations 9 and 23.

Illustrations 3, 4, 5 and 13 come from magazines in the Birmingham Central Library. I thank the library for their kindness in allowing me to reproduce these, and the staff (particularly of the Language and Literature Department) for their considerable assistance. Several rare books were consulted *via* the Inter-Library Loan system, and I am grateful to those involved for tracking down copies on my behalf.

Many thanks to the following for permission to use illustrated material in their possession: John Eggeling (dealing as Phantasmagoria Books, 8 Colwell Road, East Dulwich, London SE22) for illustrations 12 and 25; Mark Westwood (who deals in aeronautical books at Little Mill, Glasbury, Hay on Wye) for illustration 32; and to Donald Goldberg for illustration 24.

In addition, I am grateful to Brian Aldiss and Robert Holdstock for their useful and perceptive comments on the typescript of the book.

CM

INDEX